Battlegro

MONS

Battleground series:

Stamford Bridge & Hastings by Peter Marren
Wars of the Roses - **Wakefield / Towton** by Philip A. Haigh
Wars of the Roses - **Barnet** by David Clark
Wars of the Roses - **Tewkesbury** by Steven Goodchild
Wars of the Roses - **The Battles of St Albans** by
Peter Burley, Michael Elliott & Harvey Wilson
English Civil War - **Naseby** by Martin Marix Evans, Peter Burton
and Michael Westaway
English Civil War - **Marston Moor** by David Clark
War of the Spanish Succession - **Blenheim 1704** by James Falkner
War of the Spanish Succession - **Ramillies 1706** by James Falkner
Napoleonic - **Hougoumont** by Julian Paget and Derek Saunders
Napoleonic - **Waterloo** by Andrew Uffindell and Michael Corum
Zulu War - **Isandlwana** by Ian Knight and Ian Castle
Zulu War - **Rorkes Drift** by Ian Knight and Ian Castle
Boer War - **The Relief of Ladysmith** by Lewis Childs
Boer War - **The Siege of Ladysmith** by Lewis Childs
Boer War - **Kimberley** by Lewis Childs

Mons by Jack Horsfall and Nigel Cave
Néry by Patrick Tackle
Retreat of I Corps 1914 by Jerry Murland
Aisne 1914 by Jerry Murland
Aisne 1918 by David Blanchard
Le Cateau by Nigel Cave and Jack Shelden
Walking the Salient by Paul Reed
Ypres - **1914 Messines** by Nigel Cave and Jack Sheldon
Ypres - **1914 Menin Road** by Nigel Cave and Jack Sheldon
Ypres - **1914 Langemarck** by Jack Sheldon and Nigel Cave
Ypres - **Sanctuary Wood and Hooge** by Nigel Cave
Ypres - **Hill 60** by Nigel Cave
Ypres - **Messines Ridge** by Peter Oldham
Ypres - **Polygon Wood** by Nigel Cave
Ypres - **Passchendaele** by Nigel Cave
Ypres - **Airfields and Airmen** by Mike O'Connor
Ypres - **St Julien** by Graham Keech
Ypres - **Boesinghe** by Stephen McGreal
Walking the Somme by Paul Reed
Somme - **Gommecourt** by Nigel Cave
Somme - **Serre** by Jack Horsfall & Nigel Cave
Somme - **Beaumont Hamel** by Nigel Cave
Somme - **Thiepval** by Michael Stedman
Somme - **La Boisselle** by Michael Stedman
Somme - **Fricourt** by Michael Stedman
Somme - **Carnoy-Montauban** by Graham Maddocks
Somme - **Pozières** by Graham Keech
Somme - **Courcelette** by Paul Reed
Somme - **Boom Ravine** by Trevor Pidgeon
Somme - **Mametz Wood** by Michael Renshaw
Somme - **Delville Wood** by Nigel Cave
Somme - **Advance to Victory (North) 1918** by Michael Stedman
Somme - **Flers** by Trevor Pidgeon
Somme - **Bazentin Ridge** by Edward Hancock
Somme - **Combles** by Paul Reed
Somme - **Beaucourt** by Michael Renshaw
Somme - **Redan Ridge** by Michael Renshaw
Somme - **Hamel** by Peter Pedersen
Somme - **Villers-Bretonneux** by Peter Pedersen
Somme - **Airfields and Airmen** by Mike O'Connor
Airfields and Airmen of the Channel Coast by Mike O'Connor
In the Footsteps of the Red Baron by Mike O'Connor
Arras - **Airfields and Airmen** by Mike O'Connor
Arras - **The Battle for Vimy Ridge** by Jack Sheldon & Nigel Cave
Arras - **Vimy Ridge** by Nigel Cave
Arras - **Gavrelle** by Trevor Tasker and Kyle Tallett
Arras - **Oppy Wood** by David Bilton
Arras - **Bullecourt** by Graham Keech
Arras - **Monchy le Preux** by Colin Fox
Walking Arras by Paul Reed
Hindenburg Line by Peter Oldham
Hindenburg Line - **Epehy** by Bill Mitchinson
Hindenburg Line - **Riqueval** by Bill Mitchinson
Hindenburg Line - **Villers-Plouich** by Bill Mitchinson
Hindenburg Line - **Cambrai Right Hook** by Jack Horsfall & Nigel Cave
Hindenburg Line - **Cambrai Flesquières** by Jack Horsfall & Nigel Cave
Hindenburg Line - **Saint Quentin** by Helen McPhail and Philip Guest
Hindenburg Line - **Bourlon Wood** by Jack Horsfall & Nigel Cave

Cambrai - **Airfields and Airmen** by Mike O'Connor
Aubers Ridge by Edward Hancock
La Bassée - **Neuve Chapelle** by Geoffrey Bridger
Loos - **Hohenzollern Redoubt** by Andrew Rawson
Loos - **Hill 70** by Andrew Rawson
Fromelles by Peter Pedersen
The Battle of the Lys 1918 by Phil Tomaselli
Poets at War: Wilfred Owen by Helen McPhail and Philip Guest
Poets at War: Edmund Blunden by Helen McPhail and Philip Guest
Poets at War: Graves & Sassoon by Helen McPhail and Philip Guest
Gallipoli by Nigel Steel
Gallipoli - **Gully Ravine** by Stephen Chambers
Gallipoli - **Anzac Landing** by Stephen Chambers
Gallipoli - **Suvla August Offensive** by Stephen Chambers
Gallipoli - **Landings at Helles** by Huw & Jill Rodge
Walking the Gallipoli by Stephen Chambers
Walking the Italian Front by Francis Mackay
Italy - **Asiago** by Francis Mackay
Verdun: **Fort Douaumont** by Christina Holstein
Verdun: **Fort Vaux** by Christina Holstein
Walking Verdun by Christina Holstein
Verdun: **The Left Bank** by Christina Holstein
Zeebrugge & Ostend Raids 1918 by Stephen McGreal

Germans at Beaumont Hamel by Jack Sheldon
Germans at Thiepval by Jack Sheldon

SECOND WORLD WAR

Dunkirk by Patrick Wilson
Calais by Jon Cooksey
Boulogne by Jon Cooksey
Saint-Nazaire by James Dorrian
Walking D-Day by Paul Reed
Atlantic Wall - **Pas de Calais** by Paul Williams
Atlantic Wall - **Normandy** by Paul Williams
Normandy - **Pegasus Bridge** by Carl Shilleto
Normandy - **Merville Battery** by Carl Shilleto
Normandy - **Utah Beach** by Carl Shilleto
Normandy - **Omaha Beach** by Tim Kilvert-Jones
Normandy - **Gold Beach** by Christopher Dunphie & Garry Johnson
Normandy - **Gold Beach Jig** by Tim Saunders
Normandy - **Juno Beach** by Tim Saunders
Normandy - **Sword Beach** by Tim Kilvert-Jones
Normandy - **Operation Bluecoat** by Ian Daglish
Normandy - **Operation Goodwood** by Ian Daglish
Normandy - **Epsom** by Tim Saunders
Normandy - **Hill 112** by Tim Saunders
Normandy - **Mont Pinçon** by Eric Hunt
Normandy - **Cherbourg** by Andrew Rawson
Normandy - **Commandos & Rangers on D-Day** by Tim Saunders
Das Reich – **Drive to Normandy** by Philip Vickers
Oradour by Philip Beck
Market Garden - **Nijmegen** by Tim Saunders
Market Garden - **Hell's Highway** by Tim Saunders
Market Garden - **Arnhem, Oosterbeek** by Frank Steer
Market Garden - **Arnhem, The Bridge** by Frank Steer
Market Garden - **The Island** by Tim Saunders
Rhine Crossing – **US 9th Army & 17th US Airborne** by Andrew Rawson
British Rhine Crossing – **Operation Varsity** by Tim Saunders
British Rhine Crossing – **Operation Plunder** by Tim Saunders
Battle of the Bulge – **St Vith** by Michael Tolhurst
Battle of the Bulge – **Bastogne** by Michael Tolhurst
Channel Islands by George Forty
Walcheren by Andrew Rawson
Remagen Bridge by Andrew Rawson
Cassino by Ian Blackwell
Anzio by Ian Blackwell
Dieppe by Tim Saunders
Fort Eben Emael by Tim Saunders
Crete – **The Airborne Invasion** by Tim Saunders
Malta by Paul Williams
Bruneval Raid by Paul Oldfield
Cockleshell Raid by Paul Oldfield

Battleground Europe

MONS

JACK HORSFALL
&
NIGEL CAVE

Series editor
Nigel Cave

Pen & Sword
MILITARY

First published in Great Britain in 2000 by Leo Cooper
Reprinted in 2014 by
PEN & SWORD MILITARY
An imprint of
Pen & Sword Books Ltd
47 Church Street
Barnsley, South Yorkshire
S70 2AS

ISBN 978 0 85052 677 6

A CIP catalogue record for this book
is available from the British Library

Printed and bound in England
By CPI Group (UK) Ltd, Croydon, CR0 4YY

Pen & Sword Books Ltd incorporates the Imprints of Aviation, Atlas,
Family History, Fiction, Maritime, Military, Discovery, Politics, History,
Archaeology, Select, Wharncliffe Local History, Wharncliffe True Crime,
Military Classics, Wharncliffe Transport, Leo Cooper, The Praetorian Press,
Remember When, Seaforth Publishing and Frontline Publishing

For a complete list of Pen & Sword titles please contact
PEN & SWORD BOOKS LIMITED
47 Church Street, Barnsley, South Yorkshire, S70 2AS, England
E-mail: enquiries@pen-and-sword.co.uk
Website: www.pen-and-sword.co.uk

CONTENTS

Series Editor's Introduction......6
Acknowledgements......8
Advice to Travellers......10
List of Maps......13
Elements of the German First Army at Mons......14
Elements of the BEF at Mons and in the Borinage......17
The Legend of the Angel of Mons......20

Chapter 1 **The Road to Mons**......21

Chapter 2 **Sunday 23 August: The Morning**......43

Chapter 3 **Mons: The afternoon of 23 August**......69

Chapter 4 **Monday, 24 August: The Last Day**......107

Chapter 5 **Tours**......131

Selective Index......190

Kaiser Wilhelm and the Chief of the General Staff Colonel-General Helmut von Moltke (foreground) at manoeuvres in 1909.

SERIES EDITOR'S INTRODUCTION

Mons is one of those battles of the First World War that has a resonance as great as the Somme and Passchendaele for most people in Britain. They might not know anything more than the name, but it is a name that has stuck in the national subconscious.

Surprisingly enough, there is hardly anything written on the battle as such; there are excellent books on the campaign of 1914, but nothing in great detail on the fighting that took place on 23 and 24 August in this area of Belgium nestled up against the French border. Indeed there was no guide book of any great note until Michael Gavaghan's *Mons 1914* appeared a year or so ago.

This book is chiefly the result of the labour of Jack Horsfall who completed it some considerable time ago; it has been a long time in the editing. It is a fascinating read, opening up the battle and the achievement of the men of II Corps. These men were holding great lengths of front – well over a thousand yards per battalion was quite common – against a vastly superior army in numbers, an army that was at least as well equipped and, in the case of artillery, far better off in numbers and variety of gun. Then, as now, Mons was an industrialised town, heavily dependent on mining and related activities, and was built up and dominated (then more than now) by slag heaps in the surrounding countryside.

The narrative takes the reader through the narrow streets of Mons and out into the countryside of the Borinage. The one great change in the topography has been the disappearance of the Condé Canal, overwhelmed by the transport of the late twentieth century, the car, the truck and the ubiquitous autoroute.

The tours are complex and do require two people in the car to follow easily; this is inevitable in such a built up area and in following a story which covers a wide area and involving so many important small unit actions. This is a key to understanding the military events of 1914 from the British perspective. It is not the story of great masses of men engaged in enormous conflagration, such as the Somme. Rather the Retreat and later battles of 1914, such as Le Cateau, the Aisne and above all First Ypres, are often dominated by the actions of individual battalions, squadrons and batteries. Their stories are often very well written up. This combination of factors makes for an unusual guide.

Reading, checking and following the tours all provided me with considerable insights into the fighting at Mons in 1914, even though I had read about it extensively before. It certainly enhanced my admiration for the achievement of all ranks of those first formations and units of the British Expeditionary Force; it will be a worthwhile achievement if this book helps others feel the same way.

Nigel Cave
St Mary's, Derryswood

Thirsty German troops accept a drink from a monk as they march into Belgium.

ACKNOWLEDGEMENTS

First I must thank the noted author Nigel Cave who suggested that I might care 'to have a look at Mons' with the idea of writing a Battlefield Guide. 'Mons' had always seemed remote in time and place to me, overshadowed by later momentous events. I must say that the pleasure that I got from exploring Mons and the small mining towns of the Borinage, south west of Mons, where the people proved to be so extraordinarily friendly, was very great and having been 'bitten' I find that I must go back there as often as I can.

The help given to me by the curator of military museums has been invaluable, particularly Philip Dutton of the Imperial War Museum and Michael Ball of the National Army Museum. The curators and archivists of the regimental museums, those regiments that fought there in August 1914, have been most generous, sending copies of their war diaries, maps and extracts from their regimental histories telling of those three days when those few battalions and cavalry squadrons stopped and held the might of the German's First Army. I hope this guide will further enhance their stories making it possible for people to see all the battles there.

I am most grateful to Monsieur Fernand Martin, the Director of Tourism at Mons, Monsieur Andre Ceuterick the Deputy Mayor of Frameries, Monsieur Pierre Warnier of Quieverain and the Mayors of Cuesmes, Ciply, Jemappes, Tertre, Saint Ghislain and Wasmes for all their willing help, generously sending me maps of their towns that I might use, particularly the Mayor of Boussu and his Council who received me so kindly at the town hall of Hornu, telling me so much of what happened there in 1914 and 1944. To Monsieur Marcel Capouillez of Boussu who gave me permission to reproduce photographs from his splendid book, to use in this guide. To the Commonwealth War Graves Commission who have kindly helped me with their registers of the cemeteries and for their immediate response to my queries. Also to the many people in the towns and villages who must have thought I was a little mad as I asked them in my 'remarkable' French about what had happened there so long ago. Their patience and surprising knowledge of the events then was most willingly given.

However I thank most of all the two men who I can now call my friends, whose knowledge of those events at Mons and the Borinage is unsurpassed, being a lifetime's work for them. Monsieur Andre Englebert, the Royal British Legion's representative at Saint Ghislain, a Resistance fighter in World War Two and highly decorated, gave me permission to use his written material, and provided me with copies of many photographs of the old canal bridges that our men fought to hold in August 1914.

The other is Monsieur Bernard Figue of Tertre, whose maternal grandfather was an Irish soldier, Mr John Whyte, who married a Belgian girl in 1920. He is buried in Flenu cemetery close to the memorial and graves of men of the 1st Royal Scots Fusiliers. His brother, Bernard, wounded at Serre on the 1st of July 1916, was evacuated to Cheltenham, dying there of his wounds, to be buried in the local cemetery. Bernard Figue's paternal grandfather, Monsieur Leon Figue was Mentioned in Despatches in World War 1 for his intelligence gathering, sending the information through Holland, and subsequently awarded the MBE for his espionage work. He was arrested by the Germans in August 1942, taken to Wolfenbuttel in Germany and beheaded in November 1943. His body was returned in 1947 to be buried in the communal cemetery at Boussu, you will see his grave in Tour 4. A street in the centre of the town is named after him. Bernard Figue's knowledge of both wars is remarkable and he looked after me as a brother.

Finally my grateful thanks to Paul Wilkinson at Pen & Sword whose hard work made the manuscript into a readable book.

Lastly but not least the authors of the books listed below from which I drew much interest and information, reading them before I ventured out and looking at them on the battlefields with the war diaries and regimental histories sent to me.

The First Seven Divisions. *Lord Ernest Hamilton*
Mons. *John Terraine*
The Guns Of August. *Barbara Tuckman*
The Mons Star. *David Ascoll*
Before Endeavours Fade. *Rose E.B. Coombes MBE*
Great Battles of World War 1. *Anthony Livesey*
The World War 1 Album. *Ross Burns*
History of The Irish Regiment. *Lt. Col. C. Gretton*
History of The Suffork Regiment. *Lt. Col C.C.R. Murphy*
The South Lancashire Regiment. *Colonel B.R. Mullay*
INVICTA, The Queens Own Royal West Kent Regiment. *Major C.V. Molony*
History of The Duke Of Wellington's Regiment. *Brigadier General D. Bruce, CBE*
The Cheshire Regiment, 1st Battalion at Mons. *Frank Simpson*
Farewell Leicester Square. *Kate Caffrey*

ADVICE TO TRAVELLERS

Mons is some 110 miles south east of Calais, thirty miles south of Brussels; whilst the coal mining towns of the *Borinage* are two or three miles to its south and stretch some ten miles or so westwards, close by the Condé Canal. This guide tells the story of the battles there in three days of August 1914 - the 22nd, 23rd and 24th. Its main purpose is to encourage visits to those battlefields and to remember those valiant Regular soldiers that have become known to history as the Old Contemptibles; hopefully it will help to keep alive their memory for a

1. Area Map: Mons in context.

later generation. For the most part it tells the story of the infantry, cavalry, gunners, sappers and their supporting arms from their arrival in the Mons area on 22 August 1914, when the first shots were fired in the first action of the BEF, to their withdrawal from the Mons Salient on the 24th August, the initial steps of the long retreat to the Marne. These actions are then followed on the ground today by means of five tours.

Unlike other British battlefields on the Western Front, such as Ypres, the Somme and Arras, which are toured by thousands of visitors and where there is an abundance of inexpensive accommodation, Mons is a relatively expensive place in which to stay. There are few hotels in the neighbouring towns in the old coal-mining district of the *Borinage*, but the following list should be of assistance. The guide is set in a French (or Walloon) speaking part of the country.

• Le Cosaque Gourmand, 2 Rue Defuisseaux, B7333 Tertre St Ghislain. *Tel +32 65 761666.*
Autoroute Exit 25. Ideal for all of the tours described in the book. Reasonable rooms, though not palacious.

•Auberge Le XIXieme, Grand Place 4, B7378 Thulin. *Tel + 32 65 650156.*
The hotel is very comfortable but might be considered to be situated too far to the west.

•Gite a la Ferme, 1, Rue de l'Eglise, B7382 Audregnies *Tel + 32 65 430684.*
Very comfortable and particularly good for the battles of the 'left flank guard'.

There are various hotels in Mons itself, such as the Infotel (3 stars) (+32 65 366221); the Hotel le Lido (4 Stars) (+32 65 327800) and the Hotel St Georges (2 Stars) (+32 65 318671). Other possibilities are Cambrai and the various motel types of accommodation to be found on the intersection to the autoroute near that city.

Mons is approximately the same distance from Calais as Albert. The people are both friendly and helpful; the centre of Mons is attractive and there is a good range of cafes and restaurants. A striking difference to most other British battlefields lies in the built-up nature of Mons itself, and it is consequently that little more difficult to navigate and to visualise the past; on the other hand, outside the towns, the changes have been relatively few, with the exception that the Condé Canal has been built over by the autoroute. Mons boasts a small but striking museum devoted to its wartime experience.

There are detailed maps in the touring section, but visitors should find the following useful.

Michelin Map 51 (1:200000) - particularly recommended is the overprinted version available from the Commonwealth War Graves Commission, showing the location of most of their cemeteries. This is available from The Commonwealth War Graves Commission, 2, Marlow Road, Maidenhead, BERKS SL6 7DX; at the time of writing the map cost £3.

IGN (Belgian) 45/5-6 (1:25000) - Quievrain - Saint-Ghislain
IGN (Belgian) 45/7-8 (1:25000) - Mons - Givry
IGN (Belgian) 51/3-4 (1:25000) - Aulnois - Grand-Reng or the French Series Bleu 2605 E.

These maps are available from several bookshops in Mons; in case of difficulty in locating them, the Information Office on the main square will be able to direct you.

Particularly useful is Map 111 Mons-Charleroi in the Belgian 1:100000 Purple series, which will prove to be invaluable for navigation purposes.

You should ensure that your vehicle insurance is fully valid from your insurers and, if not, obtain the necessary Green Card. I would recommend that you get breakdown cover - over the years I have had to use this a couple of times, and it does provide peace of mind. You will also require a small medical kit, basic spare parts for the vehicle (most notably light bulbs) and warning triangles. Medical cover is provided to a considerable extent by Form E1 11, obtainable from most reasonably large Post Offices, but beware that it is reciprocal cover (ie you get in Belgium what the Belgians get; they get in the UK what the British get) and it is wise to take out personal insurance, which will also cover your personal possessions. It is a good idea to ensure that your tetanus jab is up to date.

The following items are likely to prove useful, if only at some stage in your trip: a camera (preferably with some sort of zoom capability) and plenty of film (this is cheaper in the UK); a notebook to record your trip as well as noting what pictures you have taken; binoculars; a compass; a corkscrew; basic picnic equipment; stout walking shoes (and a plastic bag to keep them in when they are not in use); a good waterproof jacket (and, for the determined, waterproof trousers!); a hat; bottled water; and a rucksack to take all this lot around with you.

Unlike the Salient, there is relatively little likelihood of coming across rusty but lethal remnants of the war in the shape of unexploded shells and grenades; but in the unlikely event that you do find any, leave it alone. As recently as 1999 members of the French Bomb Disposal squad were killed by old First World War ordnance in two different incidents in the old British zone alone.

THE MAPS

List of maps:

1. Area Map: Mons in context 10
2. The armies' positions at Mons 31
3. First Contact 37
4. The Battle for the Canal du Centre 44
5. The Battle at Nimy and Obourg 62
6. Developments on the right flank 70
7. The action of 2nd Royal Irish Regiment, 23 August 72
8. The action around Jemappes 82
9. The action at Mariette 85
10. The action at Les Herbieres, St Ghislain and Mariette 86
11. Action at Lock No 3 and the Railway Bridge 87
12. Battlefield of 1st Royal West Kents 88
13. Lock No 4, 23rd August 91
14. The action south of Hautrage 94
15. 1/DCLI's action along the canal bank 104
16. Smith-Dorrien's right flank: 24th August 108
17. The Battle at Wasmes 117
18. Official History Map: actions at Elouges and Audregnies .. 120
19. Audregnies: the afternoon of 24th August 122

Tour Maps

1. Mons traffic map 132
2. The Royal Fusiliers' right sector 134
3. The Royal Fusiliers' left sector 138
4. The road to Casteau 140
5. 4th Middlesex defence of the canal 142
6. The retreat from the canal through Hyon 144
7. Jemappes and the retreat through Flenu 153
8. The fight at Frameries and Ciply 160
9. Tour through Ciply and Cuesmes 162
10. Route map to Hornu and Wasmes 165
11. Town plan of St Ghislain 167
12. Town plan of Boussu 170
13. The defence of the canal north of St Ghislain 173
14. The fighting in Wasmes 177
15. Tour of the action at Elouges and Audregnies 181
16. Defence of the canal by 1/DCLI at le Sardon 187

ELEMENTS OF THE GERMAN FIRST ARMY
AT MONS
Commander: Generaloberst Alexander von Kluck

III CORPS *(General von Lochow)*: **Centre of the attack.**
Corps Cavalry: 3/Hussars
5th Division *(General Wichura)* At Baudour
9 Infantry Brigade
8/Grenadiers
48/Chasseurs
10 Infantry Brigade
12/Grenadiers
52/Chasseurs
5 Artillery Brigade
18/Regiment
54/Regiment

6th Division *(General von Roden)* At Ghlin
11/Infantry Brigade
20/Chasseurs
35/Fusiliers
12/Infantry Brigade
24/Chasseurs

General Alexander von Kluck with his staff.

64/Chasseurs
6 Artillery Brigade
3/Regiment
39/Regiment

IV CORPS *(General Sixt von Arnim)*: **Right of the attack.**
Corps Cavalry: 10th Hussars
7th Division *(General Riedel)* At Ville Pommeroeul
13/Infantry Brigade
26/Chasseurs
66/Chasseurs
14/Infantry Brigade
27/Chasseurs
165/Chasseurs
7/Artillery Brigade
4/Regiment
40/Regiment

8th Division *(General Hildebrand)* At Harchies
15/Infantry Brigade
36/Fusiliers
93/Chasseurs
16/Infantry Brigade
72/Chasseurs
153/Chasseurs
8/Artillery Brigade
74/Regiment
75/Regiment

IX CORPS *(General von Quast)*: **On the left.**
Corps Cavalry: 16th Dragoons
17th Division *(General von Bauer)* At le Roeulx
13/Infantry Brigade
75/Chasseurs
76/Chasseurs
34/Infantry Brigade
89/Grenadiers
90/Fusiliers
17/Artillery Brigade
24/Regiment
60/Regiment
18th Division *(General von Kluge)* At Casteau
35/Infantry Brigade

84/Chasseurs
86/Fusiliers
36/Infantry Brigade
31/Chasseurs
85/Chasseurs
18/Artillery Brigade
9/Regiment
45/Regiment

I (Cavalry) Corps *(General Freiherr von Richtofen)*
Guard (Cavalry) Division
5th (Cavalry) Division

II (Cavalry) Corps *(General von der Marwitz)*
2nd (Cavalry) Division
4th (Cavalry) Division
5th (Cavalry) Division

Overall there were about 135,000 German troops opposing the British forces at Mons and in the *Borinage*.

It is worth pointing out that, contrary to popular belief, a German division had just as many (or just as few) machine-guns as their British counterpart. A German infantry division at full strength numbered some 17,500 men; a British one just over 18,000. Cavalry divisions were much smaller; a German one had over five thousand men, which included at least one Jaeger (ie light infantry) battalion - which had a machine-gun company with six machine-guns.

German infantry at manoeuvres in 1909.

ELEMENTS OF THE BEF PRINCIPALLY INVOLVED IN THE BATTLE OF MONS AND THE ACTIONS IN THE BORINAGE

II Corps
General Sir HL Smith-Dorrien GCB, DSO

3RD DIVISION: *Major-General HIW Hamilton*

7 Brigade: *Brigadier-General FWN McCracken*
3/Worcesters
2/South Lancs
1/Wilts
2/Royal Irish Rifles

8 Brigade: *Brigadier-General BJC Doran*
2/Royal Scots
2/Royal Irish Regiment
4/Middx
1/Gordon Highlanders

9 Brigade: *Brigadier-General FC Shaw*
1/Northumberland Fusiliers
1/Lincs
4/Royal Fusiliers
1/Royal Scots Fusiliers

C Squadron 15/Hussars
XXIII, XL, XLII, XXX Brigades, RFA
48 Heavy Battery, RGA
56 and 57 Field Companies, RE

5TH DIVISION: *Major-General Sir C Fergusson*

13 Brigade: *Brigadier-General GJ Cuthbert*
1/KOSB
2/Duke of Wellington's
1/RWK
1/KOYLI

14 Brigade: *Brigadier-General SP Rolt*
2/Suffolk
1/East Surrey
1/DCLI
2/Manchester

15 Brigade: *Brigadier-General AEW Count Gleichen*
1/Norfolk
1/Cheshire
1/Bedfordshire
1/Dorsetshire

A Squadron, 19/Hussars
XV, XXVII, XXVIII, VIII Brigades, RFA
108 Heavy Brigade, RGA
17 and 59 Field Companies, RE

19 Brigade: *Major-General LG Drummond*
2/Royal Welsh Fusiliers
1/Cameronians
1/Middx
2/Argyll and Sutherland Highlanders

THE CAVALRY DIVISION: *Major-General EH Allenby*
1st (Cavalry) Brigade: *Brigadier-General CJ Briggs*

2/DG (Queen's Bays)
5/DG
11/Hussars

2nd (Cavalry) Brigade: *Brigadier-General H de B de Lisle*
4/DG
9/Lancers
18/Hussars

3rd (Cavalry Brigade: *Brigadier-General H de la P Gough*
4/Hussars
5/Lancers
16/Lancers

4th (Cavalry) Brigade: *Brigadier-General Hon CE Bingham*
Household Cavalry Regiment
6/DG (Carabiniers)
3/Hussars

5th (Cavalry) Brigade: *Brigadier-General Sir PW Chetwode*
2/Dragoons (Royal Scots Greys)
12/Lancers
20/Hussars

D, E, I, J, L Batteries, RHA

There were also cyclist companies, signal companies, RFC squadrons, Field Ambulances and members of the Army Service Corps.

Cavalry riding through a Belgian village during the early days of a war of movement. TAYLOR LIBRARY

THE LEGEND OF THE ANGEL OF MONS

Sunday, 23rd August 1914 had been a very hot and oppressive day and the British soldiers in their thick khaki uniforms were exhausted at the end of it. There had been little food and water and no matter how much they fired their rifles, the Germans had kept coming forward, seemingly disregarding the great piles of their dead and wounded and with an inexhaustible supply of reinforcements. Mons was on fire, as were other towns two or three miles to the south west, all wreathed in smoke, the sky red with the fires and the setting sun and spotted with small white clouds. As the British slowly and reluctantly withdrew in the face of the relentless pressure, preparing to continue the battle into the night, and with the obvious risk of being encircled by the 75th Regiment from Bremen on the right, it seemed that angels, in the form of archers, appeared in the sky bearing down over Mons onto the enemy. Suddenly the German attacks ceased and they withdrew in haste. The British defending battalions were then able to make their withdrawal into prepared defensive positions without hindrance and reorganised to continue the battle on the following day.

Variations on this vision, which included in the versions spread around St George, medieval cavalry, archers and angels continued to be recounted by numerous Old Contemptibles until the last one 'faded away'. The story can be traced back to the work of a journalist on the London Evening News, *Arthur Machen*, who wrote a fictional story at the time of Mons. Whatever the soldiers saw, it is likely to have been as a result of a combination of fatique and the conditions of the evening sky. Whatever, it was an extraordinary couple of days for the British Expeditionary Force, angels or not.

Chapter One

THE ROAD TO MONS

In the Province of Hainaut, and amongst the towns of the coal-mining district of the *Borinage*, lies the ancient town of Mons, which can trace its origins back to the eighth century. It sits on a low hill and at an historical crossroads. Eighteen miles to the north is the battlefield of Waterloo, where the decisive battle of the Napoleonic Wars was fought almost a hundred years earlier; nine miles to the south is Malplaquet. Here, in 1709, the Duke of Marlborough won an enormously bloody victory against the French who had come to relieve the siege of Mons. Marlborough eventually captured Mons in the October.

Mons retains, at its centre, much of its ancient charm; the town walls have been replaced by a ring road but the core area still has narrow, winding, cobbled streets, lined with ornate stone buildings. Nearby is the Headquarters of SHAPE [Supreme Headquarters Allied Powers Europe], the military nerve centre of NATO.

In 1914 the hill of Mons overlooked the junction of two canals: the Canal du Centre, coming from the south east connecting, through Charleroi, with the River Sambre and running round the northern edge of Mons to come down its western side where it was joined by the Canal du Condé. This went sixteen miles westwards to Condé itself and connected with the River Scheldt, coming from Valenciennes. Both canals were some sixty feet wide, six to nine feet deep and crossed by numerous bridges, both wooden and metal. There were eighteen bridges between the eastern side of Mons, at Obourg and St Aybert, three miles to the east of Condé. The wooden bridges carried pedestrians; others were metal and carried railway lines; the iron road bridges either could be raised or swung to allow the passage of large barges. At the towns large sheds had been built on the canal bank to hold goods and coal. The population of Mons was just under 30,000, whilst the smaller towns - large villages really - held about 5,000 people.

The train of events that had brought the BEF here is well known. The alliance system and unstable situation in the Balkans, coupled with political weakness to varying degrees in Austria-Hungary and Russia, had set the war off across Europe by 4 August 1914. Imperial connections (and a number of lesser alliances, such as that between

Great Britain and Japan) served to make the war global.

Behind the political situation in 1914 lay the simmering dispute between France and Wilhelmine (or Imperial) Germany, which was the consequence of the Franco-Prussian War of 1870-71 and the harsh terms that were imposed upon France on her defeat. This led to a situation whereby the military planners of both countries set about working out how to deal with the military potential of the other. Indeed von Moltke the Elder and his General Staff seriously considered a war of attrition against

Von Moltke the Elder.

The Schlieffen Plan

HOLLAND

Ostend

Ypres

Brussels

Liege Aachen

Scheldt

Lille

Intended position of German Forces by 23rd August 1914

Arras

Somme

Intended position of German Forces by 1st September 1914

Amiens

Aisne

Metz

Verdun

Paris

Strasbourg

F R A N C E

Marne

Meuse

COUNT ALFRED VON SCHLIEFFEN

France - and lamented the fact that the war of 1870 had been ended before significant fatalities could be inflicted on her - so that France would not pose a threat to the Reich for the foreseeable future.

France's isolation was dramatically reversed when she signed a defensive pact with Russia, and so the Germans had to face the prospect of a war on two fronts. From this situation emerged the Schlieffen Plan, which aimed at removing the French from any war as soon as possible - ie in about forty days, so that the German army could then turn to the Russian army, which would be much slower to

KAISER WILHELM II   GENERAL HELMUTH VON MOLTKE   GENERAL ALEXANDER VON KLUCK

French infantry going forward. TAYLOR LIBRARY

mobilise. The rebuilt French army, permeated with the offensive spirit, adopted Plan XVII, which essentially involved a mass attack along her western borders with Germany.

The British had held aloof from European entanglements until she found herself isolated at the time of the Boer War; this, combined with the threat from Wilhelm II's policy of building up the Imperial Navy, resulted in the creation of a loose alliance (the Entente Cordiale) with France. A treaty also existed with Belgium, for whose territorial integrity the British government (along with other European powers) stood as guarantor by the Treaty of London in 1839, which acknowledged the de facto creation of the country in 1830. It was not just a policy of altruism - a defence of the rights of small countries - that motivated the British. It was in her national economic interests to ensure that the coastline (and thus the rivers and waterways) offering access to the central European markets was not controlled by a great power and this had been a cornerstone of English and then British foreign policy for hundreds of years.

It was agreed that a British force, should war be declared, to be known as the British Expeditionary Force, would take its place on the French left and these troops would concentrate at Maubeuge (sometimes spelt in books as Mauberge). Kitchener, the new Secretary of State for War, was not totally convinced of the soundness of this plan, and was for concentrating his troops at Amiens, but he was persuaded by others to allow the original proposal (to a large extent compiled by Henry Wilson) to go ahead.

The war had been under way for some three weeks by the time the British arrived at Mons. The mobilisation of the British troops (note - some sixty percent of which were Reservists) had proceeded smoothly and the embarkation to France had been a model of

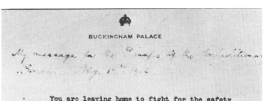

BUCKINGHAM PALACE

My message to the Troops of the Expedition Force, May. 12th 1914

You are leaving home to fight for the safety and honour of my Empire.

Belgium, whose country we are pledged to defend, has been attacked and France is about to be invaded by the same powerful foe.

I have implicit confidence in you my soldiers. Duty is your watchword, and I know your duty will be nobly done.

I shall follow your every movement with deepest interest and mark with eager satisfaction your daily progress, indeed your welfare will never be absent from my thoughts.

I pray God to bless you and guard you and bring you back victorious.

George V visiting his troops.

Cossacks camp over the border in East Prussia. The Russians launched an attack sooner than the Germans expected. TAYLOR LIBRARY

General Helmuth von Moltke.

military efficiency. Meanwhile, on the continent, things had not gone as planned for either side. The new German Chief of the General Staff, another von Moltke, had seriously weakened the original Schlieffen Plan, in many ways for good reason. Thus he almost certainly did not have the volume of troops that would be required for this daring plan to be executed successfully. The French attacks under Plan XVII went calamitously wrong, and the French casualties for 1914 were horrendous - some 35% of all their casualties in the war. The Russians, on the other hand, were able to launch a massive attack into East Prussia far earlier than anticipated; which in turn led to the (possibly fatal) decision to move two German Army Corps to the Eastern Front. By the time that they arrived there Tannenberg had been fought and the crisis was over; whilst they missed the crisis on the northern flank.

Relations between Field-Marshal French (commanding the BEF) and his neighbouring French Army commander (Lanrezac, commanding the Fifth) got off to a terrible start, largely the fault of Lanrezac, a military genius in many respects, but a flawed Army Commander. The situation was resolved to a great degree by the intervention of that

26

Field-Marshal French.

General Joffre.

Lanrezac.

significantly underrated commander, Joffre, who came up with a plan to foil the Germans, assisted as he was by the weakness of von Moltke, his opposite number. Eventually Joffre despaired of Lanrezac, even though he was one of his protegés, and he was sacked before the Battle of the Marne, a fortnight or so after Mons.

When the British arrived at Mons in that hot August the intention was to participate in an advance; they were soon to be disabused of such a thought.[1]

A new element in this war lay in airpower; in 1914 it was at its infancy - barely out of the maternity ward. The Royal Flying Corps went to war with four squadrons (Numbers 2, 3, 4 and 5), an Aircraft Park and a Headquarters under the overall command of Brigadier-General Sir David Henderson. [As a point of interest, the Royal Naval Air Service was formally established on 1 June 1914.]

The primary task of the RFC was to act as reconnaissance - part of the eyes of the army; and this function it carried out, generally, admirably, in those fraught early months of the Great War. This arm suffered some of the earliest casualties; one is struck by the lonely grave of Corporal F Geard, flying in a BE 8, who was killed in a crash over Peronne on 18 August 1914. He is buried in a grave isolated from other British troops in the Communal Cemetery in that town; just over the hedge is the large British Communal Cemetery Extension.

On 16 August the Headquarters of the RFC moved from Amiens to Maubeuge. It took the army a few days to catch up with them. An officer commented

We were rather sorry that they had come, because up till that moment we had only been fired on by the French whenever we flew. Now we were fired on by the French and the English. ...To this day I can remember the roar of musketry that greeted two of our machines as they left the aerodrome and crossed the main Maubeuge - Mons road, along which a British column was proceeding.

27

Germans surround the shattered remnants of an allied aircraft.

To safeguard against this happening again, everyone worked through the night to decorate the underside of the lower planes of all the machines with a Union Jack in the shape of a shield.

The first aerial reconnaissance by the RFC took place on 19 August; on 22 August Sergeant-Major Jillings, an observer in No. 2 Squadron, was wounded in the leg by a rifle bullet whilst flying over Maffle, south east of Ath. On the same day the first British aircraft lost to enemy fire came down. This was an Avro of No. 5 Squadron, manned by Lieutenants V Waterfall (pilot) and CGG Bayly (observer). At this stage all pilots were seconded from regiments within the army; Waterfall was in the East Yorks and Bayly was a sapper. The plane was shot down, sometime around midday, by rifle fire, quite likely by men of Walter Bloem's B Company, 12th Regiment of the Brandenburg Grenadiers.

> *Suddenly an aeroplane appeared overhead. This time there was no doubt about it: the red, white and blue rings under the wings could be seen with the naked eye. I told off two groups to fire at it, and soon everyone seemed to be firing at it. It turned back as if to return southward but too late; its nose turned down, it made several corkscrew turns, and then fell like a stone a mile or so away. Murmurs of satisfaction all round. A little later three Hussars came past and shouted out that they had found the aeroplane in a field further on. 'What about the pilot and observer', I asked. 'Both in bits, sir.'*

The plane came down to earth at the village of Marq, a mile or so away;

and a Belgian peasant managed to spirit away the observer's report before the Germans arrived. This made its way, finally, to the War Office after hostilities had ended. The Germans buried the officers in the Louviau family's plot in the cemetery of Labliau at Marcq; after the war (in 1924) their remains were translated to Tournai Communal Cemetery Allied Extension. They were the first British officers to be killed in action in the First World War.

1. An excellent and highly readable account of the British campaign up to the Battle of the Marne is John Terraine's *Mons*, first published in 1960 but reprinted recently.

Preparation for the Battle

The two corps of Field-Marshal Sir John French's BEF began to arrive in the coal-mining area south of Mons on 22 August. Lieutenant-General Sir Douglas Haig, commanding I Corps, had two divisions, the 1st (Major-General SH Lomax) and the 2nd (Major-General CC Munro). II Corps should have been commanded by Lieutenant-General Sir JM Grierson, a brilliant soldier, polyglot (speaking both French and German fluently) and probably the man who knew the German army better than anyone else (he had been Military Attaché in Berlin) and the most bemedalled man in the army. Unfortunately he died of a heart attack on 17 August - a victim of his exuberant, *bon viveur* lifestyle - on the train bringing him to his Headquarters. French wanted to replace him with Plumer, but Kitchener decided that it should be Lieutenant-General Sir Horace Smith-Dorrien. A capable soldier, commissioned into the line infantry, this was to be a fateful decision, not so much because of Smith-Dorrien's competence, but because he had been selected over French's head; friction between him and GHQ was to characterise his time with the BEF. In his Corps were two divisions: the 3rd (Major-General HIW Hamilton) and the 5th (Major-General Sir C Fergusson). In addition to these infantry divisions was the 'super-heavy' Cavalry Division (with four brigades), commanded by Major-General EH Allenby (a fifth brigade, under Brigadier-General Chetwode, was to operate independently); and also over seventy batteries of artillery and a number of RE Field Companies, along with various other support units, such as Field Ambulances.

Lieutenant-General Sir Horace Smith-Dorrien

29

Although mentioned in all the books, it still seems remarkable to me how few people have commented on the composition of this so-called Regular force of troops that arrived in those early days in France and Belgium. The majority of them had not been in uniform at all on the day war broke out. Called to the Colours were huge numbers of reservists - men who had done their time in the army and were then paid a retainer to maintain their commitment after they had left. A good example of such a man is Frank Richards, whose account of his military service in *Old Soldier Sahib* and *Old Soldiers Never Die* is probably the classic account of military service in the ranks through the Edwardian era and in the Great War. The War Establishment of a battalion in 1914 (other ranks) was 977. In the 5th Division, for example, 2/KOSB had no less than 700 reservists, 1/Dorset 595, 1/RWKents 590, 1/DCLI 650 and 1/Cheshire 555. In the 3rd Division 4/RFusiliers had 735 (!), 1/Lincoln 545, 2/RScots 500, 1/Gordon 530 and 1/Northumberland Fusiliers 640.

Rerservists preparing to join their regiment, August 1914.

LATEST ORDERS
OF THE
KAISER
TO HIS GENERALS.

It is my Royal and Imperial command that you concentrate your energies, for the immediate present, upon one single purpose, and that is that you address all your skill and all the valour of my **SOLDIERS to EXTERMINATE first, the treacherous English,** walk over General French's **contemptible little Army.**

Headquarters Aix la Chapelle, August 19th, 1914

What answer must Britons give ?

GOD SAVE THE KING.

B. B. MASON, Printer to Freattrope School, Chester

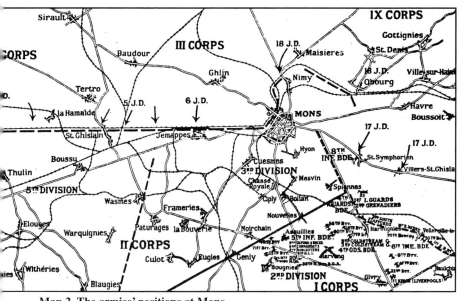

Map 2. The armies' positions at Mons.

These reservists had to be kitted out, collect new weapons, break in new boots (very hard work; the boots were hobnailed, and the pavé roads on the continent, with their concave surface, were torture) and be spread amongst the battalion's companies. They then had to be got to the station and to their embarkation ports. All went extraordinarily well.

The BEF was to fight to the left of General Lanrezac's Fifth Army, joining with it (so it was thought) in an advance to the north east, and so the BEF had brought all its equipment with them, anticipating a long march forward. Haig's I Corps wheeled to the right, with its right flank (1st Division) at the village of Grand Reng, nine miles south of Mons on the road to Beaumont and close to the French Fifth Army. The 2nd Division was on the left, almost in a straight line to the north. It was the intention of Smith-Dorrien's II Corps to extend that line through and

British infantry marching into Belgium.

31

beyond Mons, forming an attacking front to the north east, with the 3rd Division on the right at and below Mons and the 5th Division over the Condé Canal on the left flank. The Canal du Centre came in from the east and then ran around Mons, joining up with the Condé Canal to the south west. Both canals had numerous bridges (most made of iron) and bridged locks along their length, and their sixty feet width provided a considerable obstacle. The country immediately below the Condé Canal and Mons was a hilly coal-mining area, with at least a dozen industrial villages in a six mile wide strip. These stood close together and were densely populated, with narrow and winding streets, many railway lines and smoking slag heaps (many of these were burning internally) a number of which were as much as two hundred feet high, and with

Belgian refugees flee before the German army.

Belgian troops with dog teams pulling machine guns. The Belgian army was small and not well equipped and no match for the invaders.

cobbled roads between them. The scene would not be unfamiliar with those who knew the towns of east Lancashire and west Yorkshire, though the surrounding countryside was significantly flatter. The constricted ground was not a natural battle site, but then there was no intention of fighting a battle there when the soldiers arrived to be greeted by wildly enthusiastic and generous Belgians. These people had already seen the victims of war, hundreds and hundreds of refugees along with their pathetic collection of possessions, fleeing from the German atrocities to the east. Most notable amongst these was the torching of Louvain (Leuven) which started on 22 August and went on for five days. A German officer told an American diplomat who visited the town on 28 August,

> *We shall wipe it out, not one stone will stand upon another!*
> *Not one, I tell you. We will teach them to respect Germany. For*
> *generations people will come here to see what we have done!*

At Seilles fifty villagers were shot; at a small mining town (Tamines), irritated by the defence put up by the French army, soldiers shot 384 men (ranging from the ages of 13 to 84) near the church (22 August) whilst a horrendous massacre took place at Dinant on 23 August when 612 people, including a baby in arms (only three weeks old) and its mother were executed as a reprisal for an alleged attack by Belgian

As the German army swarmed through Belgium, reports of atrocities were widespread among the fleeing refugees.

civilians on German soldiers who were repairing a bridge.[1] Doubtless the atrocities were exaggerated for the benefit of propaganda, but there were some quite atrocious and indefensible acts carried out by elements of the German army in the early months of the war. In some senses one wonders why we should be surprised; the level of unacceptable acts in the Napoleonic Wars - for example in the Peninsula campaign - was very high, as was the case for other conflicts in the nineteenth century. The twentieth century has progressed with every significant conflict bringing further examples of utter contempt for the well-being of innocents

In the midst of this distress, newly arrived, was the annual departure for the summer holidays. It was felt that the German invasion would be stopped, held up by the great fortresses to the east and thrown back by the indomitable French and now aided by the brave British. Thus the railway station had recently been filled with throngs of locals heading off for their summer break.

Germans in the Belgian town of Bruges in August 1914.

The arrival of the BEF in Mons

The British began arriving on 22 August. Part of Brigadier-General Doran's 8 Brigade (3rd Division) entered Mons itself and then moved on, 4/Middx (Middlesex) on the right, on the west bank of the Canal du Centre, whilst the other three battalions were close behind. 4/RF (Royal Fusiliers), of Brigadier-General Shaw's 9 Brigade went through the town to the village of Nimy, which lay a mile to the north but was situated on the south bank of the Canal du Centre as it curved around to the south west. The three other battalions of the Brigade took up position to the west and south of the Condé Canal, which put them to the left rear of the Fusiliers.

Behind both brigades was Brigadier-General McCracken's 7 Brigade; the 3rd Division was ready to move forward.

Major-General Fergusson's 5th Division was spread out to the left of the 3rd, along the south bank of the remarkably straight Condé Canal. On the right was Brigadier-General Cuthbert's 13 Brigade; Brigadier-General Count von Gleichen's 15 Brigade in reserve and Brigadier-General Rolt's 14th on the left, at its extremity some nine miles from Mons. By the evening the troops had all found billets in factories, schools and houses; and although they only anticipated staying until the following day, they dug in, helped by enthusiastic young Belgians. Similar scenes were taking place on I Corps front, off

A Company, 4th Royal Fusiliers, resting in the square at Mons on 22 August 1914. They were to move up to the canal bank at Nimy.

to the right. Intermingled amongst the infantry corps were elements of Allenby's Cavalry Division, which had already got reconnaissance patrols on the far side of the canals. They were checking the way for the next move, which was to be an advance by II Corps to the north.

The 72 batteries of artillery had also been busily engaged in finding suitable positions, far from easy in the crowded country with its numerous mining villages. The majority had to be content with sites too far away from the canals to be effective, but a few did manage to get well forward. XL Brigade RFA managed to establish itself on the dominating hill a mile from Mons; 107 Field Battery established itself between the town and Nimy.

It was in the 5th Division area that there were the greatest problems. Major CS Holland, commanding 120 Field Battery of XXVII Brigade, managed to bring his four 18 pounders onto the canal towpath at Saint Ghislain.

Some of the Forward Observation Officers (FOO) thought they had found ideal places from which to view the enemy - when and if they came - from the top of the slag heaps. On the other hand, they were quick to discover the drawbacks: they were hot and smoking, with a thin crust that could break and through which a man could fall. Men from the coal mining areas were all too aware of this danger. Still, they were not going to be there for long.

The Royal Engineers were busy as well, examining the bridges to look at their load bearing capabilities and also how they might be destroyed if necessary. The CRE (Commander, Royal Engineers) of the two corps also discussed the recruiting of gangs of civilians to dig defences - in the light of what was soon to come they would be useful.

Early on the morning of 22 August Brigadier-General de Lisle's 2

Major C.S. Holland commanding 120 Field Battery of XXVII Brigade RFA, leading his men to the canal at St Ghislain.

Market place in Saint Ghislain.

(Cavalry) Brigade had been out covering the approaches from Brussels, well to the front of the main bulk of the army. Major Tom Bridges (eventually to become a major-general), commanding C Squadron of 4/(Royal Irish) Dragoon Guards, had his men in a wood just over the bridges at Nimy, about two miles up the road to Brussels [1]. This was in the village of Casteau, about four miles from Soignies, further up on the road to Brussels. At about 7am he saw four German cavalrymen trotting towards him. He would find out later that they were of the 4/Cuirassiers (Lancers) of the 9th (Cavalry) Division. They must have suspected something and began to turn back towards Soignies. Captain Hornby, followed by his Troop, gave chase along the pavéd road, alongside which a tram track ran. Corporal Thomas after a few moments dismounted and fired his rifle, hitting one of them [2]. The pursuit [3] continued for about a mile until, at a minor crossroads

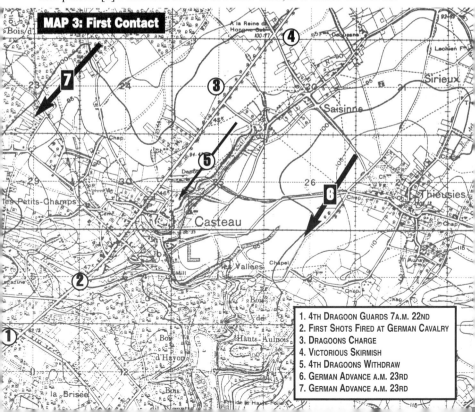

MAP 3: First Contact

1. 4TH DRAGOON GUARDS 7A.M. 22ND
2. FIRST SHOTS FIRED AT GERMAN CAVALRY
3. DRAGOONS CHARGE
4. VICTORIOUS SKIRMISH
5. 4TH DRAGOONS WITHDRAW
6. GERMAN ADVANCE A.M. 23RD
7. GERMAN ADVANCE A.M. 23RD

known as the Queen of Hungary [4], the enemy received reinforcements and a hand to hand battle of the thirty or forty cavalrymen took place. Some of the Cuirassiers were killed and a number captured - the Germans broke off the engagement and galloped off down the road.

Thomas was a regular soldier who had joined the army when he was fourteen; it is claimed that he was the first man to fire a shot in anger in the British army in the war. Hornby was awarded the DSO for his part in the skirmish. His men brought back a number of lances, helmets and other trophies; more importantly they had discovered the fact that the German cavalry were not up to their standard and that more significant numbers of Germans must be close by.

The German cavalry of the IIIrd and IXth Corps were engaged in scouting in front of the main bodies of their infantry, blissfully unaware of where the British actually were - an ignorance shared by their Army commander, von Kluck. This ignorance, and his concern about the vulnerability of his right flank, was to play an important part in the development of the Battle of Mons. At one stage he was convinced that large numbers of British troops were detraining at Tournai, well to the west, and this was to hold up the advance of vital elements of his army for several hours before it was ascertained that these troops were in fact only a brigade of French Territorials.

A Squadron of 19/Hussars, commanded by Major Parsons, accompanied by Captain JC Burnett and his 5th Cyclist Company (5th Division), were patrolling five miles north of the Condé Canal in the wooded area north of the village of Hautrage in front of 14 Brigade, when they met up with German cavalry. The engagement between the two small forces went on for most of the day. The Hussars were reluctant to retire as their Short Magazine Lee Enfield, with its long range, was causing so much damage; but the Cuirassiers received reinforcements. The Hussars' efforts to prevent the enemy reaching the outposts of 1/DCLI (Duke of Cornwall's Light Infantry), who only arrived at the canal in the afternoon, were gradually being overcome. They retired to Pommeroeul and then Le Petit Crepin; with the assistance of a troop of Life Guards from 4 (Cavalry) Brigade they came back over the canal.

Over on the right flank, in front of 4/Middx at the Canal du Centre, German cavalry were active in the late afternoon. They exchanged rifle fire with D Company from over the canal at Obourg. There were no casualties, but the Battalion was the first infantry to fire at the Germans in the Great War.

German cavalry (Lancers) watering their horses.

Very early on Saturday morning, 22 August, Field-Marshal Sir John French set out by car from his Headquarters at Le Cateau to visit General Charles Lanrezac, commanding the French Fifth Army, the left of the French army, at his Headquarters near Phillipeville some sixty miles away. Utterly fortuitously he came across Lieutenant Edward Spears, who was the liaison officer between the two Armies. Spears informed French that the Germans had broken through on the River Sambre, the French Xth Corps was falling back, the German First Army was extending out to the west and that the French Fifth Army was not advancing. French returned to Le Cateau, seeing little point in going to Lanrezac's Headquarters, especially as the latter was away examining advanced posts. A more serious reason was that the two did not get on at all well, largely a consequence of Lanrezac's singularly off-hand and rather insulting manner.

Spears returned to Fifth Army Headquarters to learn further disquieting news. The German XIIth (Saxon) Corps was advancing so vigorously that it posed the threat of cutting off Lanrezac's Army; he decided that he must continue his retreat. This would expose the British army's right flank, creating a gap of some nine miles between Haig's I Corps and the Fifth Army. Spears immediately set off along the congested roads, filled with refugees and French military all heading westwards. He reported to French who had also heard from one of Lanrezac's staff officers that his Army would not be advancing and was, in fact, contemplating withdrawal. However, he requested that the

BEF attack as originally planned. French realised the impossibility of this request but bravely offered to hold a line at Mons and along the Condé Canal for twenty-four hours, well aware of the consequences if Lanrezac's front collapsed.

General Sir Horace Smith-Dorrien had only take over command of his Corps at 4pm on 21 August at Bavai (also spelt Bavay). He now had to contemplate how to deal with the situation. Although continuing with preparations for an advance, he also set about making preparations, on his own initiative, for a battle along the Condé Canal. He considered that the canal would do fine as an initial barrier but would be difficult to hold against a large force. He instructed his divisional commanders, therefore, on 22 August, to begin preparing a second line of defence on a line amongst the hill top villages south of the canal from Paturages, five miles south west of Mons and then stretching eastwards through Frameries and Ciply. Smith-Dorrien had shown great prescience.

The Headquarters of II Corps was in the small, white Chateau de la Haie, in the hamlet of Sars-la-Bruyere, seven miles south of Mons, off the main road and without any telephone communication; it was about half way to Bavai, where French had his Advanced Headquarters. It was not a good choice of location, difficult to find in the dark and to communicate with at any time, and this was to cause Smith-Dorrien problems in due course.

At 5am on Sunday 23 August French drove there to hold a meeting with his two Corps commanders and Allenby, who had already brought

his Division back over the canal in the face of heavy German pressure. The Field-Marshal's orders were ambivalent: because of doubts about the intentions of the French they must stay where they were, prepared for any kind of move. Aircraft patrols had already started that morning and reports were awaited on the results of their reconnaissance. The BEF's Chief of Staff, Lieutenant-General Sir Archibald Murray, was to remain at II Corps Headquarters, to react to whatever situation arose whilst French set off to Valenciennes. He wanted to find out what the French were doing to secure the allies left flank and to see Brigadier-General Drummond, commanding the hastily formed (on 22 August) 19 Brigade. Its composite battalions had formed the Lines of Communication Defence troops. Drummond was to be warned that he might be needed to support the left flank, and that he was to come under Allenby's command, whose Headquarters were in Quievrain.

Whilst this conference was taking place the battalions of the 3rd and 5th Divisions were prepared for an attack. The attack would be made by three German corps, from right to left the IXth, IIIrd and IVth of Kluck's First Army. To his left was the Second Army, commanded by von Bülow; at this stage in the campaign, von Kluck answered to von Bülow, which provided potential for considerable friction. Von Bülow's Army lay directly in front of Lieutenant-General Haig's I Corps which would not be attacked: there was concern about Lanrezac's Fifth Army and it would also hold Haig in position so that von Kluck's right hook could 'put him in the bag'. The German First Army would fall like a scythe on the British, pivoting somewhere from the north of Charleroi.

Von Kluck was not happy with the deviation from the Schlieffen

General Ulrich von Bülow.

Plan, feeling that he should be kept well out to the west and leaving the BEF to von Bülow and the Third (Saxon) Army. But von Kluck could only be angry and frustrated, as von Bülow controlled all three armies. The decision by the Germans would be a fateful one; whilst the BEF performed outstandingly in the battle to come.

Two other factors, with origins buried in the past, were to help the defenders. The German army adopted a policy of attacking en masse - just as the French did - advancing shoulder to shoulder in solid blocks of companies and carrying their rifles at the trail; on approaching the enemy they would fire from the hip, regardless of finding a target or taking aim. This would have an overwhelming and terrifying effect on the enemy whilst boosting their own courage. It had worked thus far (though there had been some local difficulty at Liège). The second factor was, at least in part, the consequence of Treasury miserliness over the matter of machine-guns. Haig had been Director of Military Training when, in 1908, it was laid down that the infantry should be able to fire fifteen aimed rounds a minute in order to qualify for an extra payment. This would be stopped if a man did not maintain that standard. Many were able to fire even more quickly. This skill at arms was to be crucial. The army was also trained to march long distances - fifteen miles in full kit in what became known as 'Kitchener's Test'. This, too, was to be an important attribute over the next momentous three weeks or so.

1. See, for example, Martin Gilbert, *First World War* (London: Weidenfeld and Nicolson 1994) pp 42-43

Rows of German dead cut down by rifle fire as they attacked en masse.
TAYLOR LIBRARY

Chapter Two

SUNDAY 23rd AUGUST: THE MORNING

6am - 8am: The Scythe Starts to Swing

The 3rd Division.

During the evening of the 22nd Lieutenant-Colonel Hull had placed his 4/Middx in the positions where they would begin the battle the following day. His task was to hold the south bank of the Canal du Centre, facing Obourg on the hill in front of him, on the far side of the sixty-foot wide canal. There were three bridges that concerned him: on his extreme right flank at Lock No. 4; the road bridge to Obourg some five hundred yards towards his centre; and Lock No. 5, two thousand yards to the left of that [11]. There was a further bridge, a couple of thousand yards to the north west of Lock No. 5, which was at the junction of his left flank and 4/RF.

Immediately to the right of the Obourg road bridge was the railway station [14], on the south bank. D Company, commanded by Captain HEL Glass, would cover both this bridge and that at Lock No. 4 [13] - and for a thousand yards to the north west of the bridge, an impossibly long front. Lieutenant William Allinson was in command at the station, which had been extensively strengthened by the defenders.

To the left of D Company was B Company [10], under the command of Major WHC Davy, who was in touch with Captain Ashburner's C

Private A. F. Carter. 'D' Coy 4th Middlesex.

Lock 4, guarded by Captain Glass's D Company.

Company (4/RF) at the Bridge des Bragnons [6].

In reserve, C Company of 4/Middx (Captain Oliver) was a thousand yards behind D, in front of a large hospital and convent, and A Company (Major WH Abell) was on its left [9]. Lieutenant LF Sloane-Stanley, the machine-gun officer, had his two guns between them at the

MAP 4: The Battle for the Canal Du Centre

1. PTE. GODLEY MACHINE GUN
2. LT DEASE KILLED
3. 'B' COMPANY CAPT. CAREY
4. CAPT. FORSTER'S BRIDGE SWUNG BACK
5. 'C' COY 4TH RYL FUS.
6. LT. HOLT R.E. KILLED. BRIDGE INTACT
7. 'D' COMPANY 4TH RYL FUS.
8. HOSTAGES IN GERMAN ADVANCE
9. 'A' COMPANY 4TH MIDDLESEX
10. 'B' COMPANY 4TH MIDDLESEX
11. LOCK BRIDGE NOT BLOWN
12. GERMAN BATTERY
13. 'D' COMPANY 4TH MIDDLESEX
14. RAILWAY STATION

junction of two small roads, looking towards the woods sloping down to the south bank of the canal. Battalion Headquarters was first put into a quarry to the left of the large cemetery which was on the side of a small hill, but then moved 500 yards north west of the cemetery into the cellars of a small house on the road to Nimy.

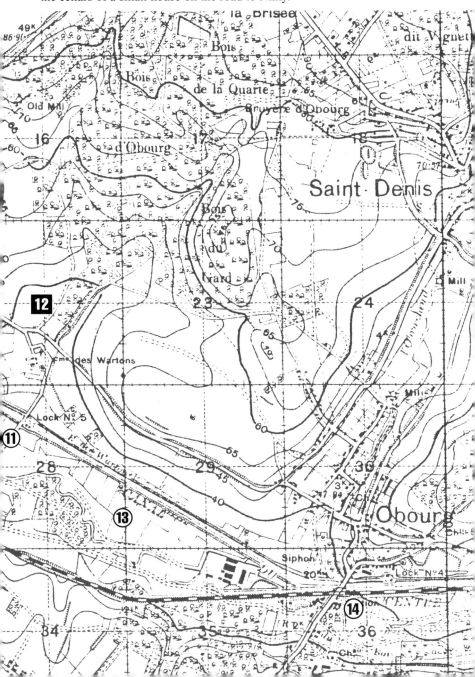

Lock No. 5.

The long stretch of the Canal from Lock No. 5 today, looking towards Nimy. The 4th Middlesex were dug in on the left bank.

Road bridge at Obourg and the Railway Station.

Lt Holt's Bridge on The Rue Des Bragnons. The lifting gear is on the Maisieres side.

At dawn a mist hung over the canal and light rain was falling. Shelling of the Battalion's positions had not yet started, but at 8am the first shots of the battle came across the canal, fired at D Company positions at the station by the German 31st Infantry Regiment. They hit Private J Parr, whom many consider to be the first infantryman to be killed in the Great War. Lieutenant-Colonel Hull had, earlier that morning, told his officers that there would be no advance over the canal, saying, 'This, gentlemen, is where we will stand and fight!'.

Lieutenant-Colonel NR McMahon, commanding 4/RF, was at Nimy, on the right flank of 9 Brigade. He commanded 26 officers and 983 other ranks, of whom 734 were called up reservists. Opposite his Battalion were troops of the German IXth Corps, two regiments (ie six battalions) of the 18th Division whose attack line stretched eastwards along the Canal du Centre to D Company's (4/Middx) position. Thus there were approximately six thousand Germans against two thousand, separated by the width of the canal. The Fusiliers had six bridges to defend: from the right there was the 'joint' one held with the Middlesex [6]; the road bridge at Nimy [4] and the railway bridge two hundred yards to its left [2]; the bridge at Lock No. 6 [7], a thousand yards further left beyond the canal bend; and the Ghlin road and adjacent railway bridges five hundred yards further along the canal, the western entry to Mons.

Brig-General N. R. McMahon, D.S.O., who commanded the 4th Royal Fusiliers from Mons to Ypres.

Captain Forester held the road bridge at Nimy, which had been swung back, with two platoons whilst two other platoons were entrenched at the railway bridge and the canal bank to its left. Lieutenant Maurice James Dease, the machine-gun officer, had placed his two guns at the railway bridge [1], one at each side, in small emplacements of sandbags built onto the stone buttresses, with fields of fire across the canal. B Company was at Nimy Railway Station with Battalion Headquarters. D Company was at Lock No. 6 and the road and rail bridges on the Ghlin road. Part of the Company was on the western side of the canal, for about a thousand yards, on flat land dominated by a large wood. A Company, under Captain Cole, was in

Swing Bridge at Nimy, looking towards Mons.

reserve on the northern edge of Mons. In fact, only two companies, C and D, were on the defensive against the six German battalions. Captain Byng of D Company had blocked the railway bridge with large drums of cable, wheeling them into position and turning them on their side, thereby forming a barricade.

Four 18 pdrs of 107 Battery of XXIII Brigade RFA had found positions close to the station at Mons from where they could support the two companies. At 8am all was still almost quiet, although movement could be heard in the woods on the other side of the canal.

To the left of the Royal Fusiliers was 1/RSF (Royal Scots Fusiliers), who had been brought by their commanding officer, Lieutenant-Colonel Douglas Smith, to the eastern end of the Condé Canal on the 22nd. He marched them over the bridge at Jemappes, along the pavéd road across the flat, marshy land to Ghlin, two miles away. This was his allotted position, on the left of the Londoners, for the Corps advance.

However, long before nightfall, he was withdrawn to take up positions on a two thousand yard length of the canal, from Loch No. 1 on the right to the iron lifting bridge, Pont Richebe, at Jemappes on the Battalion's left flank. Several hundred yards east of that bridge was Lock No. 2, also bridged and 700 hundred yards again to the east was

Railway Bridge at Nimy in 1914.

British Infantry preparing to meet the enemy with a blast of fire. For a number of years the infantry had been trained to fire 15 aimed rounds a minute – much greater than their continental rivals

a lifting road bridge leading from Jemappes to Ghlin. Lieutenant-Colonel Smith placed outposts over the canal near to the bridges. Captain Rose (B Company) and Captain Innes (C Company) shared the defence of the long length of canal on the right of the railway station, close to the southern bank. Captain Tullis (D Company) held the left flank at the Pont Richebe whilst Battalion Headquarters was in the village behind the church, where the reserve company, A, was also situated. The whole of the Battalion's position was amongst a small, heavily built-up area on the edge of the coal mining district.

As early as 6am, just north of the bridge to Ghlin, the quietness of the morning was broken by B Company when its outpost was approached by a German cavalry patrol coming out of the mist. At 500 yards the Scots' machine-gun hit the patrol, killing one and forcing the others to scatter. The fallen trooper was identified as being part of IXth Corps.

For the time being all was quiet, and soon the church bells sounded out. Many of the villagers (there was a population of about 6,000) appeared on the streets, either to go to mass or, so it seemed to the bemused soldiers, going to the station to board the holiday train that was already waiting there, to take them to their destination via Mons. They seemed quite oblivious to the imminence of fighting on their doorstep.

1/NF (Northumberland Fusiliers) were under the command of Lieutenant-Colonel HS Ainslie. When they came close to the mining area near to Frameries, B and C Companies, under the Battalion's Second in Command, Major C Yatman, were detached and marched to the left and became the left flank troops of both the Brigade and the 3rd Division. They were positioned near Quaregnon, tasked with defending the lifting bridge at Mariette, a thousand yards to the left of1/RSF. The remainder of the Battalion went into Cuesmes, some mile and a half south of Mons and a similar distance from the Condé Canal and Jemappes. Billets were found for Battalion Headquarters in the Curé's house on the village square. Just as in Jemappes, a remarkable holiday atmosphere prevailed.

Major Yatman's orders that evening had been to hold on as long as possible, so he knew that there would be no advance on the Sunday. The evening and night of the 22nd were spent in preparing the defence of the bridge, by A Company, and the canal bank to the right by C Company. The situation was somewhat complicated, for in reality there were two canals and therefore two bridges. The first was a short, twenty foot long bridge, that spanned the first narrow, but very deep, drainage canal and connected the south bank to the forty foot wide central tow path. Then came the lifting bridge (which lifted towards the far bank) over the sixty feet wide Condé Canal. On the north bank was the bridge keeper's house; Sergeant Panter with twelve men turned that

British Field Gunners. Effective guns, but too few in number and ammunition. They were also hampered by having problems in finding good fire postions.

into a small fort by loopholing the walls. The railway ran alongside the north bank, so the level crossing gates were jammed and a barbed wire barricade erected which connected the houses. A further obstacle was made on that side of the canal with some iron railings, virtually enclosing the Sergeant and his party, but leaving a small gap through which they could make their escape. The buildings on the central bank were demolished, but the ruins manned to provide support for the outpost beyond; whilst the main defence took up position in loopholed houses lining the south bank.

The men were still working on the defences when Major Yatman was summoned at about 7am to the station in Quaregnon. There he spoke on the telephone to a man who spoke in perfect English; he was a British agent who told him that he was near the Bois de Badour, some four miles north of the canal, and that various German units were near him, which he identified. Suddenly the voice fell silent and Yatman never did discover either who the brave man was or his fate.

The 5th Division

The first battalion of Sir Charles Fergusson's Division to arrive at the Condé Canal on the 22nd was 1/RWK (Queen's Own Royal West Kents). Lieutenant-Colonel A Martyn's Battalion was to defend the three bridges at Saint Ghislain, 3,000 yards west of Quaregnon. There was a fixed iron railway bridge on the right, not quite 2,000 yards west of the Northumberland's bridge at Mariette; a wooden one at Lock No. 3, barely a hundred yards to the left of the railway; and another lifting road bridge a thousand yards to the west of that. The Battalion's front was about 3,000 yards. D Company (Captain RGM Tulloch) would hold the railway bridge whilst C Company (Major P Hastings) was to guard the two to the left of it. These two forward companies were commanded by Major PM Buckle, the Second in Command. A and B Companies were in reserve in Hornu, two miles south.

The companies at the canal set about turning the buildings close to the canal into strong points, loopholing walls, erecting barbed wire barricades and digging trenches on the far bank. C Company had moved across because buildings on the north side obstructed their view beyond. The situation for the defenders was not helped by the ground round about consisting mainly of water meadows, useless for artillery.

Reports of the enemy by the Divisional Cyclists on the 22nd after their skirmish led to a decision to send men northwards to make contact with the enemy. At 5.30am A Company (Captain GD Lister) received instructions to follow a cavalry patrol of 19/Hussars and the

Cyclists over the canal and make a reconnaissance towards Tertre, two miles to the north; and to take up a position as far as the fork in the road on the southern edge of that village.

Shortly after 8am the Company went over the canal and within half an hour had reached their objective. The men dug themselves in on either side of the road, about 400 yards from the village.

2/Duke of Wellington's was in support to 1/RWK and were billeted in and around the market square of Hornu. The Battalion had hardly settled in when Captain WM Ozanne, the machine-gun officer, was ordered to take his two guns forward to support 1/RWK at the railway embankment on the north side of the bridge. It was a dark night and no easy matter to drag the gun limbers over the tow path; however at 10.30 pm he met up with Captain HD Buchanan-Dunlop at Lock 3 and determined to stay with the Kents until daylight.

At 4am on the Sunday morning some Belgian cyclists came through their position and said that they had seen large numbers of the enemy with field guns approaching the canal. The 2/Duke of Wellington's machine-gunners then went over the canal to the embankment; Captain Ozanne positioned one each side of the twenty foot high mound, the gun team on the right being commanded by Sergeant Smith. They were firmly in position by 7.30am.

The left flank battalion of 13 Brigade was 2/KOSB (King's Own Scottish Borderers), which had seven hundred reservists in its ranks.[1] It had arrived (under the command of Lieutenant-Colonel CM Stephenson) at Boussu, two miles south of the Condé Canal and two miles west of Hornu, in the afternoon of the 22nd; after a short rest it marched north to the canal, to the left of 1/RWK, and stopped at the hamlet of Les Herbieres. The Battalion's task was to hold the iron road bridge of Les Herbieres at Lock No. 4 and the thousand yards plus of canal bank that lay between there and 1/RWK. 200 yards west of the Les Herbieres road bridge was a fixed railway bridge which was the responsibility of 1/E Surreys of 14 Brigade. As in 13 Brigade sector on their right, a deep drainage canal ran alongside the main one, separated

1st East Surrey's on their way to Les Herbieres.

2nd K.O.S.B at Boussu on their way to the canal.

by the wide tow path and beyond it the lifting bridge. On the north bank was a short row of houses.

B and D Companies of 2/KOSB under Majors ES D'Ewes Coke and Chandos Leigh were moved up to the canal and began digging trenches. They, too, were aware that there would be no advance. General Smith-Dorrien's orders to prepare a second line of defence had dispelled that idea. Opposite the short row of houses a tall white house on the south side of the bank was turned into a machine-gun post. Lieutenant JBW Pennyman, the machine-gun officer, used the top floor to give him good observation. Houses were knocked down or fortified and barricades built. Over the bridge, some 400 yards north, the road forked to the right, the road to Tertre, a village soon to be occupied by the Germans. By dawn on the 23rd, B Company (Major Coke) was in position half a mile north of Lock No. 4 to cover the approaches. The defence of the bridge and the bank lay in the hands of D Company. To the right A (Captain LD Spencer) and C (Captain EW Macdonald) Companies had their men stretched out toward the 1/RWK position. The machine-guns of the supporting battalion, 2/KOYLI (King's Own Yorkshire Light Infantry), under the command of Lieutenant Pepys, had been brought up to cover these companies.

At 7.30am things were quiet to their front, although sounds of battle could be heard to the right. It was not until midday that things began to happen on this part of the battlefield.

As the morning progressed Major Coke and some others continued to examine buildings for their defensive potential. They found in one the occupants who had remained despite the obvious preparations for a battle. They were made most welcome and fed omelettes and given coffee to drink. One of the ladies of the house suggested that all the visitors - and there were many by now - should write their names on the tablecloth. Four years later, in November 1918, Coke, who was by then a Brigadier-General (he commanded 169 Brigade of the famous 56th (London) Division from its formation in France in February 1916 to the end of the war), found himself near Les Herbieres. He went to see if he could find the house once again. It was only a ruin, but on hearing his voice two ladies came out of the cellar. In minutes they were drinking coffee and he was answering questions about the officers the ladies remembered, such as Captains Smith and Spencer and they were telling him of their experience under German occupation. In due course they produced the tablecloth, safeguarded despite the vicissitudes of the war, and presented it to Coke; it is now the cherished possession of the Regiment's Officers' Mess.

The last battalion of 13 Brigade, 2/KOYLI, with the exception of its machine-guns, were in support in Boussu; they would see no action until Sunday midday when enemy shells began to fall around the brewery where they were billeted and having their lunch.

In touch with 2/KOSB on the left were 1/E Surrey of 14 Brigade. Their commanding officer, Lieutenant-Colonel Longley, had brought the Battalion over from Dublin via Kingston upon Thames, where 499 reservists were added to the strength. The Battalion reached the Condé Canal on the Saturday afternoon, having made an eighteen mile approach march. It was to defend the railway bridge at Les Herbieres, which carried the major Mons to Tournai line, and a lifting road bridge, the Pont d'Hautrage, almost a mile to the left of that. South of the canal the land was a vast water meadow and to the north, on either side of a five hundred yard long railway embankment, were small woods. Nearly two thousand yards away was the large and scattered village of Hautrage. A mile south of the canal flowed the narrow River Haine. Lieutenant-Colonel Longley had also been told that there would not now be an advance over the canal, and so he placed his companies accordingly. C Company (Captain JP Benson) went over the canal and

The Brewery. 2 KOYLIs billets in Boussu.

deployed either side of the embankment, taking with them the machine-gun section under Lieutenant TH Darwell. On the left flank was B Company (Captain EM Woulfe-Flanagan), at the road bridge; part of the company was put over the canal to guard the fork in the road to Hautrage, a couple of hundred yards beyond the north bank, with two platoons guarding the southern end of the bridge. Between these two was D Company (Captain MJ Minogue), spread out along the south bank, and nearby was Battalion Headquarters. A Company (Captain HP Torrens) was held in reserve about 500 yards to the rear of Headquarters, in a small wood. The Battalion Second in Command (Major HS Tew) took up post to the south of the railway bridge and held responsibility for that flank. The dressing station and transport lines with the reserve ammunition were well behind Major Tew, to the left of the railway line. The East Surreys had probably the best position of all the units in the 5th Division, with good fields of fire, and Lieutenant-Colonel Longley had positioned his men very effectively.

At dawn on the 23rd a patrol under Captain Campbell went forward as far as the railway station at Hautrage (blissful, happy days, before the arrival of the Belgian Dr Beeching, when every settlement seems to have had a station) and found the railwaymen busily engaged getting steam up and removing the engines and carriages south over the canal and into the British lines.

Lieutenant-Colonel Longley came forward and decided that he needed better fields of fire, which could be achieved by clearing the undergrowth. He sent A Company forward to do this, and asked 2/Suffolk, the Brigade reserve, to lend him a company to help. Except for hard work in the hot and humid morning and the clank of pick and shovel, all was quiet and uneventful, at least until shortly after noon.

The left flank battalion of the whole of II Corps was 1/DCLI (Duke of Cornwall's Light Infantry). They had to guard over 3,000 yards of canal. The front extended from left of the Pont d'Hautrage to Lock No. 5, 2,000 yards away. Nearby, to the east, there was a lifting bridge which connected Thulin, two miles south of the canal, to Le Petit Crepin, five hundred yards on the north side and beyond that the large village of Pommeroeul. The frontage extended a further thousand yards to the west, but at least there were no more bridges or locks to defend along this stretch.

1/DCLI's commander, Lieutenant-Colonel Martin Turner, was an extraordinary man. He was born in 1865 to middle class parents and left home at the age of 19 to enlist as a private. He was immediately bought out by his father, but left home again and this time joined the

Gordon Highlanders, probably thinking that this would take him far enough away from his father this time. He served on the North West Frontier in India and was commissioned in due course into the DCLI. He went to Burma and fought in the war there and then saw service in 1897 in the Tirah campaign on the North West Frontier. He returned to Burma as Adjutant of the Burma Rifles and then returned to command the DCLI depot at Bodmin. In 1911 he took command of the 1st Battalion. He was severely wounded on the Aisne in September 1914 and ended his war as a Brigadier-General, having been given command of a brigade in 1916.

Turner concentrated his Battalion along the road bridge and its approaches. The obvious line of attack would be down the long, wide and straight road from Ville Pommeroeul - the land on either side of it was water meadow.

He faced another potential problem if the enemy should breach the canal defences. Behind the canal, at its southernmost point perhaps a mile away, was the River Haine; not a particularly wide feature, but it could complicate matters if a retreat had to be made in haste, and certainly could affect the cohesion of the Battalion.

Most of the defences were put over the bridge, on the north side of the canal. B Company sent a platoon under Lieutenant Saville to take a position some four hundred yards forward on the road leading to the

These two photographs were taken by British soldiers who took part in the battle of Mons. The photograph on the left shows a canal barge converted into a bridge as a means of retreat across the canal.

east side of Le Petit Crepin. He in turn sent three men, under Private Sambrook, a couple of hundred yards forward along this road. C Company took up a position over the bridge, whilst the remainder of B was concentrated at the southern bridgehead. A Company was deployed along the bank to connect with the troops to the right. D Company (Captain Woodham) were in reserve, but were spending their time preparing the defences of the bridge over the Haine, just north of Sardon. Lieutenant-Colonel Turner, with his adjutant, Lieutenant AN Acland, made their advanced Headquarters in this hamlet, whilst the main Battalion Headquarters were in Thulin, several hundred yards further south - which was also the location of 5th Division Headquarters.

The two other battalions of 14 Brigade, 2/Suffolk and 2/Manchester, were deployed around Hainin, a couple of miles south of the canal; the Suffolks in support of the East Surreys and the Manchesters of the DCLI.

At 6am on Sunday morning Private Sambrook and his two comrades were surprised to see riding slowly towards them a number of German cavalry. These men were from the 9th (Cavalry) Division, part of Marwitz's IInd (Cavalry) Corps. Von Kluck had continued to push his cavalry westwards, rather than concentrating them with his main army, as von Bülow wished. The dissipation of his cavalry force could well have had a crucial impact on the Retreat a few days later if they had been more readily available.

The cavalrymen were in no hurry, chatting as they rode, with no idea of the proximity of the British - or, indeed, the French. The three DCLI men held their fire, keeping well down in the ditch that ran alongside the road. The Germans came alongside them and one, an officer, glancing down, saw them. He fumbled for his revolver but he was too late and Private Sambrook shot him at close range. The patrol wheeled about and made off up the road, but one of the soldiers

grabbed at the reins of the wounded officer's horse. He did not manage to stop it, but in all the excitement the officer's helmet fell off. In the meantime the other soldiers get up their fire, causing casualties, but the Germans got away. The three men of the outpost

German cavalry (Lancers).

Wounded German cavalrymen being bandaged by their medical corps.

scrambled out of the ditch and back to Lieutenant Saville's position, carrying their helmet trophy with its bullet hole with them. It is now in the regimental museum in Bodmin.

Shortly before 7am the Germans returned and looked for the Cornwall's outpost; not finding anyone there they continued their progress along the road towards the platoon's position. At less than a hundred yards Saville's men opened fire and once again the cavalry beat a hasty retreat, returning whence they came. Saville did not know how many he had hit, but there were a number of dead horses on the road and later in the morning villagers came in with various trophies such as swords, pistols, lances and items of uniform.

At 8am one of the German Dragoons, badly wounded, was brought in by the villagers. He could stand, but was in abject fear, expecting to be shot. He was put on a stretcher and sent back to Battalion Headquarters. After he was examined the medical officer reported that all the man's stomach contained was oats; obviously he had been sharing the horse's rations.

The Germans had still not given up, and shortly after 8am another cavalry patrol came up, this time along the Ville Pommeroeul road, probably oblivious of earlier events. This time the advance was taking the cavalry directly under Lieutenant Benn's machine-guns, positioned at the bridge with several hundred yards of straight road along which to fire. Unfortunately, before they could be brought to bear a rifleman to the right of the bridge fired a shot, which was enough to send the cavalry back. Nevertheless, a dead horse could be seen lying in the road and shortly afterwards the wounded rider was brought in. He too was in fear of his life and begged for mercy. He was sent back to Headquarters at Thulin. The Germans were now well aware of the

British left flank; but it was not until Sunday afternoon that any fighting returned to Lieutenant-Colonel Turner's Battalion.

15 Brigade was put in reserve behind 13 and 14, towards the centre and west of the Condé Canal, in and around the villages of Boussu and Elouges.

The Royal Engineers had also been having a busy time. The CRE (Commander Royal Engineers) of 3rd Division was Lieutenant-Colonel CS Wilson, who controlled the Division's two Field Companies, 56 and 57; the CRE of the 5th Division was Lieutenant-Colonel JAS Tulloch, with his Field Companies, the 17th and 59th; they had been very industrious.

Gangs of Belgians had been recruited to assist with the construction of II Corps' second line of defence, and these needed to be supervised. However, the first priority was the bridges and their preparation for demolition.

The sappers faced a real problem. There was a severe shortage of explosives - but more acute was the insufficient number of fuses. A short time before mobilisation the fuze instantaneous had been withdrawn (due to store changing). The speed of mobilisation meant that they had not been replaced. They would have to rely upon safety fuse and electrical firing, and these exploders were only issued on the basis of one per section. It would mean that to explode more than one charge simultaneously would require each length of fuse to be of the same length and all to be fired at the same time. As the iron girder bridges required multiple charges, much ingenuity would be required. There were eighteen bridges in total, more than there were officers to take charge, so much of the work fell upon junior NCOs.

At 2.30am on the 23rd the sappers of the 3rd Division were told to prepare the bridges in their area for demolition but were further instructed at 8.53am that nothing must be destroyed until the Division's retirement became necessary. The engineers of the 5th Division were busily engaged in preparing houses to be used as strong points; though the bridges had been reconnoitred, nothing as yet had been done about preparing them for destruction.

It took some time to get the men of the 56th and 57th on to the bridges, broadcast as they were on the task of preparing the second line. Nothing could be done until 6.30am; Major NJ Hopkins of the 56th Fd Coy sent men into Mons in search of more explosives, but they returned empty handed. By 8am the task had begun, but in the curve of the canal from the top near Nimy and down to Obourg firing had already commenced, so that it was impossible to work on these bridges.

59

8am - Midday: The Battles of the Mons Salient Begins

At about 8.30am the attack by the 85th and 86th Fusiliers under the protection of a heavy bombardment began against the Middlesex on the right of the salient's tip at Mons. They were firing from across the canal and some of them got into houses on the hillside of Obourg and put strong pressure on D Company in the station. It was in this initial attack that Private Parr was killed.

On the left of the Battalion, opposite B Company, machine-gunners saw a German battery unlimbering their guns almost a mile away across the flat land below the hill; these were put under heavy fire and the gunners departed to seek an alternative site.

Gradually the German infantry attack spread further around the bend towards the bridge at Rue des Bragnons. At about this time, Major Hopkins was ready to send his engineers to demolish the bridges on 4/Middx front; two platoons of C Company of 2/RIrR (Royal Irish Regiment) went with the section to the bridge over the Canal du Centre at Obourg. However, when Captain Fitzgerald arrived it was already too late, the enemy were positioned on the far side of the bridge, making it impossible for the sappers to operate. The engineers also tried to get to the Rue des Bragnons bridge, but again the Germans had arrived first. The commander of the RE section, Lieutenant HW Holt, was killed when the Germans rushed his section; he has the dubious

British machine gun section. Each battalion was equipped with two of these guns. TAYLOR LIBRARY

German field battery, preparing to engage in very open positions.

distinction of being the first Royal Engineer officer killed in the War. Sergeant Miles and the rest of the section were captured. Thus, all the bridges in front of 4/Middx were intact and available to the enemy.

The German infantry began to come towards the canal at about 10am, advancing in solid blocks with rifles at the trail, firing from the hip. The intention was to storm by sheer impact of numbers. The rifle and machine-gun fire of 4/Middx tore great gaps in the compact ranks; but still they came on and, despite their awful losses, the sheer number of them forced the bridges and by 10.30am they were over the canal.

At the railway station almost all of the defenders had been either killed or wounded, including the detachment's commander, Lieutenant

German dead – the lines of them are indicative of the infantry attack methods adopted in the early days of the war. TAYLOR LIBRARY

ABW Allistone, wounded and captured. An unknown last man at the barricade on the station roof remained at his post; although wounded, he could still fire his rifle. By his action he helped those who were physically able to make good their escape; in due course this nameless hero was killed.

Captain Glass was wounded by the time his D Company withdrew to the convent; whilst Major Davey was killed by the time that B Company was forced back to the railway cutting. At 11 am 4/Middx's line had not been broken, but it had been squeezed back so that it was well south of the canal and surrounding the group of buildings in front of the communal cemetery, including the convent and the hospital. Lieutenant-Colonel Hull called on 2/RIrR (commanded by Lieutenant-Colonel St.J Cox) to come up in support, which was done promptly.

4/RF stood to at daybreak after a gruelling night of digging and

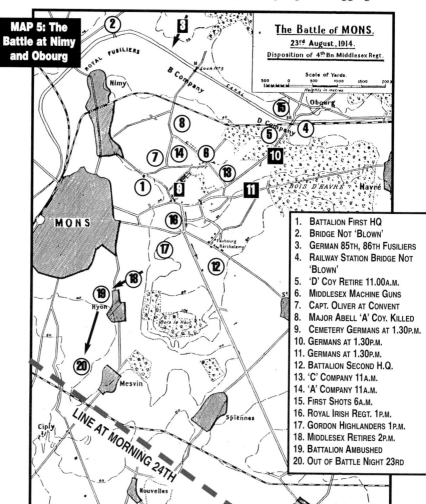

MAP 5: The Battle at Nimy and Obourg

The Battle of MONS.
23rd August, 1914.
Disposition of 4th Bn. Middlesex Regt.

Scale of Yards.

1. BATTALION FIRST HQ
2. BRIDGE NOT 'BLOWN'
3. GERMAN 85TH, 86TH FUSILIERS
4. RAILWAY STATION BRIDGE NOT 'BLOWN'
5. 'D' COY RETIRE 11.00A.M.
6. MIDDLESEX MACHINE GUNS
7. CAPT. OLIVER AT CONVENT
8. MAJOR ABELL 'A' COY. KILLED
9. CEMETERY GERMANS AT 1.30P.M.
10. GERMANS AT 1.30P.M.
11. GERMANS AT 1.30P.M.
12. BATTALION SECOND H.Q.
13. 'C' COMPANY 11A.M.
14. 'A' COMPANY 11A.M.
15. FIRST SHOTS 6A.M.
16. ROYAL IRISH REGT. 1P.M.
17. GORDON HIGHLANDERS 1P.M.
18. MIDDLESEX RETIRES 2P.M.
19. BATTALION AMBUSHED
20. OUT OF BATTLE NIGHT 23RD

Germans assemble in a wood ready to attack. TAYLOR LIBRARY

preparing their defences. They had heard the Germans moving about in the large wood on the far side of the canal. Shortly before 8am a cavalry patrol was seen coming towards the opposite bank of the road bridge, which had been swung back. Galloping straight towards it, unaware of the proximity of the Fusiliers, the officer and six men were brought to an abrupt halt when the Londoners opened fire, killing four of them and wounding the officer, knocking him off his horse. The remaining two members of the patrol escaped, fleeing back into the wood. Quickly men dashed across the bridge and brought the officer in; he turned out to be Lieutenant von Arnim, the son of Sixt von Arnim, commander of IVth Corps, whose troops would soon be engaged against 14 Brigade. The Lieutenant was a member of the 'Death's Head' Hussars, and his notebook showed that he had been observing the British positions from the wood, yet had no idea of the scale of the force on the opposite side of the canal.

The Germans began their attack against 4/RF at about 10am, led by the 84th Regiment in solid blocks, who advanced under a barrage of artillery fire. At a thousand yards the targets could not be missed and their leading sections of four abreast were destroyed, causing the whole regiment to retire back to the wood. After a heavy bombardment on the Fusiliers' trenches they came on again; the Royal Artillery could not reach them from the awkward firing positions that they had been able to find. Casualties began to mount, particularly amongst the officers. Lieutenant Mead was sent up from Nimy railway station to assist but was almost immediately wounded in the head. He returned to have it

Lieut. Maurice James Dease.

dressed and then went back without hesitation, whistling as he went, to be shot again through the head, this time fatally. By this time Captain Ashburner was wounded and Captain Fred Forster had been killed.

The Germans were still being held at bay, the two machine-guns on the railway bridge in particular doing great execution, though suffering losses amongst their crews as well. By 11am the machine-gun officer, Lieutenant Maurice Dease, had been wounded twice. Each time one of the guns stopped firing he went forward from his trench on the embankment some fifty yards back to find out why; and then returned once more with replacements or more ammunition.

C Company remained under constant bombardment; the road bridge was impassible because it had been swung back, but the valiant Germans still came forward to try and force a crossing over the railway bridge. Casualties amongst C Company continued to mount despite reinforcements; Captain Bowden Smith died of wounds and Lieutenant EC Smith was killed outright.

Major Howard had not given up all hope of destroying the railway and road bridges at Nimy. He sent one of his section commanders, Lieutenant AF Day to deal with them; but Day found that he had not got enough explosive to do both. In any case, the enemy fire was devastating and he could not get into suitable positions to lay charges. Nevertheless, he remained close to the railway bridge to await his opportunity. Further to the left things were altogether quieter, even though the men of 4/RF here did come under sporadic rifle and shell fire from across the canal. They had sunk the barges and other craft; and now they simply awaited their turn to be attacked. Corporal A Payne (later to become a Major) of 57 Fd Coy, with his six sappers, had laid his charges carefully at the road bridge to Ghlin and the nearby

German medium battery. The range and number of guns available to the Germans put the BEF at a severe disadvantage.

railway bridge. He did not have an electric exploder and so would have to set the charges off simultaneously with equal lengths of safety fuse. He waited the word of command to destroy the bridges.

Over to the left, before Jemappes, at the start of the Condé Canal, 1/RSF could hear the battle raging to their right but before them all was relatively quiet. At 10.30am the artillery of IIIrd Corps opened fire on them, soon to be followed by the densely packed columns of infantry belonging to the 6th Division coming across the water meadows from the wood behind Ghlin. After being received with the accurate and rapid fire of the Scots, they spread out and came forward in rushes in small units. Some company commander had had the sense to abandon the suicidal formation used in most places that morning.

Lieutenant-Colonel Smith had already withdrawn his posts north of the canal, and his Battalion's concentrated fire stopped the enemy not more than 200 yards from the Pont Richebe, in the built-up area to the left of the railway station. They would succeed in holding the 6th Division until early in the afternoon.

The sappers of 57 Fd Coy were here as well; Lieutenant PK Boulnois had left Corporal Jarvis and Sapper Neary to deal with the bridge over Lock No. 2, 800 yards east of Pont Richebe, when it was time so to do. Boulnois had with him four NCOs and four sappers on bicycles, with a forage cart loaded with explosives and a drum of cable. His responsibilities were the bridges from the right of Jemappes station to the lifting bridge at Mariette, the latter defended by 1/NF on 9 Brigade's left flank. The party was divided into pairs, one to each bridge; leaving explosives and cable at each, he arranged that he would return with his exploder and blow each in turn. Because the Mariette Bridge promised to be the most difficult, that was entrusted to his senior NCO, Sergeant Smith, and Sapper Dabell. The senior engineer officer at 9 Brigade's bridges was Captain Theodore Wright, the adjutant to 3 Division's CRE. He had a car and a roving commission from Mariette to the two bridges at Nimy. The morning for all these sappers was busy and dangerous, though they were constricted by the requirement to await orders before they could blow their bridges. Nevertheless, all the barges and boats, some of them homes, were sunk, to the misery of some of the owners who could only stand and watch it happening.

Cpl. Charles Alfred Jarvis.

At midday, all the bridges in the 3rd and 5th divisional areas were still intact.

Capt Theodore Wright.

By 9am Sergeant Panter, 1/NF, had seen nothing from his strongpoint in the bridge keeper's cottage north of the canal. Sergeant Johnson was with a small party in a coal shed on the central bank, equally alert. C Company were busy improving their trenches on either side of the road crossing the south bank of the canal; whilst B Company was engaged in similar activity at the road junction a hundred yards further south. Major Yatman put his detachment's Headquarters 300 yards further down the road at the railway station. At mid-morning the sound of gunfire could be heard to the right; whilst two miles to the west, where 1/RWK held the canal at Saint Ghislain, a large battle was obviously taking place. Not a shell had fallen on Mariette before 10.30am, almost as though the Germans had forgotten about the bridge here and were concentrating on those to the left and at Jemappes.

Sergeant Panter suddenly saw a column of German infantry entering the main street in front of them, four abreast, and proceeding as if unaware of the British presence. Within minutes the fire of him and his men had scattered the enemy, leaving many dead and wounded lying in the street. At 11am Panter withdrew his small garrison back over the canal into C Company's trenches; as he did so the enemy artillery began to shell the northern bank where he had been. The fire lifted and the bombardment passed over the canal and also onto the central bank between the two canals, killing Sergeant Johnson. The three men who were with him were unable to make their escape due to the crossfire across the bridge. They took shelter in the cellar, where they remained until the battle had passed over them completely. They then emerged and managed to catch up with their battalion five days later when it had marched many miles to the south.

1/Lincoln, the fourth battalion in 9/Brigade, was in reserve in Cuesmes, a mile and a half south west of Mons; on Sunday morning they were prepared to move to whatever part of the battlefield needed their assistance. At midday they were called upon to block the roads

Much of the fighting at Mons took place in built up areas from which much of the civilian population had not had the time (or inclination) to escape.

from the town at the south west corner, erecting four barricades. Whilst engaged in this they were not aware of how grateful 4/RF would be for their assistance an hour or so later.

1/RWK (13 Brigade) found themselves engaged in fighting soon after 8am. They had entrenched themselves and covered the three bridges in their sector. Did they but know it, they were only three miles from the concentration area of the German 5th Division. To the north of the canal was A Company, not far from Tertre, covering the approaches from Badour and waiting for the enemy which Cyclists had reported seeing in large numbers in and beyond the village. Meanwhile four 18 pdrs of 120 Battery had been brought forward to just south of the canal. At 8.15am four of the Divisional Cyclists came down the road from Tertre at full speed and flung themselves down into the ditch where Lieutenant Gore's men were digging in. [Gore himself would be killed at Neuve Chapelle two months later.] They reported that the rest of the detachment had been blown to pieces by the enemy's artillery. Within minutes of this some hundreds of infantry began to come towards the Kents from the open land between the village and railway embankment on the right. As everywhere else, this was the first time 1/RWK had seen solid ranks of infantry steadily marching towards them; Captain Lister's men could not miss. These Germans were from 3 Battalion, 12th Brandenburg Grenadiers; their brave advance was brought to a halt with fearful casualties. The Germans then brought a battery of artillery into action and another body of infantry began to advance; in the meantime more of them, 1 Battalion, began to advance out of Tertre down the left hand side of the road through the wooded area.

See also map on page 88

(For an outstanding account of this battle from the German perspective, you should make every endeavour to get hold of a copy of *The Advance from Mons* by Captain Walter Bloem, who commanded B Company, 1 Battalion, 12th Brandenburg Grenadiers in the battle. It is a quite remarkable book; Bloem comments on this day's fighting:

> *A bad defeat, there could be no gainsaying it; in our first battle we had been badly beaten, and by the English - by the English we had so laughed at a few hours before.*

What is even more remarkable about this book is that it was published in Germany, by this well-established novelist, in 1916.)

Over on the railway embankment Captain Ozanne, commanding the two 2/Duke of Wellington's machine-guns, had come across his first German. At 10am, before he went into action against the Brandenburger's assaulting 1/RWK to his left, he had gone 200 yards in front of his emplacements and found a track that ran underneath the embankment; where he came face to face with a German cavalryman.

See also map on page 87

Equally shocked, the German bolted off on his horse and Ozanne raced back the way he had come, neither having the presence of mind to draw a weapon. On returning to his guns he opened fire on more of the cavalry that had emerged from the wood, 500 yards to his left. Later in the day he would be wounded and have a remarkable escape from capture when, at 11pm, he found a train about to leave a siding from Saint Ghislain station, arriving in Amiens some hours later.

A Company had now become so depleted that it was unable to withstand the pressure from the overwhelming number of Brandenburgers; shortly before noon the men retired, Major Beresford then brought B Company over to replace them, whilst the field guns got right up to the canal to support them. A Company had lost severely in the morning's fighting: one officer dead, two wounded and 93 other ranks killed, wounded or missing. During the withdrawal of A Company, Private Donovan of C Company saw Lieutenant Bell struggling to bring in a wounded man of A Company. He went forward to help, regardless of the lead mayhem around him; in due course he received the DCM for this action, the first won by the Battalion in the War.

The battle at Saint Ghislain continued throughout the afternoon, only ending at nightfall.

2/KOSB could only sit tight and listen - the men of von Kluck's army, his human scythe, did not reach their position until shortly after midday. 2/KOYLI were in the rear, but their lunchtime at the brewery in Boussu was to be rudely disturbed by enemy artillery. It was to be the last hot meal, disrupted or not, that the Battalion was to enjoy for some days to come. One man was hit and the rest bolted their food down. Lieutenant Pepys hurriedly returned to his machine-guns at the canal embankment; the rest of the Battalion would not see action (apart from being shelled) until 2.30pm. 1/East Surrey also spent a quiet morning - nothing at all happened on their front; they could only listen and wonder as to what was taking place on their right. 1/DCLI also had a quiet morning, after the initial early morning flurry of excitement with Private Sambrook and German cavalry.

15 Brigade's four battalions were employed in digging defences two and three miles south of the canal, at Wasmes, Elouges and Paturages. Shells had not fallen far from them, but they would not see the real war until the following day.

1. The reason for the huge number of reservists in so many units of the original BEF is simple. The battalions of which it was composed were home based, often supplying men to garrisons across the Empire. These latter battalions and units were generally kept up to strength. Somewhat ironically, therefore, Mons was hardly a battle of the Regular Army - more a battle of the Regular Army and Reservists. Divisions that arrived later on, in the early months of the war, tended to be far more regular in composition, as they were formed from full strength battalions and regiments returning from overseas.

Chapter Three

MONS: THE AFTERNOON OF 23rd AUGUST

8 Brigade and 4th Royal Fusiliers

The German infantry were now pouring across the Canal du Centre bridges in the Middlesex sector and were working their way round the

right flank of D Company, moving out of Havre Wood, threatening to encircle the Company. On the northern, left, flank the Germans had reached the railway cutting where Major Davy, commanding B Company, had already been killed. Major Abell, taking A Company towards it, hoping to prevent the Battalion from being encircled, was also killed [9]. The machine-gun officer, Lieutenant Sloane-Stanley, was wounded, but still there in the centre of the two front line companies, north east of the cemetery [13], with his surviving gun. In front of him he calculated that six enemy guns were in action. With six volunteers he intended to stay until overrun and captured. The German artillery had brought up more guns to the slopes on the far

German infantry advancing 'shoulder to shoulder'.

side of the canal and the whole of the sector east of Mons was being saturated with shell fire.

2/RIrR received the call for help from Lieutenant-Colonel Hull whilst they were in the midst of their lunch, the last prepared one they would have for some time. They had heard the battle drawing closer and had been under shell fire since the middle of the morning.

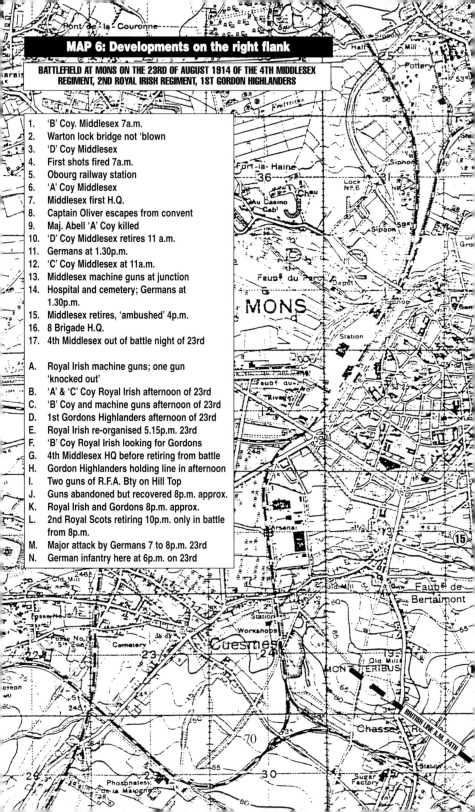

MAP 6: Developments on the right flank

BATTLEFIELD AT MONS ON THE 23RD OF AUGUST 1914 OF THE 4TH MIDDLESEX REGIMENT, 2ND ROYAL IRISH REGIMENT, 1ST GORDON HIGHLANDERS

1. 'B' Coy. Middlesex 7a.m.
2. Warton lock bridge not 'blown
3. 'D' Coy Middlesex
4. First shots fired 7a.m.
5. Obourg railway station
6. 'A' Coy Middlesex
7. Middlesex first H.Q.
8. Captain Oliver escapes from convent
9. Maj. Abell 'A' Coy killed
10. 'D' Coy Middlesex retires 11 a.m.
11. Germans at 1.30p.m.
12. 'C' Coy Middlesex at 11a.m.
13. Middlesex machine guns at junction
14. Hospital and cemetery; Germans at 1.30p.m.
15. Middlesex retires, 'ambushed' 4p.m.
16. 8 Brigade H.Q.
17. 4th Middlesex out of battle night of 23rd

A. Royal Irish machine guns; one gun 'knocked out'
B. 'A' & 'C' Coy Royal Irish afternoon of 23rd
C. 'B' Coy and machine guns afternoon of 23rd
D. 1st Gordons Highlanders afternoon of 23rd
E. Royal Irish re-organised 5.15p.m. 23rd
F. 'B' Coy Royal Irish looking for Gordons
G. 4th Middlesex HQ before retiring from battle
H. Gordon Highlanders holding line in afternoon
I. Two guns of R.F.A. Bty on Hill Top
J. Guns abandoned but recovered 8p.m. approx.
K. Royal Irish and Gordons 8p.m. approx.
L. 2nd Royal Scots retiring 10p.m. only in battle from 8p.m.
M. Major attack by Germans 7 to 8p.m. 23rd
N. German infantry here at 6p.m. on 23rd

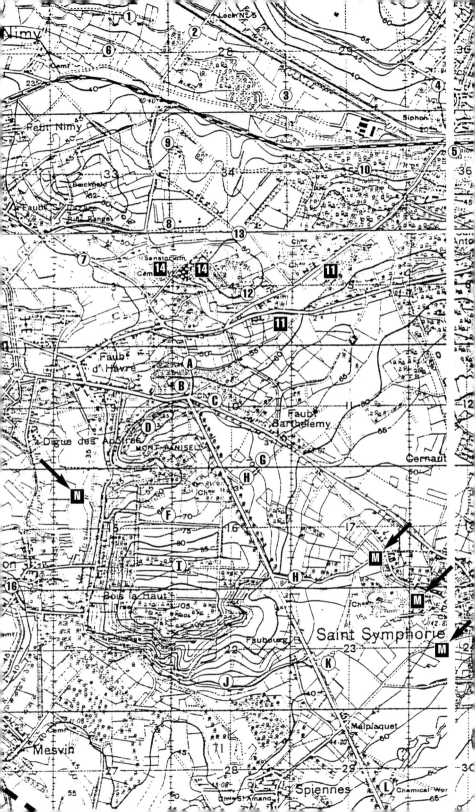

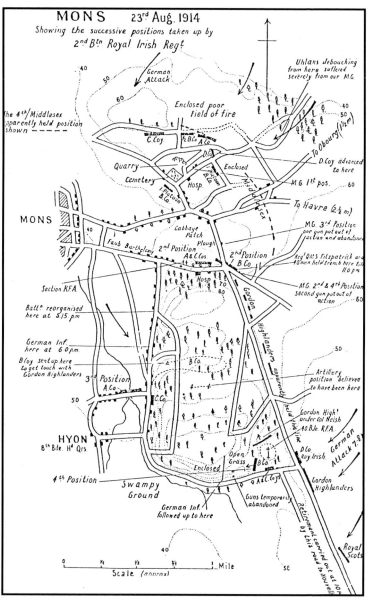

Map 7: The action of 2nd Royal Irish Regiment, 23 August.

Lieutenant-Colonel Cox sent A Company and two platoons from each of B and C, under the command of Major St Leger, at the double to the quarry above the cemetery [14]. D Company under Captain Elliott moved to the cemetery, where C Company of 4/Middx were hanging on to their position. Two sections from A Company of 2/RIrR were put

72

in the hollow at the western exit of the cemetery and at the major crossroads 200 yards beyond. Lieutenant FL Rushton, the Transport Officer, took the Irish machine-guns well forward, close to the remaining one of 4/Middx, between A and C Companies.

The battlefield of 4/Middx gradually became that of 2/RIrR. Already the commander of A Company, Captain Mellor, had been killed by a shell burst as he went forward with Major St Leger. The whole Battalion, by 2pm, was involved in an arc covering the crossroads at the Faubourg Barthelemy and the road to Binches and Harmignies. To the rear was the large Bois la Haut [I], the trees covering the hill which rose some five hundred feet high.

The battered remnants of 4/Middx who had survived the enemy onslaught thus far attempted to withdraw from in front of the cemetery. The Mental Hospital [14] in front and to the right of the cemetery had caught fire, and hundreds of terrified inmates fled across the fields into the British defence lines, adding a macabre dimension to the confusion. Numbers were killed, whilst behind them came the advancing Germans, only a few hundred yards away and now dominating the battlefield; they were managing to infiltrate the Irish and Middlesex positions through the confusion of streets surrounding the cemetery. Captain Oliver withdrew with the remnants of C Company after the Middlesex machine-gun was finally silenced and made for the large building which was the convent [8], a few hundred yards to the north of the cemetery. He wanted to get his horse out of the stables, but found that the Germans were already there. He took his men to the high wall at the back, but the gate was locked; one of his men blew it off, but injured himself in the process. Emerging from the gate on the Nimy Road, he and his men ran into crossfire; some fell, but the survivors crossed the road and went into the hollow where they found Lieutenant Ferguson with some men of the Irish A Company.

By 3.30pm Lieutenant-Colonel Hull's survivors had left the battlefield, though there remained some who were unable to move back with the rest and who were eventually overrun as they became isolated. Unfortunately the trials were not over for 4/Middx. They took the narrow road behind the west side of the hill [15] and marched towards the tiny village of Hyon [16]; the Germans were already there. They had managed to work their way from Nimy between the Middlesex and 4/RF. Here [N] the Middlesex fought their last battle of the day and another sixty men became casualties. Eventually they reached Nouvelles, a few miles further south [17], and the roll call on that summer's evening showed that they only numbered 275. Fifteen

Corporal Payne's Road Bridge - leading to a park on the west side of the canal. Destroyed.

officers were casualties, of whom five were killed and ten wounded and taken prisoner (including the Battalion Medical Officer, Captain Terry, who was himself wounded but opted to remain behind to look after the casualties). 453 other ranks were casualties, of whom ninety were killed; but a hundred of these reappeared over the next days as II Corps proceeded with the retreat. Still, given that the total British casualty count for the Battle of Mons was some 1,600, this was a very significant proportion of the total, well over 20%.

By 1pm the situation of Lieutenant-Colonel McMahon's 4/RF was desperate. Although the railway bridge had still not been forced, C (also known as Y) Company had almost eighty casualties. Lieutenant Dease, twice wounded, had lost almost all of his machine-gun section and the left hand gun had been knocked out.

Round the corner at Lock No. 6 and the two bridges, the railway running under the Ghlin road bridge, Captain Byng and D (Z) Company had been under fire and direct frontal attack from the woods (about a mile away) and the open land in front for some hours. The defenders' fire had kept the (initially) massed ranks of Germans at bay, but by 1pm the Germans had learnt their lesson and Byng had moved his men back to the canal. Corporal Payne of 57 Fd Coy had everything prepared to demolish the bridges as soon as the Fusiliers got across. The enemy artillery fire fell on the men of D Company as they ran back over the bridge, covered by Major Mallock's rearguard from A (W) Company. As the last man stumbled across, Corporal Payne and his men lit the six lengths of safety fuse and ran across the railway lines under the bridge. Because of the noise of bursting shells and the general sound of battle, Payne could not hear if his charges had exploded, but some evidently had as large pieces of the bridge came hurtling down behind him as he ran.

At 1.10pm the Battalion received its first order to retire.

At Nimy Dease realised that both his guns had ceased firing; he went forward once more and was hit for the third time, mortally wounded. There was no one left alive at the guns, and only one in the

74

machine-gun section. Only the right hand gun was fit to use, and that had bullet holes in its water jacket. Lieutenant Steele asked for volunteers who could use the gun, and Private Sidney Frank Godley of the machine-gun section, already wounded, said that he could. Moving forward he cleared out the position and set to work firing across the water into the enemy infantry. Lieutenant Day of 57 Fd Coy had remained close by the bridge in the hope of getting a chance to fix demolition charges, but the opportunity never came and during the morning he was wounded and, in due course, captured. With the sole machine-gun still firing, Lieutenant Steele carried Dease back to the rear, where he died.

At 1.40pm McMahon received the order to retire; with Godley remaining at his gun the survivors of the 4th Royal Fusiliers withdrew back into Mons.

A brave German, Musketier Oscar Niemeyer, went into the canal, swam over to the road bridge and operated the machinery to swing it back into position over the canal. He was shot and killed by the British in the process. But nothing could now stop the hordes of German infantry from pouring over the canal, especially as Godley had been wounded again and his gun had become too damaged to fire.

They harassed the Fusiliers as they fell back and set fire to the housing; they also herded a large number of civilians in front of them. This forced a number of Fusiliers, who were manning a barricade across the main street, to fall back into Mons, as they could not fire into that crowd. The four guns of 107 Battery also withdrew from Mons. The first battalion of Brigadier-General Shaw's 9 Brigade to withdraw from Mons fell back through the winding and narrow streets towards the small village of Ciply, two miles away. Their retreat was covered by 1/Lincoln, who were dug in at the southern exits of Mons.

4/RF suffered more than 150 casualties. In the course of their fighting at Mons they had the honour to win the first two of the war, VCs, Dease and Godley. Maurice Dease's was gazetted first. He was educated by the Jesuits at Stonyhurst; that establishment has the honour of providing the first officer VC of the Second World War, Ervine-Andrews. Godley heard about his VC when he was recovering from his severe wounds as a prisoner; the news was given to him by the Commandant of the PoW camp.

**Sidney Frank
Godley.**

At 10 am on 24 August 4th Royal Fusiliers withdrew from the Mons salient.

Now that all the bridges from Nimy to Obourg were

available to the enemy, and with two battalions out of the fight, the full force of the enemy fell on 2/RIrR and 1/Gordons (Gordon Highlanders), commanded by Lieutenant-Colonel FH Neish. In front of their curved perimeter line of only 800 yards radius from the major road junction at the Faubourg Barthelmy were the 85th (Bremen) and 35th Infantry Regiments; coming down through Mons, after 4/RF's withdrawal, was the 84th (Schleswig) Regiment. The Gordons had entrenched themselves along the main road to Harmignies [H] in a position running south easterly from the road junction and on the forward slope of the hilly Bois la Haut. Their Headquarters were on the western slope in a large house. The whole area was thickly wooded. On top of the hill [I] and at both ends were the three batteries of artillery from XL Field Brigade RA, the 6th, 23rd and 49th. A mile below the Gordons, and along the same road, was Lieutenant-Colonel McMicking's 2/RS (Royal Scots). There were still three battalions of 8 Brigade to fend off the German attack on the Mons Salient.

Since 1.30pm, when the Middlesex had begun to withdraw, the machine-guns of 2/RIrR had been out of action [A]. Sergeant J Whittington recovered one and brought it back to the crossroads [C] and got it into action. D Company, after their first advance to the quarry, had been so badly mauled that it was withdrawn back to Hyon, behind the hill, neither the Germans or the Middlesex having yet got there. When Quarter Master Sergeant Fitzpatrick saw this happening he collected about forty men from the Transport Lines - drivers, cooks, orderlies - and placed himself under the orders of Major Simpson. This officer commanded a company of Gordons at the crossroads and Fitzpatrick's men were put into a trench on the right hand side of the road, looking down the slope towards the right hand side of the mental hospital. Despite all that happened later in the day he remained in the position until 11pm. When the position was invested by the enemy he scattered them with rapid fire and withdrew with eighteen survivors of his party. He was awarded the DCM.

Major St Leger brought his men back to the left hand fork of the crossroads [B] in front of Gendebien Chateau. This building was being used by the medical officer (Major Long) as a first aid post; Red Cross flags hung from the windows and one was placed on the roof. Notwithstanding this it was hit by shells in the early afternoon and set on fire. All the casualties were evacuated into the surrounding woods, though the wounded commander of 49th Battery, Major JS Maidlow, and Private CH Jackson died in the ruins. Major Lyon, 6 Battery, was hit whilst galloping along the road towards his battery on the hill, and fell from his horse. Private Redmond of the Royal Irish and two gallant Gordons leapt out of their trench near to the crossroads, despite the shelling and heavy firing, and carried him to the makeshift hospital; he survived the subsequent fire.

A Company had by now lost all of its officers; Major St Leger, gathering all the men that he could, put them on the edge of the road looking down the slope of the ridge and across the shallow valley towards the cemetery a thousand yards away, and through which hundreds of Germans were pouring. Major Panter-Downes (commanding C Company) arrived and was directed to hold the position. The leading ranks of the enemy began swarming up the slope, firing from the hip as they came. Panter-Downes ordered his men (only about thirty of them) to fix bayonets and with Lieutenant Shine, who had previously been down in the valley, they charged at the Germans, who were now less than fifty yards away, and routed them. This had a cost, there were thirty or so casualties, including Shine, who was mortally wounded.

200 yards to the right Fitzpatrick's party, with the aid of the machine-gun rescued by Sergeant Whittington on the right, was causing havoc in the valley. At about this time the Battalion's adjutant, Lieutenant REG Phillips, was severely wounded. Impossible to move him because of the extent of his injuries, he was taken prisoner in the evening.

There were some buildings on the eastern side of the road junction where some of the men had taken cover, firing from holes in the walls. At the road junction were two of the guns of 23 Battery, but the bombardment forced their withdrawal up the hill.

By the middle of the afternoon the Battalion had become scattered and depleted, so it was necessary to leave the crossroad position and retire behind the hill. Fitzpatrick remained, as did the Gordons, whose turn it now was to stop the Germans, helped considerably by the fire from 23 Battery on the hill; the advance of the enemy suddenly provided excellent targets. Between them the enemy was halted some 300 yards from the foot of the hill.

The land at the western side of the hill is flat and marshy, with a thin stream running through it. The Irish re-formed here [E]; Lieutenant AMS Tandy and the survivors of A Company lined the road along each side of the narrow bridge and looked north towards Mons, as the last of 4/Middx came through en route for Hyon. B Company of the Irish had also come down the narrow road behind the hill and proceeded to climb up the very steep wooded slope in a fruitless search for the

Gordons, who were mistakenly thought to be at the top. B Company returned down the hill, exhausted.

In Hyon [16] it was becoming clear to Brigadier-General Doran that he would have to move his Headquarters back. On the other hand he wanted to ensure that his Brigade was relatively safe, and he was desperate to make contact with the Gordons. Sometime before 5pm he came up to 2/RIrR and led B and C Companies back up the narrow, cobbled lane at the foot of the hill. They could hear the battle going on to the left as the withdrawing 4/Middx ran into the Germans coming down from Mons. Within a couple of hundred yards of setting off along the lane they saw the Germans ahead of them. There was no room for manoeuvre, so the Irish had to return to the bottom of the hill and to the open land between it and the main road.

At 6pm the Gordons were still holding their line on the main road [H], defying the enemy who seemed to have reverted to their tactics of pressing forward in massed, closed ranks. But the pressure was telling. The 18 pdrs on top of the hill had to be rescued; a platoon of Gordons under the command of Lieutenant IBN Hamilton was sent to extricate them, but these men did not realise that Hyon was in German hands.

The only way to extract the guns was down the back of the hill and along the narrow road, but as they moved along the lane they ran into a road block where a similar narrow lane crossed the bridge from Hyon to join the lane they were using. The leading horses were killed and the guns fell off the road into a ditch on the right. Nothing daunted, one group of Gordons chased off the Germans at the point of the bayonet, whilst another helped the gunners drag the horses and guns back up onto the road and then got away to join the Irish further along.

To the right of the Gordons were 2/RS (Royal Scots). They had been in position all day some two miles down from the crossroads, spread out along the main road. Facing them was open and flat land, looking eastwards towards St Symphorien and Villers Ghislain. On their right were 1/IG (Irish Guards), of 4 (Guards) Brigade, 2nd Division, part of Haig's Ist Corps. They had an excellent field of fire, but except for the occasional shot at German cyclists, they had had a very quiet morning, in stark contrast to the raging sounds of battle coming from their left. Late in the afternoon, as the enemy attacked the Gordons to the north, a long line of German infantry came towards the forward companies, A and D, under the command of Major Tweedie. They were assisted in the defence by the Battalion machine-guns under Lieutenant Laidley. The storm of defensive fire destroyed the German attack, bringing it to a halt 300 yards from the road in the flat and treeless fields. These soldiers from Bremen would wait until dusk before their next attempt.

With dark the Gordons withdrew, as did Fitzpatrick and his remnant; Major St Leger entrenched the survivors of the Irish along the track running from the bottom south east corner of the hill to the main road from Harmignies to Mons [K]. This position was adopted to protect the guns of XL Field Brigade that were now gathered there, having escaped from their positions at Bois la Haut; and to stem any further German advances.

At 8pm the Germans attacked [M] the two Scottish battalions again, both from across the main road and from the flattish slopes coming down from the eastern edge of the hill. The attack from this latter point, especially as it was almost dark, was so sudden that four of the guns were temporarily lost, though a bayonet charge [J] recovered them.

Shortly after this scrap the defenders could hear bugle calls. They were German, calling a halt to the fighting of the day. German losses had been tremendous; one estimate put them at more than 6,000 in Mons alone. The 75th (Bremen) regiment had lost six officers and 376 other ranks in one attack.

At 10pm the British finally withdrew from these positions, bringing the guns with them, none of which had been lost during the day. The column passed on unhindered by the Germans and arrived at Nouvelles at 4.30am on Monday 24 August. The Royal Irish had suffered 225 casualties, including five officers killed and five wounded. The Gordons (with 24 casualties) and the Royal Scots had got off very lightly. However, the battles in this part of Mons, involving five battalions and 1/Lincoln on the western fringes, had cost IInd Corps a thousand men. This was not a large number - indeed by comparison with later figures (even on 24 August) lost at Le Cateau, the Aisne and

The close formation of the German troops led to heavy losses. The corps of officers were also reduced considerably by these tactics. The photograph shows three German officers, from the 36th Regiment.

First Ypres, not to mention the vast battles later on in 1915 at Loos and the cataclysms on the Somme and in the Salient and the Hindenburg Line it is small - but the battle had been enormously significant for the well-being of the allied cause.

Mons: the afternoon at the eastern end of the Condé Canal (Jemappes - Mariette)

Since before noon 1/RSF had been involved in fighting with IX Corps; all posts on the north bank had been forced back over the bridges, but fire from the positions on the south bank kept the Germans from coming too close. At Pont Richebe [1] they were kept 200 yards away by D Company. By 1pm the CO was aware that the Germans had crossed the canal and knew that his time at Jemappes was limited. The bridges were prepared for demolition, the sappers awaiting the word to continue. The fixing of the charges was not without hazard. Whilst the Scots fired away over their heads, at Lock No. 2 [2], Lance Corporal Jarvis and Sapper Neary, assisted by Private Heron of 1/RSF, fixed charges underneath the lock bridge from a boat. It also entailed running and dodging along the bullet-swept bank to bring up explosive and stretch out cables. They had been encouraged in their work by Captain Wright, the CRE's adjutant, himself wounded in the head [8], but who continued to travel along the bank to supervise the various RE parties.

At 2.30pm Lieutenant-Colonel Smith received orders [4] to withdraw his Battalion; only now would he permit bridges in his sector to be destroyed. The Battalion was still in position when Lieutenant Boulnois and Sergeant Smith of 57 Fd Coy cycled past Lance Corporal Jarvis en route to the road bridge to the right of the station; the leads were connected to the exploder which Boulnois had with him. The bridge was successfully collapsed.

Because the Royal Scots were still in position and holding the enemy [3], Boulnois and his companion headed westwards to see Captain Wright. They met him halfway and it was determined that Sergeant Smith, the exploder and the drum of cable would go in

1st RSF Road Bridge (Gas Poste) blown up by Lt Boulnois and Sgt. Smith RE.

Wright's car and they would destroy the bridge at Mariette. Lieutenant Boulnois would go and set off the charges at Pont Richebe. Whilst this plan was being discussed they came across a despatch rider who was in search of the RSF to inform them that there was to be a general retirement. They faced the difficult task of blowing up several bridges with one exploder in a very limited time.

Boulnois cycled back to Pont Richebe; a ride difficult to imagine, as the bullets swept all round him. Somehow, one does not associate riding a bicycle with being in the middle of a battle! Whilst on his way to Pont Richebe he heard a loud explosion, which was Corporal Jarvis's bridge at Lock No. 2 'going up'; Jarvis won the VC for his actions and Private Heron the DCM.

At Pont Richebe [1] Boulnois and Corporal Halewood managed to get the charges connected and in desperation connected them to a circuit in a nearby house, hoping that by switching on the lights they would ignite the charges. On the point of doing this the power supply to the village failed; Pont Richebe remained intact.

At about 3.15pm the Germans began to come across it and the Fusiliers were faced with a difficult withdrawal [5] and lost many men as they made their way back to Frameries [10], over two miles from the canal. It entailed fighting down narrow streets and up the long hill through Flenu [9] and in the course of it the Battalion lost a hundred men. Amongst these was Captain TA Rose, who was wounded and died in enemy hands, and Captain John Erskine Young, who was killed. Civilians still in the village witnessed the fighting retreat; one of them was an Englishwoman, living in Jemappes, who later wrote to the Regiment to tell them of the fight and what she saw. Another witness was the commanding officer of the Germans, Colonel Heubner, who extolled the obstinate resistance which caused heavy losses to his men in a book on the campaign. That night 1/RSF found billets in the brewery at the north of Frameries, next to the cemetery. In contrast to the considerable casualties suffered by the Fusiliers, 1/Lincoln, which had been in reserve, suffered only two wounded.

To the left of Pont Richebe Major Yatman's large detachment of 1/NF was well aware of the heavy fighting taking place on his left and right. His position at Quaregnon and Mariette had continued to remain relatively quiet, only disturbed by the occasional shell and shots from snipers. At 3pm Captain BT St. John, commanding C Company, saw movement along the main street ahead of him, beyond the canal. Enemy infantry were gathering to come around the corner a hundred yards or so away from him. He ordered his men to open fire, but no

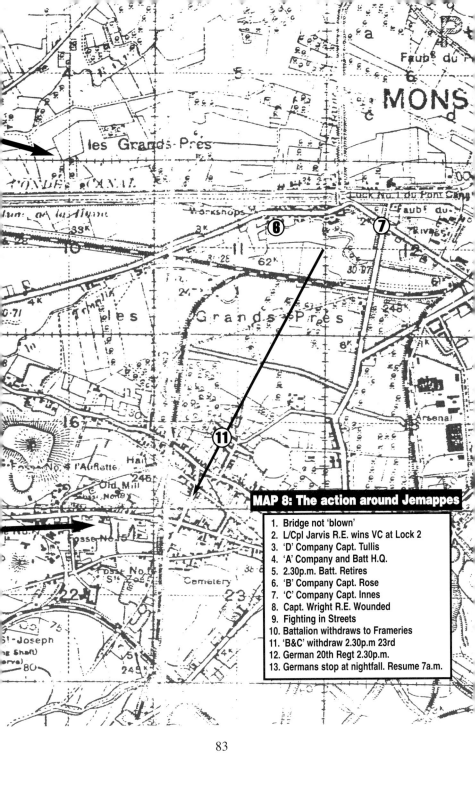

MAP 8: The action around Jemappes

1. Bridge not 'blown'
2. L/Cpl Jarvis R.E. wins VC at Lock 2
3. 'D' Company Capt. Tullis
4. 'A' Company and Batt H.Q.
5. 2.30p.m. Batt. Retires
6. 'B' Company Capt. Rose
7. 'C' Company Capt. Innes
8. Capt. Wright R.E. Wounded
9. Fighting in Streets
10. Battalion withdraws to Frameries
11. 'B&C' withdraw 2.30p.m 23rd
12. German 20th Regt 2.30p.m.
13. Germans stop at nightfall. Resume 7a.m.

Lock No 2 at Jemappes blown by Corporal Jarvis RE and Sapper Neary. Jarvis wins VC.

sooner had firing commenced than he saw a group of crying and terrified little girls, school children, running across the road in panic [4]. His men ceased firing, and the children then proceeded to run back again, and then repeating this a number of times, obviously in considerable distress. This did not last more than three or four minutes; and it might well be that the Germans did it deliberately. Whatever, they took advantage of the situation and came forward and cut the wire that the Northumberland Fusiliers had strung up and gained the shelter of the large coal sheds on the far side of the canal. They then brought up a field gun, protected by rifle fire from the coal sheds, and opened fire at point blank range. Lieutenant Boyd's men, on the opposite side of the canal from the sheds, came under intense fire.

In fact Brigadier-General Shaw had issued orders at 2.30pm that all units of his 9 Brigade should withdraw from the canal; Yatman did not receive the order.

Also close to 3pm Captain Wright and Sergeant Smith arrived at the Mariette Bridge; they had two bridges to deal with - the short twenty foot one over the subsidiary canal and the main lifting bridge beyond. The charges had already been fixed by Smith earlier in the day, but Wright, his head swathed in bandages, had to connect the electric leads to the explosives. Time and again Wright swung underneath the bridge, trying to reach the leads that were already there. Each time his head or hands showed he was fired at by the enemy, who were only a few yards

Lock No. 1 west of the station at Mons. Not blown.

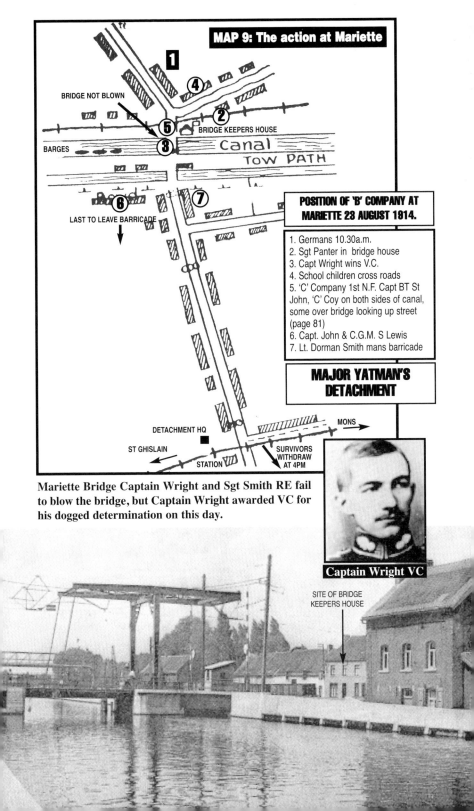

MAP 9: The action at Mariette

BRIDGE NOT BLOWN

BRIDGE KEEPERS HOUSE

BARGES

canal

TOW PATH

LAST TO LEAVE BARRICADE

POSITION OF 'B' COMPANY AT MARIETTE 23 AUGUST 1914.

1. Germans 10.30a.m.
2. Sgt Panter in bridge house
3. Capt Wright wins V.C.
4. School children cross roads
5. 'C' Company 1st N.F. Capt BT St John, 'C' Coy on both sides of canal, some over bridge looking up street (page 81)
6. Capt. John & C.G.M. S Lewis
7. Lt. Dorman Smith mans barricade

MAJOR YATMAN'S DETACHMENT

DETACHMENT HQ

ST GHISLAIN

STATION

MONS

SURVIVORS WITHDRAW AT 4PM

Mariette Bridge Captain Wright and Sgt Smith RE fail to blow the bridge, but Captain Wright awarded VC for his dogged determination on this day.

Captain Wright VC

SITE OF BRIDGE KEEPERS HOUSE

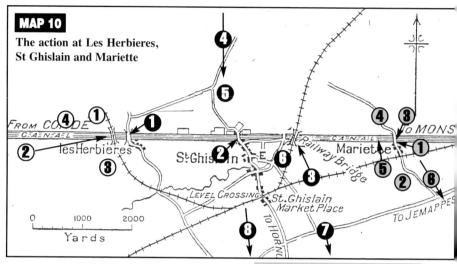

MAP 10

The action at Les Herbieres,
St Ghislain and Mariette

Yards

14 BRIGADE
1. 'C' Company Capt. Benson
2. Lt. Darwell's Machine guns
3. Major Tew's HQ 21/C 1st East Surrey
4. Lt Ward, with his sword, charging enemy

13 BRIGADE
1. Lock No. 4 road bridge not 'blown'
2. Lt. Godsell R.E. blows up road bridge
3. Road and railway bridges 'blown', Sgt. Payne R.E.
4. German Infantry arriving 9 a.m.
5. Lt. Anderson R.W.K. killed
6. Major Townsend, 'A' Coy Duke of Wellingtons'
7. Late p.m. 23rd 'Dukes' retire to Wasmes
8. Late p.m. 23rd R.W.K. go to Wasmes

9 BRIGADE
1. Captain Wright R.E. wins VC trying to blow up road bridge.
2. Major Yatman's detachment of the 1st Northumberland Fusiliers at road bridge.
3. Sgt Panter's garrison of 12 men in bridge house.
4. Children crossing road, obstructing line of fire.
5. Lt. Boyd on south bank 3pm. Germans on the other side.
6. Major Yatman withdraws south to Frameries 4 p.m.

from him. Exhausted, at one time he fell into the water, to be dragged out by the valiant Sergeant Smith. In the end he could not connect up the leads as they were too short, and it was utterly impossible to cut and bring up more. Captain Theodore Wright was awarded the Victoria Cross for his outstanding efforts. In performing a similar task a few weeks later, on the Aisne, he was mortally wounded and is buried at Vailly.

At 4pm Yatman decided that he had to withdraw. As soon as it was clear that Captain Wright's efforts had failed, the troops giving him what covering fire they could on the north side of the canal came back to Dorman-Smith's lines on the south bank. As the men prepared to retire through Quaregnon a cyclist arrived from Brigade Headquarters with the orders to fall back; the survivors threaded their way through the mining town and headed for the hill-top village of Frameries, three miles to the south. The Germans had already got over the canal at Pont Richebe; the Fusiliers were aware of this and made a detour to the west,

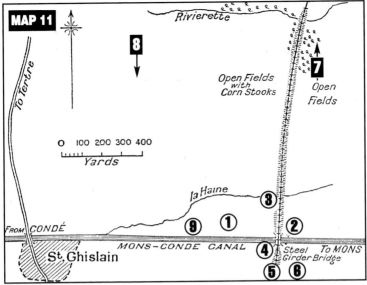

Action at Lock No 3 and the Railway Bridge.

1. Captain Ozanne. MG officer, wounded and escaped
2. Sgt Smith, Senior Machine Gun Section Sergeant
3. Captain Ozanne comes face to face with German Lancer
4. Captain Ozanne and other wounded shelter under bridge
5. Railway embankment. Corporal Marsden R.E. killed, bridge blown
6. Major Tulloch's company Royal West Kents
7. 10am 23rd German Cavalry
8. German Infantry held at distance by machine guns
9. Site of Lock No.3 and 'B' Coy. Duke of Wellingtons

towards Paturages, thereby avoiding a clash with a much greater force; so that it was dark by the time that they reached their destination.

The 12th Brandenburg Grenadiers of the German 5th Division had come no closer to the canal since 1/RWK had brought them to a halt in the morning; they remained some 300 yards from the canal, shocked by their heavy casualties, which included Major Praeger, a battalion commander. The Brandenburgers had suffered some 3,000 casualties, inflicted by little more than 300 of the West Kents and the 2/Duke of Wellington's in support near the railway embankment. However, 1/RWK had not got off lightly itself - only ninety men out of the 200 or so who had crossed the canal managed to return.

The four field guns were brought from their forward position into one closer to the village for the rest of the afternoon. Another group of guns at a slag heap a thousand yards to the east maintained its fire for most of the afternoon as well. The German infantry was content to spend most of the time firing from their positions, but made a further effort at about 6pm, but with no success, and that ended their attacks for the day. 1/RWK casualties for the day numbered about a hundred.

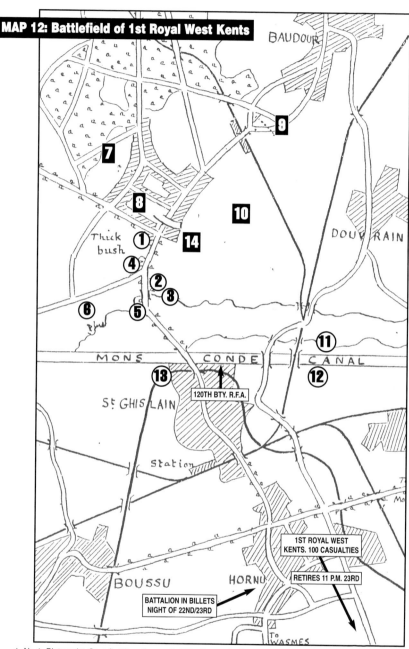

MAP 12: Battlefield of 1st Royal West Kents

BAUDOUR

DOUR RAIN

Thick bush

MONS CONDE CANAL

St GHISLAIN

120TH BTY. R.F.A.

Station

1ST ROYAL WEST KENTS. 100 CASUALTIES

RETIRES 11 P.M. 23RD

BOUSSU HORNU

BATTALION IN BILLETS NIGHT OF 22ND/23RD

To WASMES

1. No 1. Platoon Lt. Gore first in action against Fusiliers
2. No. 2 Platoon Lt. Wilberforce Bell
3. No. 4 Platoon Lt. Anderson killed on withdrawing
4. No. 3 Platoon Lt. Chitty
5. Pte Donovan wins D.C.M
6. Lt Gore's Platoon retires and evades capture
7. German Fusilier Battalion

8. German and Fusilier Battalion
9. German Artillery and Machine guns
10. Brandenburg Grenadiers
11. Trench (dummy) dug across railway embankment
12. Corporal Rogers shot and killed whilst observing
13. Lt. Godsell R.E. blows up road bridge
14. 3,000 Brandenburgers 'knocked out' by 1st R.W.K

Mons: the afternoon from Saint Ghislain to Les Herbieres and the action of 13 Brigade.

To the immediate right of 1/RWK were the 2/Duke of Wellington's. Captain Ozanne with his machine-guns [1 and 2] at the railway embankment had helped Lieutenant-Colonel Martyn's men halt the attack of 12/Brandenburg; and for their efforts spent most of their time under shellfire. They could see the Germans sheltering behind corn stooks [8] in the fields and fired on them intermittently; at 3pm a shell burst in front of his emplacement, shattering his arm and wounding others.

Map page 87

He was able to make his way, along with the other wounded, back to the railway bridge and sheltered under it until nightfall. The bridge [5] had already been prepared for demolition and nearby was Corporal Marsden of 17 Fd Coy ready to do the task. Whilst Ozanne was taking shelter there the Germans shelled the railway line and its bridge heavily, blowing off some of the gun cotton charges. The Corporal, despite the heavy bombardment, replaced them and the connecting leads. His work done, he returned to the south side, waiting for the exploder to arrive. Later on, whilst watching the action through a telescope, he was hit by shell fire and killed.

Lieutenant O'Kelly took a platoon of fifty four men up to the canal on the right of the embankment at 1.30pm. He came under fire from the direction of Mariette, where shortly the Northumberlands were to begin their retirement. Apart from some shelling, which generally went over their heads, these men came to no harm, but at 3pm O'Kelly saw a mass of infantry coming towards him across the open fields. Opening fire into the closed ranks, the enemy suffered fearful casualties, but 'as fast as they fell others came to take their place; each of my men must have fired hundreds of rounds'.

By 5pm they had come within 300 yards of O'Kelly's platoon and he ordered his men to fix bayonets. But then the Germans stopped and shortly afterwards the men heard the sound of bugles and the attackers started to melt away - for the moment at least, they had had enough. At

Captain Ozanne shelted in a barge under bridge. Corporal Marsden RE killed. Bridge blown by Lt Godsell RE and Sgt Payne.

6pm he was ordered to retire, having suffered three killed and twelve wounded.

Captain RC Carter had taken B Company over the canal at about the same time as O'Kelly had gone forward. He put the men into buildings to the right of the road bridge near Lock No. 3. The Brandenburgers had slowed down since their battle with the Kents and Carter's orders were to fire at only good targets and not to give their position away in order to avoid artillery retaliation. Lieutenant-Colonel Gibbs had come up to examine the positions in the front line close to the canal; his orderly, Private Shellabear, was killed just a few yards from him at 3pm. At 4.30pm Brigadier-General Cuthbert sent an order to strengthen the right flank of his 13 Brigade, Major EN Townsend took A Company towards Mariette and told Captain EV Jenkins to stay with D Company in reserve on the square at St Ghislain. 2/Duke of Wellington's stayed where they were, the Brandenburgers having given up their attack for the day; the Battalion had only suffered three casualties amongst the officers thus far, all wounded.

1/RWK and 2/Duke of Wellington's were responsible for four other bridges in 13 Brigade's sector. There was a lifting bridge at Lock No. 3, 200 yards to the left of the railway where Corporal Marsden was killed; a large lifting bridge carrying the main road from St Ghislain to Tertre, in the centre of 1/RWK's sector and where B Company of 2/Duke of Wellington's held the sheds on the north bank; only six feet to its left was a wooden bridge; and there was a lifting bridge 500 yards further on. Lieutenant Godsell was responsible for all of these bridges.

At 2pm Brigadier-General Cuthbert sent for him and said that he wanted them all demolished. The road bridge was a problem because it was constantly in use carrying orderlies, ammunition, wounded men and everything required by the infantry on the north side. The adjacent foot bridge could not deal with this sort of traffic, whilst to complicate matters it would be necessary to raise the road bridge in order to fix the charges.

Lock No. 3 Captain R.C. Carter's men in the building on the right. Bridge blown by Lt Godsell RE.

LT O'KELLY'S MEN LINING SOUTH BANK

Godsell made Corporal Gerachty and two men responsible for the Lock bridge; whilst Corporal Taylor was sent to the bridge west of the main one. Because of the heavy firing none of the bridges could be blown in the afternoon; in any case there was only one exploder and that would be used, as a priority, at the railway bridge. The road bridge and its small neighbour had to be blown at the same time, for fear of creating a mutual explosion; and they could not be destroyed until the men on the far bank had been withdrawn. Lieutenant Godsell had to wait.

2/KOSB had been waiting for their turn to get involved in the fighting all morning; they were not to be kept waiting overlong as the German IIIrd and IVth Corps moved around to swing against Smith-

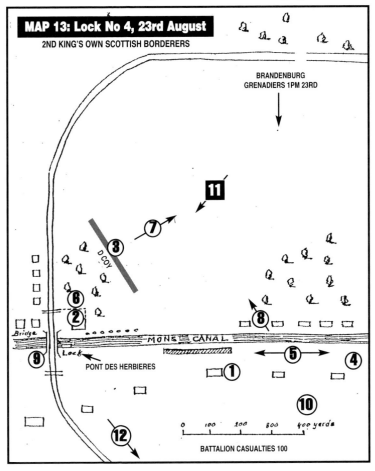

MAP 13: Lock No 4, 23rd August
2ND KING'S OWN SCOTTISH BORDERERS

BRANDENBURG GRENADIERS 1PM 23RD

MONS CANAL

PONT DES HERBIERES

BATTALION CASUALTIES 100

1. Lt. Pennyman's Machine Guns
2. Major Coke's Tablecloth House
3. Major Chandos Leigh 'D' Coy
4. Lt. Pepys. KOYLI machine guns
5. 'A' and 'C' Companies Capts. Spencer and MacDonald
6. Lock House 'Hit' and demolished
7. Lts Dalrymple and Jones lead counter attack
8. Capt Spencer with two platoons to help 'D' Coy
9. Lt Pottinger R.E. 'cut off'. Bridge fails to 'blow'
10. 2nd KOYLIs relieve KOSBs
11. Germans final assault stopped at copse
12. 8pm 23rd KOSBs retires

Dorrien's flank. Major AE Haig, the Second in Command, had his observation post alongside Lieutenant Pennyman's machine-guns at the top of the white house [1]. At 1pm he saw Germans moving diagonally across his front [11]. They were coming in a south westerly direction from Tertre, heading for the bridge; they were a party of Brandenburg Grenadiers, led by an officer who stood out because of his bandaged head. Haig could see that they were being cautious, but they also seemed to be unaware that there was anybody in front of them. They advanced in small groups over the water meadows, cutting the barbed wire fences as they came, Haig quickly informed Major Chandos Leigh's B Company [3] on the far side of the canal as to what was happening; they brought the advance to a halt by their rifle fire. Haig reinforced their position, whilst the Germans commenced to bring their artillery to bear.

In the course of the bombardment the lock house [6] and the cottage [2], whose occupants had welcomed the Borderers earlier, were hit; Haig saw the people, carrying a canary (strange what the memory recalls) disappear into the Battalion's lines.

Haig reinforced D Company with some of A Company [5]; D Company moved forward to get clear of the houses now under heavy shellfire. This, unintentionally, became a counter-attack, and men began to fall as the Grenadiers opened up with machine-guns and the artillery showered them with shrapnel. In addition, the machine-guns in the white house which had been searching the woodlands from which the Germans had emerged with their fire, came under artillery fire; Pennyman was forced to take them out to a less obvious position.

At 3pm Major Haig ordered a retirement from the advanced positions to the canal; Major Leigh, who had won the DSO in South Africa, and had been wounded somewhere in the water meadows, could not be found and had to be left behind. He died shortly afterwards in German captivity. Other casualties included the Medical Officer, Captain Gibbon, and Captain Kennedy, both wounded; CSM Wilson was mortally wounded and Sergeants Adair and Murray were

Lock No. 4 Road Bridge at Les Herbieres. Lt Pottinger RE failed to blow it with his pistol.

wounded - the latter would be killed on the Somme. Corporal Field was shot through the forehead but made a miraculous recovery in a German hospital; in all the Battalion suffered about a hundred casualties.

Lieutenant Pottinger of 17 Fd Coy had been waiting at No. 4 Lock bridge [9] since the early afternoon, waiting for the infantry to retire and for permission from Lieutenant-Colonel Stephenson to blow it. This was not forthcoming until later in the evening and when the Germans were almost on the bridge. To Pottinger's dismay the charges would not go off; resourcefully, and using his skill as one of the army's best shots, he fired his revolver at the primer. The Germans were on the bridge and firing at him at this point; unfortunately the charges remained dead. He managed to make his escape, with his men, in the gathering gloom; in any case the enemy had stopped for the night and were not prepared to set off into the unknown in pursuit.

Lieutenant-Colonel Bond's KOYLI moved out of the brewery at Boussu after it had been hit by shell fire at midday and moved up towards the canal. The machine-gun officer, Lieutenant Pepys, was on the left of the St Ghislain road bridge, where he had been all day. The Battalion took up position 500 yards to the left of the road bridge and about a hundred yards south of the canal. At 2.30pm Captain Lowther took C Company up to the canal to strengthen the Borderers firing line; at about the same time Pepys was killed by a German sniper from the north bank and his place in charge of the machine-guns was taken by Lieutenant BN Denison.

The battalions of 13 Brigade were still at the canal at 6pm.

Mons: the afternoon at the west end of the Condé Canal (Railway Bridge at Les Herbieres to Thulin Road Bridge) - 14 Brigade.

Lieutenant-Colonel Longley's 1/E Surrey had been watching and hearing the action of their right in 13 Brigade's sector; at 1pm C Company, in position close to the Borderers on either side of the railway embankment, came under fire. Before this Major Tew had sent Lieutenant Schomberg to Major Leigh of the Borderers to arrange that neither battalion would withdraw from the canal without informing the other. Lieutenant-Colonel Longley extended this so that neither would retire until dark, an arrangement also made with Lieutenant-Colonel Turner of the DCLI. Unfortunately matters were altered by the German attack on the left flank as regards the latter agreement.

As soon as the enemy attack commenced, Captain Benson went forward with the officer commanding the front platoon of A Company

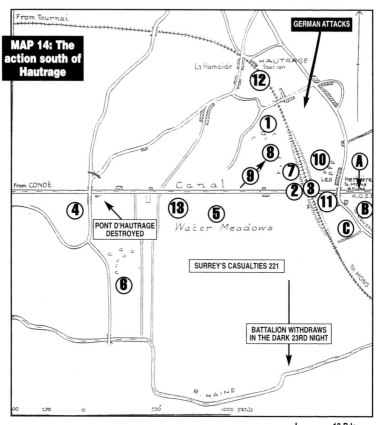

MAP 14: The action south of Hautrage

GERMAN ATTACKS

From Tournai

La Hamaide

HAUTRAGE Station

⑫

①

⑧

⑨ ⑦ ⑩ Ⓐ

From CONDÉ Canal Les He were To Mons 2 miles K.O.S.B

②③ ⑪ Ⓑ

④ ⑬ ⑤ Ⓒ

PONT D'HAUTRAGE DESTROYED

Water Meadows

SURREY'S CASUALTIES 221

⑥

BATTALION WITHDRAWS IN THE DARK 23RD NIGHT

R. HAINE

00 250 0 500 1000 yards

---

14 BRIGADE: 1ST EAST SURREY'S

1. 2nd Suffolk's clearing brush for Surreys
2. Barges under Railway Bridge
3. Lt. Darwell's machine guns
4. Capt. Woulfe - Flanagan 'B'
5. Capt. Minogue 'D' Coy 'Surreys'
6. Capt. Torrens 'A' Coy. 'Surreys'
7. Capt. Benson killed

8. Capt.Campbell hit
9. Lt Ward charges with sword
10. Lt. Wynward attacks at embankment
11. Bridge (railway) blown by R.E.s
12. Capt. Cambell's patrol to Hautrage
13. Lt. Col. Longley's Batt. HQ

13 Bde:
2nd KOSB - 2nd KOYLI

A. 2nd K.O.S.B.'s at Bridge
B. Lt. Pepys KOYL machine gun officer killed
C. KOYLI relieves KOSB at canal between 6p.m. and 7p.m on the 23rd

(Lieutenant Wynward), crossed the canal by a barge they had moored under the railway bridge and moved into the nearest trench on the left of the railway embarkment. They soon came under machine-gun fire and Benson was mortally wounded [7]. Wynward put him on a stretcher that was brought over with them and had the Captain taken back over the canal. It was all in vain, for although Benson was taken to the dressing station established in the convent at Boussu, he died there.

Captain Campbell, who earlier that morning had seen the railwaymen getting up steam in Hautrage station [12], took over

94

command of C Company. For some reason, Tew ordered Campbell back to the south side of the bank; he had hardly arrived when it became apparent that the battle on the far side was escalating and he sought permission to return to his Company. He returned safely, heading for the men on the left of the embankment first. On the other side of it the German attack had become heavier - the thrust of the enemy action was against the Borderers; and that part of C Company had no idea that there might be a withdrawal later that afternoon.

The German infantry now advanced in extended order and attempted to climb and cross over the railway embankment. They were struck heavy blows by Lieutenant Darwell's machine-guns [3] on the south side of the bridge, which fired straight up the railway line. At 4pm Lieutenant Wynward took fifty of his men and launched a bayonet charge [10] against the Germans, who had occupied his front line trenches, and recovered the position. In the process he was severely wounded in the arm and forced to come away, but his men held their recaptured ground.

Tew could see that 2/KOSB were being forced to give ground, regardless of the agreement, and so at 6pm he ordered all of his men north of the canal to fall back across it. With the railway bridge coming under intense fire, he also withdrew Darwell's machine-guns from their exposed position. The men to the right of the embankment got the message and withdrew successfully by means of the barge; but the platoons to the west did not move - they were unaware of the order.

The Germans were no longer threatened by the machine-guns and were thus able to get onto the embankment and attack the remaining part of C Company, who had successfully repelled German attacks on the left, west side of the embankment all afternoon.

Captain Campbell was hit in the neck almost immediately this new German assault began; picking himself up, he was hit again, struck in the face by a shot that almost severed his tongue. He struggled on towards Lieutenant Ward's trench, but was wounded twice more, and added a broken arm to his other injuries. He finally fell to the ground and stayed there, though he was to survive the war as a German

The original railway bridge at Les Herbieres. It shows the positions of Lt Darwell's machine guns (1/East Surreys) in the right foreground.

prisoner, the last eleven months of which were spent interned in the Netherlands. Ward was stirred into action by seeing the fate of his Captain and by the proximity of the enemy; he got his men together and drew his sword, leading them in a charge [9]. He was shot and killed. Lieutenant Morritt, nearest to the embankment, could see what was happening on his left and the danger of his position being cut off by Germans coming down the slope between him and the canal. He led his men in a charge to the canal, which a few managed to reach. Morritt was not one of them; he was shot in the knee and brought down. Whilst lying wounded he saw a German aiming his rifle at him from a range of twenty yards, but fortunately the shot only broke his sword. Morritt was taken prisoner, but did not survive the war; he was shot whilst trying to escape on 27 June 1917.

By this stage it was 7pm; the Germans were close to the canal, but did not attempt to cross it until dawn.

2/Suffolk had taken part in the Surreys battle. Captain LF Hepworth had taken two platoons of C Company over the canal to support the bridgehead and stayed there until they were ordered to retire by Major Tew. The Battalion suffered its first casualties in the desperate hours preceding 7pm, with several killed and Lieutenant VMG Phillips wounded and a prisoner. The survivors of these two platoons withdrew with the East Surrey men.

At nightfall the bridges were intact but the Germans were still on the north side of the canal.

1/DCLI had spent the afternoon preparing for the inevitable German attack whilst, if they only knew it, the German IVth Corps completed its movement to the south. In front was the 7th Division and, to the DCLI's left, was the 8th Division. As the situation unfolded before him, Lieutenant-Colonel Turner became increasingly concerned about his open left flank, the edge of his Battalion, of Smith-Dorrien's II Corps and of the whole BEF.

The Royal Engineers of Major G Walker's 59 Fd Coy had completed their demolition preparations at the bridge and had also constructed a bridge over the River Haine in the rear of the position. They simply had to await events.

Turner withdrew Lieutenant Benn's machine-guns from north of the canal, concerned that they might be lost in a determined attack. They were replaced by the construction of a stone wall built with paving stones from the road, a sangar right across it, similar to the ones that they had built in India on the North West Frontier. A section of ten men were placed behind it with orders to remain until relieved. Turner had carried out his fine tuning of the Battalion's preparations,

At 4.45pm the Germans advanced out of Ville Pommeroeul, about 1300 yards up the perfectly straight road, four abreast and densely packed. Behind the infantry could be seen cavalry, the whole seeming to be on parade. The light infantrymen were astonished - what they had witnessed in the morning was nothing compared to this. The men at the newly constructed barricade waited until the enemy reached a point 750 yards away (it had been measured and marked early in the morning) and then opened fire simultaneously, shooting as fast as they could reload. The result was devastating, and in a moment the road was empty of Germans except for the many who would never move again. The enemy infantry at the railway level crossing, some way further back than those who had taken the full blast of rifle fire, began to fire towards the bridge, but the range was too great to do any damage.

Major Petavel, the Second in Command, went over to the north side and ordered the men back - B Company to come over the bridge, C Company further to the right by the means of two barges which Lieutenant Acland, the Adjutant, had moored there for the purpose. The last man over cast them adrift.

Before the infantry left the canal, but with every man over, the sappers destroyed the lifting road bridge and then went to the left and blew the one at Lock No. 5 and a wooden one, outside of Lieutenant-Colonel Turner's sector.

At 6pm the DCLI withdrew from the canal to take up defensive positions on each side of the road behind the bridge over the River Haine, at the hamlet of Sardon, a thousand yards or so south of the canal.

2/Manchester came into action for the first time in the late afternoon when the Germans, surprised at seeing the bridge destroyed and correctly assuming that the British had withdrawn, came down to the bridge to be met by the Manchesters machine-guns. These

A brief rest period in the early part of the retreat from Mons.

eloquently dissuaded them from such an idea; the enemy would wait until dark to cross the wreckage.

In fact Lieutenant-Colonel Turner's fear of being left out on a limb on the left was not accurate. 19 Brigade, under Brigadier-General Drummond, formed from lines of communication troops, arrived in the area around Hensies, two and a half miles west of the Thulin road at 3.30pm. 1/SR (Scottish Rifles) went to the left of St Aybert; 2/RWF (Royal Welsh Fusiliers) moved behind them in support; 2/A&SH (Argyll and Sutherland Highlanders) to their right and 1/Middx actually on the canal in and about St Aybert. This latter Battalion was the closest to the DCLI.

Men of the German 8th Division attacked the lifting bridge east of the village at about 4.30pm when B Company was just arriving; they got there in time to prevent their crossing and protect that of a squadron of the 2nd Dragoons, part of 1 (Cavalry) Brigade, moving under shellfire.

At 5pm a heavy attack was launched against B Company's position, but the Germans were driven off, aided by the mounting of a machine-gun in a house overlooking the bridge. The Royal Engineers blew up the bridge (preparations had been made in the afternoon) in the middle of this firefight. The Germans decided against any further attempt that day, but tried again in the early morning of the 24th, only to be driven off again. 1/Middx had got off very lightly, suffering eight casualties, of whom two were killed.

Brigadier-General Count von Gleichen's 15 Brigade remained almost entirely aloof from proceedings. At 10am 1/Dorsets held a church parade, but although the parade happened, the service was abandoned. At midday C and D Companies, under Major Saunders and Captain Davidson respectively, were ordered to go forward towards the canal, to Wasmuel, and dig in. The remainder of the Battalion watched the battle progress through binoculars. At 5.30pm enemy artillery began to fire over the forward companies' heads and Captain Davidson reported that many Germans could be seen coming towards them, about a thousand yards away; they were obviously following up the battalions of 9 Brigade. One of the platoons opened fire, unaware of the CO's order forbidding this; the Germans scattered and took cover. Nothing further occurred until later in the evening.

1/Cheshire had been engaged in digging trenches near Boussu, a safe distance away. However all was not peace and tranquility; a salvo of six shells passed by, as one commented, 'so close if I'd put my hand up I could have touched them'.

Darkness now obscured the battlefield of Mons.

Mons: the critical last hours of the first day

Field-Marshal Sir John French had courageously agreed to hold the canal line for twenty four hours whilst Lanrezac reorganised his line; the time was nearly up.

Smith-Dorrien faced some severe problems. 3rd Division's 8 Brigade had withdrawn from Mons into the pre-prepared second line defences, looking north just below Mesvin, two miles south of Mons. 7 Brigade, so far uninvolved in the battles, lay in and around Ciply, a mile south of Cuesmes, on the left of the 8th. The three remaining battalions of 9 Brigade, 2/RS, 1/Lincoln and 1/NF, the last of Hamilton's Division to withdraw from the Condé Canal, were in the process of going into positions on the left of the 7th. The fourth Battalion in the Brigade, 4/RF, was also near Ciply, badly hurt in the fighting that day and would take no further part in the fighting around Mons.

Major-General Fergusson's 5th Division was preparing to retire from its positions along the Condé Canal and to carry on its fight as the left flank of II Corps; Smith-Dorrien was increasingly concerned about the gap that might be created between his men and I Corps, and so asked Haig for assistance. The nearest available help could come from Major-General C Monro's 2nd Division, his reserve formation, 5 Brigade (Brigadier-General RCB Haking commanding 2/Worcs, 2/Ox and Bucks, 2/HLI and 2/Connaught Rangers). They were marched north to take up position to the left of 9 Brigade between Frameries and Paturages.

1/RWK were still at the canal. At 6.30pm the Brandenburgers made what Bloem described as 'a supreme effort' that was utterly frustrated by the burst of rapid fire which greeted it. On the right flank, after the Northumberlands' withdrawal, a party of Germans crossed the canal and moved westwards. They attacked the two gun section of 120 Field Battery on its slag heap and captured one of the 18 pdrs; but they were unable to progress further. They were halted by Captain Tulloch's D Company that was holding the railway bridge under which Lieutenant Ozanne, 2/Duke of Wellington's machine-gun officer, had sheltered after being badly wounded.

Captain Buchanan Dunlop had dug a trench across the line north of the bridge and he still had two platoons there. Thus far their casualties had been light, though Dunlop himself had been wounded when he had rescued Ozanne earlier. At 7pm there was no thought of retiring from their positions; Dunlop came over to discuss with Captain Tulloch arrangements for holding the bridge through the night and asked

2/Duke of Wellington's for some assistance. They sent a party up from M Company. Dunlop then went to Battalion Headquarters to get his head wound dressed and brief his CO; but at 9.30pm, just before he arrived, Lieutenant-Colonel Martyn had just received an order to retire. Returning to Tulloch, Dunlop told him that the signal to withdraw back across the canal and towards Wasmes would be the blowing up of the road bridge. At midnight the Battalion withdrew to its new position; it had suffered 96 casualties during its stubborn tenure of the St Ghislain position.

Lieutenant Godsell had been waiting most of the day for the order to blow the bridges, on tenterhooks as to whether the arrangements would actually work, He had the two bridges to destroy simultaneously (the small wooden one alongside). He used equal lengths of safety fuse to light nine charges, each fuse with a sapper to light it. The charges fired; however, Sergeant Fittal of 1/RWK had never received the order to withdraw and his section was left abandoned on the wrong side of the canal. At dawn a number of Germans cautiously approached his position, calling on him to surrender. The party opened fire and drove the enemy away; and then quickly fell back across the ruins of the bridge, leaving four wounded men behind to be taken as prisoners. The railway bridge was blown by Sergeant Payne and his party of five sappers; before they set the charges off they could hear the Germans singing around their camp fires.

2/Duke of Wellington's had heard the activity at the canal; late in the afternoon Lieutenant-Colonel Gibbs had been told by Brigadier-General Cuthbert that his Battalion would probably be falling back to Wasmes sometime that night and that he thought the Germans were not the small force he had been led to believe but must be two or three corps at least. The Battalion had suffered relatively lightly, having 32 casualties that afternoon.

At 9.55pm Gibbs was ordered to retire to the prepared positions on the Wasmes - Bois de Boussu line after 1/RWK had passed through his position. Captain TM Ellis (killed at Ypres on 18 April 1915) took his company, B, to the market place in St Ghislain and there joined Captain Jenkins. Messages were sent to the other company commanders to collect their men and make straight for the railway station at Wasmes. Captain Jubb (killed the following day) was to move off with the remaining men as soon as the last man of the Kents had come through. Meanwhile the Colonel and the medical officer, Captain Graham, went to the hospital to see if any of the wounded had been evacuated. Only the horse ambulances had gone. Dismayed, they

The road bridge, at top of Rue du Pont at Lock 3, with the wooden foot bridge on the far side. Lt Godsell's bridges.

went to the railway station with a train ready to leave, with the wounded Lieutenant Ozanne on board. Running back to the hospital, he told those who could to make their way as quickly as possible to the train, which advice a few followed. 2/Duke of Wellington's moved into Wasmes and Smith-Dorrien's second line; Monday would be a very costly day for the Battalion indeed.

2/KOSB were the next to get away. The orders came as darkness fell; 2/KOYLI came up to provide cover for the withdrawal. The Battalion got away without incident, although some of the wounded horses had to be shot. Lieutenant Pottinger's lattice girder bridge over Lock No. 4 was left standing, as the engineers' (of 17 Fd Coy) charges had failed to explode. The Battalion marched through the night, finding it difficult to maintain direction on the winding roads, and arrived before dawn at the large village of Dour within the lines of 15 Brigade.

2/KOYLI was the sole remaining battalion from 13 Brigade on the canal bank as night drew on. When they arrived it was discovered that the right hand battalion of 14 Brigade, 1/E Surrey, were also retiring. Major Heathcote's A Company were sent, in the dark, to the left of the standing road bridge at Lock No. 4 and he put his men, with a machine-gun, onto the railway embankment - the scene of such bitter

The first replacement bridge with an iron foot bridge - replacing the destroyed wooden one.

fighting earlier in the day. Heathcote knew that his left flank was in the air; to his right the companies were stretched out in the order B, D and C.

The Germans had, however, seen enough for the day; their casualties all along the Condé Canal had been far greater that they could have envisaged, and indeed there were serious concerns about a possible British counter-attack. The advance had been significantly held up, but reinforcements from IIIrd Corps would continue to arrive, making an advance the following day a practical option.

The Yorkshiremen, however, fully expected an attack and swept the small woods on the far side with bursts of machine-gun and rifle fire. Later in the war a German colonel, who had been wounded there, visited the prison camp at Torgau and sought out men of the British battalions who had been on the Condé Canal. He told them of the unexpected casualties his men had received that night, which had stopped them making an attack on the bridges at Les Herbieres.

Just before midnight Lieutenant-Colonel Bond gave the order to withdraw; the last to leave the canal was Captain Luther's C Company. Before he could move his position was lit up by a German rocket, which told his men that the enemy were not far away and were lying quietly and waiting. Those on the left, by the railway embankment, brought the body of their machine-gun officer, Lieutenant Pepys, and buried him on the outskirts of Wasmes.

Before 1/East Surrey had withdrawn in the dark from its position the two bridges on the left of Major Heathcote had been blown by No 1 Section of 59 Fd Coy. The small lifting bridge was totally destroyed, but unfortunately the exploder only partially destroyed the iron plate railway bridge; however the Hautrage Bridge, which B Company of 2/KOYLI were guarding, successfully went up.

Not all of 2/KOYLI got away before midnight; Sergeants Mullins and Walker had gone asleep in their position over the canal, near the lock, and did not hear the call. When they awoke at dawn they saw parties of the enemy crossing by the broken bridge, but they somehow managed to evade them and rejoined the Battalion later in the morning.

On Monday 24th 2/KOYLI marched out of the salient, the first of the 5th Division. Their casualties at the Condé Canal had been 28 - light in comparison to most. Greater excitement would follow. Two days later, in their march to the south, at Le Cateau, Major CAL Yate would win the VC (as would Corporal Holmes) and the Battalion would lose twenty officers and 600 men. Yate was severely wounded, taken prisoner and shot whilst attempting to escape from Torgau Prison on 21 September 1914 (he told the Germans that he would never consider himself their prisoner). He is buried in Berlin.

Although Major Tew thought that he had got everyone back from the other side of the canal when the bridge was destroyed in fact they were not. On learning that some of A Company of 1/East Surrey were unaccounted for he returned to the wrecked bridge, but all he could hear were orders being shouted in German; the men must be either dead or captured. By midnight the Battalion had marched away to Boussu and then went further south to Dour. Back at the canal Lieutenant Morritt and eight of his men, all wounded, were carried by villagers to the convent in Boussu before being sent on to Germany as prisoners. Morritt made his name for repeatedly trying to escape, and was killed whilst attempting to make off from Schwarmstadt.

1/East Surrey lost 221 men killed, wounded and missing.

2/Suffolk withdrew from the canal at 10pm, a short time before the Surreys. The Battalion arrived at Dour in the early morning of Monday and withdrew from the salient later that day, almost unscathed during their time in it. It was but a reprieve, for they suffered over 600 casualties at Le Cateau.

1/DCLI had withdrawn to the bridge over the River Haine; D Company on the left looked over the water meadows before them and waited in the gloom for the Germans, who were about to cross the canal. 2/Manchester were entrenched on the right hand side of the bridge. At approximately 11pm the Germans came down the long straight road behind a barrage of shrapnel shells; but were met by the machine-guns of both battalions and incessant rifle fire. None of the infantry could see the other side's men, and the German firing was largely ineffectual.

However, they proceeded to bring up a field gun to the destroyed road bridge and fired it at the bridge over the river. Lieutenant Flint of 59 Fd Coy was working on it with his men to fix the charges; the bridge could safely be blown as all the British troops were over the river. To deal with the danger caused by the gun whilst he and his men worked at their task he posted a man to shout a warning whenever he saw the flash from the gun's muzzle. The men would drop into the ditch before the shell arrived. This extremely risky business did result in the bridge being blown, and for his bravery Lieutenant Flint won the Legion of Honour. In due course his work on the Aisne three weeks later was to result in the award of the DSO; but he was killed in January 1915.

The Germans did not advance further down the road that night and both 1/DCLI and 2/Manchester withdrew towards Elouges with few casualties - the DCLI had one killed and five wounded whilst

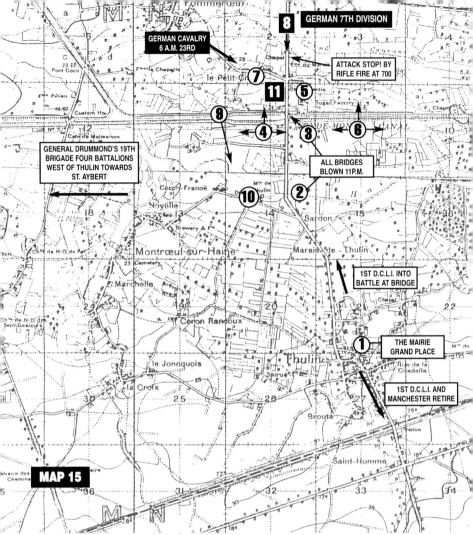

1/DCLI's action along the canal bank.

1. D.C.L.I. HQ Lt Col Turner
2. Extra River bridge built by R.E.s
3. Lifting road bridge at canal lock
4. 'C' Coy 1st D.C.L.I. in trenches
5. Lt. Saville 'B' Coy. road block
6. 'B' Coy D.C.L.I. in trenches
7. First fight Pte Sambrook 6a.m. 23rd
8. 4.45p.m. first big attack
9. 'C' Coy retires over moored barges
10. 'D' Coy D.C.L.I. Capt. Woodham
11. German field gun brought up

2/Manchester suffered a loss of twelve men. They assisted 123 Field Battery to make its escape with all of its guns after it had become a particular target of the German artillery.

Sunday night on the Condé Canal from Jemappes to St Aybert, in 19 Brigade's sector, ended on a quiet note, at least from the fighting point of view. But German bugles could be heard all along the line, signalling preparations for the following day.

The sixty-eight year old von Kluck was far from happy. His First Army had suffered an estimated ten thousand casualties at the hands of an army that had been thought contemptibly small. He was quite convinced that there were at least six divisions against him (he remained convinced of this even after the war was over, as his memoirs of the campaign illustrate - and was aghast when he eventually accepted that there were only two). He resolved to adhere to the original Schlieffen Plan. Von Bülow (another sixty-eight year old general), tired of his nagging and the personality struggle, allowed him to do as he wished. Kluck then made the possibly fatal mistake of detaching von der Marwitz's II (Cavalry) Corps from the battle and sent it west against the Territorial divisions that Joffre had placed there to protect the British left. The French Territorials put up a brave fight (assisted by, in due course, General Sordet's Cavalry Corps), barred the way and prevented Kluck's attempt to come down the British left flank and drive the two British corps into the trap of the fortress at Maubeuge fifteen miles to the south.

General Sir Horace Smith-Dorrien's last thirty six hours must have been quite exhausting; at midnight on Sunday 23 August he could afford to be reasonably satisfied with the way the day had gone. His men had fought magnificently; and he now had a very fair idea of the scale of the massive forces opposite him. He had withdrawn, with a high degree of success, his II Corps from the Condé Canal into prepared positions on the higher ground and he was in line with Haig's I Corps. He had filled the gap between the 3rd and 5th divisions with one of Haig's brigades. On his far left there were now the troops from Brigadier-General Drummond's 19 Brigade and four cavalry brigades providing a screen. Joffre had moved French infantry and cavalry to provide a further flank guard. Two of his brigades (7 and 15) were still unscathed and he had lost almost none of his artillery. However, he remained apprehensive, appreciating Kitchener's accurate view of what the Germans were likely to be about, an attitude not helped by reports from Haig's right flanking division, the 1st, that French troops were moving away from them.

Lieutenant Spears, the BEF's liaison officer with the French Fifth Army, had spent a miserable day. Since meeting French at the roadside he had been at Lanrezac's Army Headquarters witnessing the increasing desperation there as the French were sorely pressed; he learnt on the evening of the 23rd that Lanrezac was going to break off the battle and retire to the south west. This would leave the BEF's right utterly exposed and its position untenable. Spears set off for Le Cateau and arrived there at about 11pm. He was sent back to Mettet to tell Lanrezac that the Field-Marshal felt himself under no obligation to stay where he was and that he would act as circumstances dictated.

Field-Marshal French's day had also been a long one. He had been on the road since the early morning and eventually arrived back at his Headquarters at Le Cateau in the evening. The reports that awaited him indicated that his Corps commanders were satisfied with their positions and were ready for the morrow. French had not been prepared for a battle at Mons - his thoughts ever since his force had been put together had been centred on attack. He had disagreed with all Kitchener's cautionary points, and was one of the great majority who thought that it would be a short, sharp campaign.

French was a not inconsiderable soldier, though as with all his counterparts in high command he had his faults. His situation was not helped by the fact that he disliked Lanrezac and had good reason to distrust him; this personality clash was potentially calamitous for the allied cause. French realised that Kitchener might well have been right in his suggestion that the great bulk of the German army would be coming over the Meuse. Kitchener, for his part, made the vital decision of reinforcing the BEF by sending Major-General TD'O Snow's 4th Division, which arrived in France on the night of 22/23 August. It arrived on the left flank of the BEF on 26th August.

At 1am on Monday morning Sir John French sent for staff officers from the two Corps to tell them that they were to withdraw from the Mons salient as early as possible on that day, and to avoid at all costs the town of Maubeuge. Despite its obvious (all too obvious) attractions of security, food and water, it was a death trap - as events at Liege had shown - and the corps were to retire to the west of it. This stage in von Kluck's plans was, therefore, foiled.

Haig's Headquarters had received these orders by 2am via telegram; owing to the unfortunate location of Smith-Dorrien's Headquarters, utterly lacking in any form of telegraphic equipment, his orders did not arrive until much later.

At 5.30am French went to his Advanced Headquarters at Bavai and called in on Haig at Bonnet to observe the fighting going on further north. He then visited General Sordet, commanding a French Cavalry Corps, at Avesnes and then returned to Le Cateau to see the first of 4th Division's men arriving amidst the flood of refugees heading south from Mons. At his Headquarters in the Hotel de Ville where his staff was beavering away, he issued instructions for it to be moved to St Quentin.

Chapter Four

MONDAY, 24th AUGUST: THE LAST DAY

The First Hours

The 3rd and 5th Divisions anticipated a long battle in their new positions in Smith-Dorrien's second line; Ist Corps also expected that it would be in a big battle on this day. Kluck had no intention of doing this, other than to engage them with enough strength to hold them; his opponents were to be swept into a trap by his manoeuvring right wing.

8 Brigade was on the right of Hamilton's 3rd Division; 4/Middx and 2/RIrR had suffered much the previous day, but they had hardly rested during the night, working instead at the trenches and defences of the new position. These men were the first beneficiaries of the new order, as Brigadier-General Doran's 8 Brigade moved south out of the salient, heading towards Bavai[1].

To the right Haig's I Corps had a relatively easy time disengaging from its position. He too was cluttered with all his equipment up forward in hundreds of vehicles, carts and anything else that would carry the furnishings that go with an army on the advance. But he was able to start his move early in the morning and before the German artillery bombardment of the day had begun. He also set off towards Bavai, with 1st Division leading the way, followed two hours later by the 2nd. The route led them around the north of Maubeuge and down the very large - nine miles long by four miles wide - Mormal Forest. This feature was a major concern for all the senior commanders of the BEF, as it was inevitable that the two corps would have to pass either side of it, and they would therefore be forced apart for a significant period of time. This is not the sort of situation that forces in a withdrawing army appreciate.

On top of this straight forward topographical fact, other difficulties were considerable. Road discipline was completely absent. The limited roads available - foot-destroying pavé - were congested with French troops heading south, pathetic hordes of refugees and French cavalry moving across the flow, heading for the BEF's west flank. There were problems at the few bridges across the wide River Sambre; there were some clashes with German cavalry patrols; it was very difficult to keep in contact with other elements of the BEF - but, in general, the retreat went smoothly enough in the circumstances.

The six brigades of IInd Corps were fortifying their new positions,

Map 16: General Smith-Dorrien's right flank 24th August.

German cavalry attempting to cross their own pontoon bridge, caught by British artillery.

confident of their ability after seeing the German infantry convincingly repulsed in their attempts to cross the canal the previous day. True, some had managed to make it across, but at a terrible cost and at a price that prevented them following through immediately. Now the British were in positions on hills with better fields of fire and with the likelihood of more effective artillery support. Besides their feverish work, many had their first food for eighteen hours.

Smith-Dorrien received the surprising, but not altogether unwelcome, order to retire his Corps at about 4am. However he had the major problem of withdrawing two divisions on very limited roads, already congested with refugees, and beside the infantry there would be transport, guns and the bulk of Allenby's cavalry.

He resolved that the 3rd Division should go first; it had taken the heaviest punishment on the first day, and his left flank was the more secure. The 5th Division should be able to follow afterwards, especially as he had some support in the form of 19 Brigade and the cavalry on his left, whilst Haking's fresh 5 Brigade was on his right.

Brigadier-General Doran received his orders to retire at 4.30am, just as the German IIIrd and IXth Corps artillery began their bombardment. Fortunately the infantry had learnt their lesson well, and was leaving it to the artillery to soften the British positions. Thus the Brigade was uninterrupted as, 4/Middx leading, it slipped away from the salient without further loss.

To the left of 8 Brigade was Brigadier-General McCracken's 7th. It had not taken part in the battles of the preceding day, but was now

109

placed across the line of any German advance from the south of Mons. The four battalions had spent much of Sunday in preparing their defences around and to the north of the small hilltop village of Ciply. On the high ground to the right, overlooking Mesvin and guarding 8 Brigade's flank, were 2/RIRifles. To the left and directly in front of the village were 3/Worcesters; behind them were 1/Wilts. On the left of the village, between it and situated slightly north of Frameries, also on a hill, were 2/South Lancs. Also in Ciply were the survivors of the fighting at the Nimy bridges, 4/RF.

Ciply had only suffered damage from the occasional shell. The village of Cuesmes, a mile and a half to the north west had been bombarded, and the night was lit up by the fires raging there as a consequence. The narrow and winding connecting roads between the two villages had been filled all night with terrified civilians fleeing, intermingled with whom were some men from the Royal Scots Fusiliers, wounded in the fighting at Jemappes and Flenu.

At about 4am the enemy artillery opened up on the positions at Ciply, but the German infantry remained in their own positions. By this stage there had been no new orders for Brigadier-General McCracken.

To the left rear of 7 Brigade was 9 Brigade - or at least its three remaining battalions. Two of these, 1/RSF and 1/NF, had made a fighting withdrawal to get into the second line defences at Frameries. Lieutenant-Colonel Douglas Smith's Battalion had spent a quiet night in the brewery to the north of the village after fighting through Flenu. Smith was astonished to get the Brigadier-General's order to retire. Whilst the enemy bombardment was falling on Frameries, the Fusiliers marched up the hill and through the village soon after 8am, away from the salient where so many of their comrades had been lost.

Apart from the skirmish at the barricades south of Mons covering the withdrawal of 4/RF, 1/Lincoln had been uninvolved. The Battalion now took over the positions to which the Royal Fusiliers had retired, on the right of the railway embankment and the road to Cuesmes, several hundred yards north of Frameries.

1st Northumberland Fusiliers had worked without ceasing during the night, erecting barricades at the crossroads in the village, having taken little food and even less sleep. During the hours of darkness, when the streets should have been empty of all but soldiers, a number of civilians were found wandering the place. Spy scares were at their height, and a number were arrested, despite some pleading to be allowed to go to Cuesmes to rescue British wounded who had been left in houses there.

In the same vicinity was Brigadier-General Haking's 5 Brigade. 2/Worcesters were in Frameries; to their left and slightly forward, in front of Paturages, were 2/HLI and behind and to their left were 2/Ox & Bucks and 2/CR (Connaught Rangers). They had arrived at 1am from the reserve area of the 2nd Division near Bougnies, three miles south east of Frameries. When 2/Worcesters reached the village, not knowing what they might encounter, they had bayonets fixed and the officers had drawn their revolvers. They found it unoccupied, as the men of 9 Brigade had not then reached it. The German shelling in the early hours of the morning caused them some casualties before they, unexpectedly, withdrew.

Fifth Division Area

2/KOSB, ordered to retire from the canal in the late evening of Sunday, made for Petit Wasmes. This involved a march of four miles through the confusing and narrow road system, taking them through the hilly and densely built up coal mining area west of Colfontaine. There was little to eat, and in any case they were exhausted, when they arrived at their billets in a field between 1 and 2am; they slept as soon as they could. The Battalion was to see no further action in the salient and received orders to withdraw south to Blaugies and Bavai later in the morning after the 3rd Division had passed through.

2/Duke of Wellington's left the canal just before midnight; they were marching into a major battle at Wasmes which would begin in the morning of the 24th. Wasmes, three miles south of the canal, is a hollow at a multi-road junction south of Hornu, surrounded by coal mines and slag heaps and crossed by a railway line. It was part of the second line of defence. The Battalion arrived at 3am and took up positions in an arc to the north of the village; Battalion Headquarters were located with C Company a thousand yards north of the village church, close to a wood. The move to this position had not been without incident; at 3am Major Townsend's A Company were heavily shelled before they took their place to the north west of the village centre.

1/RWK were also withdrawn to Wasmes. They were in the village square when the German artillery began its shelling, preparing to take on responsibility for the left flank defences of the village. They would be engaged in fighting once more by 10am.

2/KOYLI were the last to withdraw from the canal and did not arrive at Wasmes until 7am. They went to the left of the RWKs near to the railway line; apart from suffering from the shelling, they took no active part in the battle for the village. Two companies of 1/Dorsets had been sent from Paturages to Wasmes. Part of 15 Brigade, they had been sent forward to hold the line until 13 Brigade arrived, and were to get involved in the battle here.

14 Brigade all withdrew late on Sunday six miles south of the canal, to Dour. The place became so full of troops that the CO of 2/Manchester, Lieutenant-Colonel James, had to take his men over three miles to the east, to the south western outskirts of Wasmes, arriving there at 5am in time to receive some of the German bombardment.

1/Norfolk and 1/Beds were at Dour; 1/Cheshire were south of Boussu, digging trenches and preparing for 'two thousand Germans' that were reported to be coming their way. They did not materialise, but a great many local inhabitants came through their lines, fleeing before the Germans and getting away from the imminent battle. Shortly after dawn Major Wetherall, the Brigade Major, arrived to tell Lieutenant-Colonel Boger to take his Battalion to Dour. The Cheshires were surprised and disappointed at being withdrawn; later in the day they were to have more than their fill of combat.

Battle was expected, but life was going to get unexpectedly more complicated for IInd Corps.

German 17th Division entering Boussu on 26th August 1914.

Mons: The last hours of the battle.

1. The Battles of Frameries and Ciply

The fight for the hilltop village of Frameries began with the enemy's bombardment of it which started soon after dawn. It fell on the centre of the village and 2/Worcesters's position. Within an hour it lifted and with an increased ferocity was put onto 1/NF's position, moving up towards the crossroads. The enemy infantry assault started at 7.30am when the 24th (Brandenburg) Regiment advanced to the attack from the valley dividing the village from Flenu, a mile and a half to the north.

At this critical period when Major-General Hamilton's 3rd Division came under attack as it was about to move out of the salient, 9 Brigade suddenly found that its neighbour, 5 Brigade, was withdrawing without warning. This was dismaying news for Smith-Dorrien and Hamilton, but it might have been expected as it was known that Haig's I Corps (2nd Division) were already on their way out of the salient. Nevertheless, it was a blow to their plans and would later cause 13 Brigade sever problems, but at this time it was 7 and 9 Brigades that were suffering; 8 Brigade had already moved off unscathed before the battle commenced.

At the crossroads in the centre of the village, where the street ran down steeply towards Cuesmes, was A Company manning three barricades. These blockaded the roads south, east and west and had been constructed during the night by the RE and were then being strengthened by 1/NF. At the foot of the hill, straddling the road to Cuesmes, were C and D Companies and in echelon on the right was 1/Lincoln. There were four guns from 109 Battery near the railway station on the south eastern edge of the village. The Germans may well have thought that the village was empty, having seen some British troops pulling out earlier. They were to get a rude awakening when they approached the crossroads and the railway crossing at the northern edge of Frameries. Private Tebbut of 1/Lincoln later reported,

I just kept firing my rifle until it got too hot to handle. At four hundred yards you could not miss and I never thought I would ever see so many dead men in such a small space

However, the Northumberlands and Lincolns casualties were also mounting up; both battalions slowly withdrew up the hill into the built up area. The Brandenburgers arrived at a point some hundred yards short of the barricade across the road to Cuesmes when Captain Sandilands witnessed an extraordinary incident. He was wounded, but

113

still with his Company at the barricade, when an elderly lady approached in the midst of the mayhem. She insisted on going through the barricade to fetch a doctor to attend to the wounded who were being take into the hospital at the crossroads in the middle of the village. She could not be dissuaded, despite the bullets and flying shrapnel; she proceeded to go into a house beyond the barricade and soon reappeared with a little man carrying a black bag. No sooner had they emerged when a shell landed on the house opposite; they rushed back into the house. After a short while they came out once more, and ran back up the road to the barricade and on into the hospital.

Meanwhile the German effort had increased on the right; loud banging could be heard in the houses on the Cuesmes road as the enemy made passages through them to get at A Company.

At 8.45am Major-General Hamilton ordered Brigadier-General Shaw to withdraw from the salient, increasingly concerned that otherwise his Brigade would be cut off on its left because of the withdrawal of 5 Brigade. The two battalions in Frameries began to disentangle themselves from the battle. On the left of A Company some Germans were seen attacking the western barricade fifty yards along the Paturages road. These were killed; and small rear parties kept the enemy at bay as the two battalions withdrew up the hill, *en route* to Eugies and Bavai. Their casualties had been considerable: 1/Lincoln had lost four officers and 134 other ranks, some of the wounded being taken prisoner in the convent hospital. Captain Ross, who was thought to have been killed, was later discovered to have been wounded and captured. 1/NF had suffered about fifty casualties, many of the wounded too badly hurt to move. A doctor, Captain M Leckie DSO, who was attached to the Northumberlands, died of his wounds in the hospital at Frameries on 28 August.

It was expected that Brigadier-General McCracken's 7 Brigade at Ciply would have been able to withdraw before being attacked by the German 6th Division's attack began. Two battalions did - 2/RIRifles, which came down from the ridge a mile south of Mesvin and passed through 3/Worcesters; and the remnants of 4/RF.

2/South Lancs and 3/Worcesters in their positions on either side of main road into Cuesmes, five hundred yards south of the great, embanked railway system, had seen hundreds of Germans crossing their front since the early morning. The advance of the 24th Brandenburgers extended to this position and was met by equally effective rifle fire as they swarmed down the slope of Mount Eribus, a small hill between Ciply and Mons. The enemy was halted before they reached the triangle of railway lines and the station two hundred yards in front of 3/Worcesters' A Company.

On the left Lieutenant-Colonel Wanliss' 2/South Lancs were equally under attack from the Brandenburgers; the Germans lined the railway embankment on the left, swarmed under the railway bridge and formed up behind the few houses that stood there. Facing them was D Company and Captain Travis-Cook with his machine-gun officer, Lieutenant Fulcher. They simply mowed down what they estimated to be two battalions armed with eight machine-guns; they continued firing until ordered to retire. Travis-Cook, wounded seven times, finally fell with a bullet in his neck. Fulcher and his Sergeant, Harrison, shouldered the machine-guns and took them away. However a shell blew the guns off their backs and, it was feared, killed both of them. However, it was later learnt that Sergeant Harrison had not been killed but was badly wounded and taken prisoner. He was awarded the DCM and in due course served as RSM in the 5th Battalion. Fulcher was killed in November 1914 at Ypres.

Brigadier-General McCracken became increasingly worried about his three battalions in the line - they should have retired long ago - and ordered them to get away as quickly as practicable and disengage from what was obviously an overwhelming force. 3/Worcesters were the first to move, covered by D Company (Captain de Salis) from a position at the railway, five hundred yards south of the sugar factory. The shell fire poured onto the escape route to the south, the Genly road, was so heavy that when it became D Company's turn the men had to retire in small sections to avoid destruction.

2/South Lancs acted as the rear guard, although 1/Wilts (Lieutenant-Colonel Halstead), positioned at their road junction a mile south of Ciply and who had not been committed, would be the last to leave. As 2/South Lancs retired from the battlefield the enemy, with their machine-guns on the railway embankment, raked the retreating columns of men. They had to move across the 2,000 yards of open land on either side of the Cuesmes road until they got into the shelter of the buildings on the east side of Frameries. The Battalion lost more than 300 men killed, wounded and missing - the great majority of the latter became prisoners. The RSM, Mr Robert, was found to be missing, but as happened in a large number of cases, he turned up - in this case five days and a major battle later. 3/Worcesters got off lightly with 21 casualties and 1/Wilts with thirty, amongst whom were Captain Dawes and Captain Rowan, the Adjutant. Halstead was fortunate to escape with only having his horse shot from under him.

The engagements at Frameries and Ciply in the four hours since the bombardment commenced and the last man retired cost 7 and 9 Brigades almost 500 casualties; but the Germans had suffered far more. Colonel von Brandis stated that he had lost three company commanders, every second officer, every third man; Captain Liebenow of the 64th Regiment said that his Battalion had lost every fourth man and every lieutenant. The total German casualties were over a thousand, all dead or wounded; over half those of the British were prisoners, though many were wounded.

The Germans, crossing the Condé Canal at both its east and west ends, could now turn their attention to the left of the British line south of the canal. There seemed that there was still the prospect of driving Smith-Dorrien's IInd Corps into the trap of Maubeuge.

The Battle at Wasmes

Essentially this battle involved 13 Brigade, with the addition of part of 1/Dorset from 14 Brigade. When the battalions were withdrawn in the very early hours of Monday morning, it was in the confident expectation that they were going into positions from where they could hold the enemy off for as long as need be. Their casualties thus far had not been heavy and they knew that they had inflicted a very heavy toll on the enemy in his attempts to cross the canal.

The village was packed with troops from the Brigade. 2/Duke of Wellington's were dug in on an arc a mile long around the northern edge, its peak at the crossroad a thousand yards to the north west of the village square at a point called La Justice. 500 yards east on the Binche road was an area known as Le Bosquet; 500 yards further to the east was D Company [7 and 8], at a large slag heap which marked the limit of the Battalion's right flank. On the left were three companies (A, B, C) of 1/Dorsets [17]. They looked down the slope to Hornu, a thousand yards to the north; south of them, on the western perimeter of the Wasmes defences, was B Company (Major CG Pack-Beresford) of 1/RWK [11]. Elements of all three battalions were inside the village perimeter, whilst the KOYLIs were in Paturages [16], to the south.

Until about 11am the Germans contented themselves with bombarding Wasmes and the various positions of the infantry. Although Frameries had long since fallen, they were in no hurry to lose more men than they needed. They were content to hold the Brigade whilst the threatening sweep from the right developed.

Major-General Fergusson gave the order for 14 Brigade to retire from the salient towards Bavai, to be followed by the 13th, which he knew would cover the former's withdrawal. They would be followed by 15 Brigade, which would cover the rear of the 5th Division. In turn, they would be followed by Allenby's cavalry and 19 Brigade. The salient was to be empty of British troops by the early afternoon. However, almost as soon as the order was given, Fergusson learnt that Allenby's cavalry had already gone, unable to find any signs of a great German advance, at 8am. Drummond had withdrawn his 19 Brigade for the same reason. Smith-Dorrien's left flank was 'in the air'; the 5th

1. Battalion HQ with 'C' Coy	11. Major Beresford + 15 buried here
2. Germans attack all morning 24th	12. 'B' Company Royal West Kent
3. Capt. Jubb (adjutant) buried here	13. Lt Russel buried here
4. Battlefield burials	14. Field Ambulance
5. Railway level crosssing	15. Field Artillery battery
6. Germans surrounding platoon	16. 2nd K.O.Y.L.I. retires 1.30 p.m.
7. 'D' Company battlefield burials	17. Dorsets retire midday 24th
8. Battlefield burials	18. Royal West Kents retire 1pm. 24th
9. Battlefield burials	19. D. of Wellingtons withdraw suffering
10. Sgt Spence bayonet charge	323 casualties on 24th

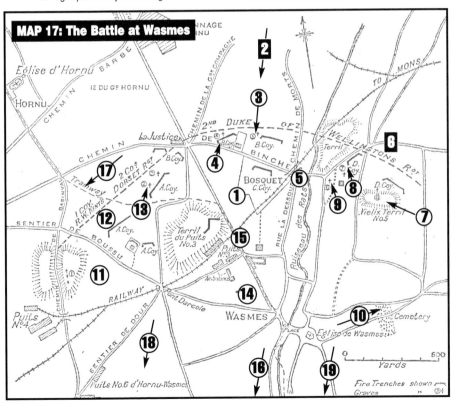

Division had a long way to go before it could be clear.

To make matters worse, the Germans began to attack Wasmes in strength; and the 8th Division began to drive through Crespin to cut off the exodus of IInd Corps.

Fergusson asked Allenby to stop his withdrawal if he could and give some support to his left flank. He then formed a 'task force' from 15 Brigade to act as a left flank shield until he could extract 13 Brigade from the fighting at Wasmes; finally the 15th could move out - what was left of it, as 1/Dorset was fighting with 13 Brigade and 1/Bedfords with 14 Brigade, and these units would withdraw with them.

Before midday the German infantry had advanced against Wasmes in great strength. On the right flank was No. 12 Platoon of C Company, 2/Duke of Wellington's, who could see the enemy coming across a corn field carrying stooks as shields. Lieutenant LE Russel was down to twelve men (he had started with thirty). He ordered them to fix bayonets and to empty their magazines into the advancing Germans. They then stood up and charged into their foe, fighting a bitter hand to hand battle until all the Dukes had been killed [13]. A platoon of D Company was near them; its commander, Sergeant Spence, ordered his men to fix bayonets and fight their way back into the village centre. A survivor, Corporal Williams, wrote

The bodies of Germans were piled up all around. I bayoneted a German, but before I could withdraw it I was clubbed on the head with a rifle, knocked out and became a prisoner.

German infantry advancing in the hot summer sun. TAYLOR LIBRARY

Williams had been previously wounded in the foot. Lieutenant-Colonel Gibbs, lying badly wounded and soon to be made prisoner, saw Sergeant Spence - also seriously wounded - gather his handful of men together and charge up the street near the church [10]. They cleared the street, the Germans fleeing from the shouting, cursing men coming up the road at them, which enabled two platoons to retire. Spence earned a DCM for his actions, but was made prisoner.

At 4pm the battle continued, but the village was invested by the enemy, with hand to hand fighting taking place amongst the winding narrow streets and the many slag heaps that were such a feature of the landscape here. On the left flank the battle had been no less intense. Major Pack Beresford, Captain Phillips and Lieutenant Broadwood of 1/RWK and many of their men were killed. The Dorsets gradually fell back south of the railway [17] running through Wasmes. By 4.30pm the Germans had removed any possibility of the men still in the village escaping capture. The casualties were high. 1/Dorsets lost three officers wounded and taken prisoner and 132 other ranks casualties; 1/RWK five oficers and twenty other ranks; but it was 2/Duke of Wellington's that suffered the most. The Adjutant, Major PB Stafford, Captain Denham-Jubb and Lieutenant Russel were killed; four other officers were wounded and captured, including the CO, whilst Lieutenant Thompson was to die of his wounds on 14 September. Captain Jenkins and Lieutenant Price were missing and 316 other ranks were casualties. The holding action at Wasmes had cost almost five hundred casualties.

The Royal Artillery had also suffered losses - including Major CS Holland, who commanded 120 Battery. For the most part, however, the guns were got out by midday and were able to play their vital part in the retreat.

The Belgians had helped as much as they could with the wounded. Captain Taylor (2/Duke of Wellington's) was wounded and was then taken into hiding by the Barbier family. In September he felt fit enough to make a run for home (it should be borne in mind that there was far from being anything resembling a solid line between the opposing armies at this stage in the war - that would not come to pass until November). Madam Barbier found him some clothes, money and provisions and also found a reliable man to act as his guide. The Captain set off, taking a large suitcase with him in which was his uniform, so that he could put it on if the situations arose and prove that he was not a spy. He alternately walked and hid through an area that was filled with Germans. He succeeded in making it to the small town

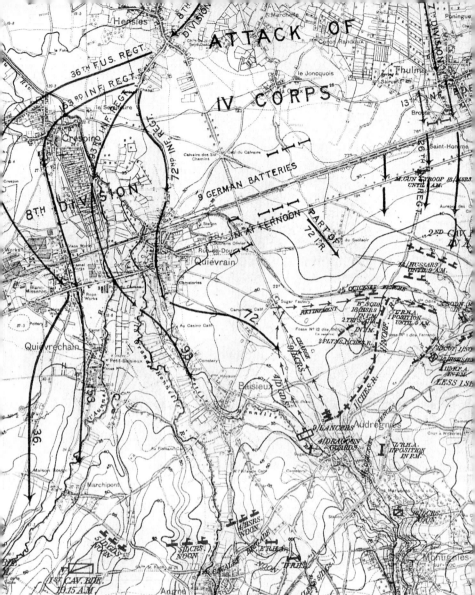

Map 18: Official History Map, actions at Elouges and Audregnies.

of Peruwelz, fifteen miles to the north west of Wasmes and managed to catch the last train to Tournai and Ostend.

Captain Ellis and fifty men (also 2/Duke of Wellington's) were cut off in a wood; in the various encounters with the enemy the group was scattered until Ellis and Corporal Kerman were the only ones left. Still wearing their uniform, for twelve days they walked south at night and hid by day as they were amongst the advancing German army.

Eventually a man found them and took them to a priest's house. The priest took them to a Belgian man who had worked in London to act as their guide. Armed with a card from the priest, asking all who could to help them, the two (now dressed in civilian clothes) with their guide set off. On the way they picked up two men from the Manchesters, and continuing their cat and mouse act with the Germans, they eventually made it through to Leuze, some thirty miles from where they had started. There they caught a train to Ostend and boarded a British destroyer, which took them to England, arriving there on 5 September. They returned to France in due course and rejoined their Battalion. The two officers from 2/DoW who escaped were to be killed on Hill 60, near Ypres, on 18 April 1915.

The Battle at Audregnies: The Glorious Last Stand of the 1st Cheshire Regiment (22nd of Foot).

The left flank guard of the 5th Division consisted of 1/Norfolk (Lieutenant-Colonel CR Ballard) and 1/Cheshires (Lieutenant-Colonel DC Boger). With the two battalions was Major Alexander's 119 Field Battery and Brigadier-General de Lisle's 2 (Cavalry) Brigade: 4/DG, 9/Lancers and 18/Hussars. The Dragoons and Lancers took up positions on the left flank, on the western side of the small hill top village of Audregnies and looking out to the north. Allenby also sent them Major Sclater Booth's L battery of the RHA (Royal Horse Artillery). Ballard, the senior officer, commanded the small force. They began to get into place at 11am; facing them, not more than 3,000 yards away, were 5,000 German infantry approaching quickly from the left, from Quievrain, whilst at a similar distance 2,000 men were advancing from Thulin, to the north. Only 5,000 yards away there were nine batteries of artillery and a further fifteen battalions of infantry coming up behind this force. This was an overwhelming force, the sharp end of von Kluck's scythe that was to drive Smith-Dorrien's IInd Corps into Maubeuge. The British had a real fight on their hands.

The position at Audregnies was a good one. The German line of attack had to come across fairly level, low-lying and open ground to a ridge running north east from Audregnies towards Elouges, two miles away. The fields were scarred by coal mine workings, and the main railway line ran across them from the south east to the north west. There was a minor railway line that ran from a spoil heap in the middle of the German attack line and yet another main line from Mons ran through the south edge of Audregnies. On the left flank, coming out of Audregnies, a pavéd, narrow Roman road ran perfectly straight towards

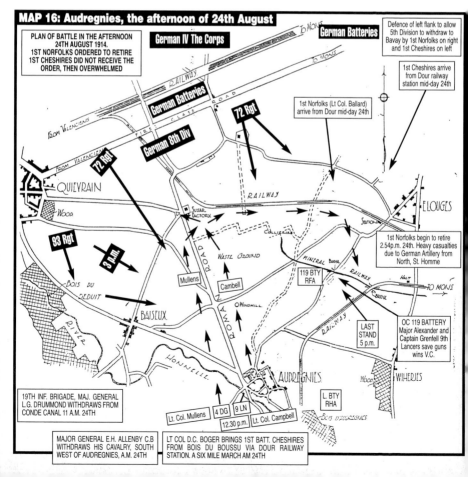

MAP 16: Audregnies, the afternoon of 24th August

PLAN OF BATTLE IN THE AFTERNOON
24TH AUGUST 1914.
1ST NORFOLKS ORDERED TO RETIRE
1ST CHESHIRES DID NOT RECEIVE THE
ORDER, THEN OVERWHELMED

German IV The Corps

German Batteries

Defence of left flank to allow
5th Division to withdraw to
Bavay by 1st Norfolks on right
and 1st Cheshires on left

1st Cheshires arrive
from Dour railway
station mid-day 24th

German Batteries

72 Rgt

German 8th Div

1st Norfolks (Lt Col. Ballard)
arrive from Dour mid-day 24th

72 Rgt

QUIEVRAIN

ELOUGES

1st Norfolks begin to retire
2.54p.m. 24th. Heavy casualties
due to German Artillery from
North, St. Homme

93 Rgt

3 mm

BOIS DU DEDUIT

BAISEUX

Mullens

Cambell

119 BTY
RFA

LAST
STAND
5 p.m.

OC 119 BATTERY
Major Alexander and
Captain Grenfell 9th
Lancers save guns
wins V.C.

AUDREGNIES

WIHERJES

L. BTY
RHA

19TH INF. BRIGADE, MAJ. GENERAL
L.G. DRUMMOND WITHDRAWS FROM
CONDE CANAL 11 A.M. 24TH

Lt. Col. Mullens | 4 DG | 9 LN | Lt. Col. Campbell
12.30 p.m.

MAJOR GENERAL E.H. ALLENBY C.B
WITHDRAWS HIS CAVALRY, SOUTH
WEST OF AUDREGNIES, A.M. 24TH

LT COL D.C. BOGER BRINGS 1ST BATT. CHESHIRES
FROM BOIS DU BOUSSU VIA DOUR RAILWAY
STATION. A SIX MILE MARCH AM 24TH

Quievrain and beyond. Some 2,000 yards along it was a sugar factory, a collection of brick buildings on either side of the road. From there two roads branched to the left, forming a letter V. Initially the 72nd Regiment would attack across and down either side of it.

The two batteries positioned themselves behind the ridge top road from Elouges to Angre, a village a mile and a half south west of Audregnies; Major Alexander's 119 Battery took the right flank, near the mineral railway and L Battery the left, in the low ground behind Audregnies. The two cavalry regiments that took part in the action were in the hollow behind Audregnies at the beginning of the Roman road - 9/Lancers on the right and 4/DG on the left. Their subsequent full-blooded charge would be the first such made by the British during the war. One other cavalry regiment would see significant action this day, when the Germans, frustrated by the flank guard, tried to get around it by coming through the hamlet of Marchipont. They were stopped by 5/DG [1 (Cavalry) Brigade] and D and E Batteries RHA.

At 11.30am Lieutenant-Colonel Ballard began to place his Battalion in position. They were spread out along a track that ran parallel to the main road from Elouges, 800 yards north of it and crossed the main railway line. Lieutenant-Colonel Boger deployed in a similar fashion, dividing the line from the left flank of the Norfolks to Audregnies (about a mile) between his companies. They were behind the main road, with some of the platoons following the same track as the Norfolks, which came gradually closer to the main road until they joined two hundred yards north of the village. He put his two machine-guns in a deserted cottage on the bend at this road junction; they had

German heavy artillery, a 210mm cannon.

an excellent view over the ground and the Roman road before them. The major landmarks to their north were a windmill a few hundred yards ahead and the sugar factory well beyond it.

The men had no time to dig trenches but made use of ditches and hollows, making them deeper if they could. Because the road undulated, no company could see another. At a few minutes after midday the German artillery began its bombardment; the British replied as the German infantry advanced on a 5,000 yard line.

Almost immediately the Cheshires suffered their first casualty. CSM Meachin (of Captain Shore's B Company) was struck in the head by a bullet as he went to his position on Farm House, some 200 yards down the road from the machine-guns' position. Beyond C Company were, in order, A (Captain Dyer), C (Captain Dugmore) and out on the right, D (Captain Jones) - the extreme part of which was commanded by Captain Rich, whose men were spaced out at five pace intervals. Jones would be killed and Dyer and Dugmore wounded during the day's fighting. The Cheshires were taking casualties from the artillery (Lieutenant Bolton and Private Thorpe hit by shell splinters) before they had even fired a shot in reply.

Lieutenant Randall, commanding the machine-gun section, was the first to open fire; setting the guns range at 1800 yards he opened up on German aircraft hovering over the British position. They were too high to be dealt with by such fire, and the Germans obviously registered their location, for all too quickly one of the guns was hit and put out of action.

The Norfolks received the same sort of treatment. A platoon that was perilously positioned forward of the spoil heap (marked 'collieries' on the map) between the railway line and the main road was in danger of being cut off. The Battalion soon lost two officers killed, Captain Cresswell followed by the Second in Command, Major JB Orr.

Boger then advanced some of his men further forward towards a sunken road that crossed the Roman road, so that they could get to a better range. Enemy shelling increased, now from a range of only 2,000 yards, and Captain Jackson was badly wounded (he was captured where he fell) and one of his sergeants, Walden, was killed.

Because of the lack of visual contact, Dugmore sent men to make contact with other companies and Battalion Headquarters in the village - none returned. The tremendous volume of fire falling on the road almost precluded movement. CQMS Pitt (D Company) saw a section of 119 Battery galloping furiously down the road to go into position behind the company, but it received the full force of a shell, piling men, horses, limber and 18 pdr into a broken mass on the road. With the Cheshires mules madly stampeding, the scene was of utter confusion and mayhem, to which was added flying shrapnel and bullets.

Fortunately the Germans chose to advance in the same reckless fashion so often employed in the battles in and around Mons - en masse and firing from the hip, with only an accidental chance of actually hitting someone. A captain of the Norfolks arrived with some reinforcements for D Company, but the shelling was so heavy that they had to take up position behind the railway embankment. Two German regiments, the 72nd and 26th, were now coming in close order behind the barrage, and were heading straight for the forward elements of the two battalions between the Roman road and the curving railway line.

It was now about 1pm. Brigadier-General de Lisle, seeing the serious situation facing the Cheshires, ordered his cavalry forward. There was to follow one of the bravest of cavalry charges, one of the epic moments of the war. Two squadrons of 9/Lancers, led by Lieutenant-Colonel Campbell along with Captain Lucas Tooth and Captain FO Grenfall, charged up the right hand side of the Roman road, jumping the deeply sunken road crossing it a thousand yards ahead. Meanwhile two troops of 4/DG attacked up the left hand side of the road, led by Lieutenant-Colonel Mullens and Major Tom Bridges; the latter had been involved in the first British cavalry charge of the war. Nothing then was more fear inspiring than 400 men mounted on horses, armed with lances and sabres, yelling and screaming in a mad charge towards you. A vague idea can be obtained by standing on the Mall in front of the Household Cavalry as they move to or from their public duties - one is more than happy to get out of the way as the sheer size of the force approaches.

Spearing or cutting down all who got in their way they raced closer to the sugar factory, scattering the terrified infantry, who had seen nothing like it, but losing men and horses all the time from the batteries of artillery, firing point blank at them, and from machine-guns. The

British lancers on patrol.

cavalry had met its historic fate with the advent of numerous machine-guns, but it still had an important role to play in the war - there was no other land means of transport that could move so quickly and with such versatility during the whole of the conflict; whilst Flowerdew was to lead a full scale cavalry charge as late as Spring 1918 against defended positions with vital consequences for a battle.

On the left of the Roman road Major Bridges was one of the first to go down, his horse shot from under him. Kicked in the face and unconscious, he was rescued by two RAMC men and taken to a cottage on the edge of Baisieux, 500 yards from where he had fallen. When he came round he looked through the window and saw lines of German infantry marching towards the village. He climbed through a window at the rear and found a wounded horse and made his way to Audregnies. He was deprived of speech by the blow in his face and was still disoriented and so sat down by the side of the road. Some time later he saw, to his complete disbelief, a blue and silver Rolls Royce being driven by an officer, 'having a look round'. The Major got aboard and was whisked away, thereby avoiding certain capture. He survived to become a lieutenant-general, a knight and to have a chestful of decorations.

The Dragoons' charge was brought to a halt in front of the sugar factory - a charge whose cost was awful. 9/Lancers suffered similarly heavy casualties. On approaching the sugar factory they found that barbed wire divided the fields there, leaving them no alternative but to swerve to the right in front of the German guns massed in the area. The three officers (all wounded) with the survivors and riderless horses raced along the south edge of the railway embankment towards the spoil heap workings and main road, where the British infantry lines were. The Colonel and his few remaining men dismounted and fought with the Norfolks' platoon at the workings. Grenfell, still on his wounded horse, found shelter under the embankment. Campbell wanted to get fresh orders and so left Lucas Tooth in command and galloped across open ground and through the hail of steel to see de Lisle. Captain Lucas Tooth remained fighting with the infantry but eventually withdrew his men; his actions that day won him the DSO, but he was to be killed on the Aisne. The cavalry lost about 300 horses and 250 casualties in their day's fighting.

Captain Grenfell was not yet finished with the battle, however. He tried to return to his squadron, which was a mile away, on the other side of Audregnies. He came to Major Alexander's 119 Battery, which had been ordered to withdraw because of the proximity of the enemy. Only

Major Alexander remained amongst the officers and some two dozen men, most of whom were wounded. There were no horses remaining. Grenfell walked his horse through the storm of steel to see where the guns had to be taken. On his return, on the track to Wiheries, he found a number of his officer comrades and returned with them. The total number at the battery was now forty and the four guns were manhandled over the fields until they reached the Elouges to Wiheries road, some 1400 yards away. Wounded again, Grenfell stayed with the battery until it was safely away from the action. Both he and Major Alexander were awarded the Victoria Cross and Sergeants Davids and Turner won the DCM. Grenfell was killed at Ypres nine months later; other members of his family killed in the war included his twin brother, and two of his cousins. His elder brother had been killed at Omdurman and another cousin in the Boer War. The military history and sacrifice of the Grenfall family is quite remarkable. Another member of the family was the outstanding comedienne, Joyce Grenfall.

Major Alexander VC.

Captain F.O. Grenfell VC.

The time was now about 4pm. Boger's orders had been to hold on at all costs, and this is what he had achieved thus far. The Germans had got through his forward defences and were close to the road. He could see the Germans massing for a second assault on the left, coming out of Bois du Deduit, south of Quievrain. This was the 93rd Regiment whilst to the north, on his right flank, the 66th Regiment were fast approaching. Boger sent a cyclist to Lieutenant-Colonel Ballard for his view of the situation - and then three more - but none of them returned. Similarly, Ballard had sent him three messages, informing the Cheshires that as the last of IInd Corps had withdrawn he was about to retire, and so should the Cheshires. None of these messages got through.

1/Norfolk retired. They had lost three officers killed, four wounded and 250 other ranks of whom a hundred had been left behind at Elouges, too badly wounded to be moved. Some of the Battalion was left behind with the Cheshires, near the spoil heap, as they had got detached from their own men and never received the order to pull out.

Boger's Battalion, did he but know it, was very much on its own. The cavalry had withdrawn after their fight at Marchipoint and L Battery had gone with them.

Both flanks of the Cheshires came under increasingly heavy

pressure. Lieutenants Matterson (Scout Officer) and Campbell of B Company, who could see the pressure on A Company coming from the other side of the Roman road, took some reinforcements towards it; Campbell was killed almost instantly. The Battalion was now gradually being pushed in towards the village, with the enemy seemingly everywhere. Captain Dugmore, with eight men, retired to the small bridge at the light railway and put up their final resistance. Private Rich of B Company with some of his men and Sergeant Blackwell and a few Norfolks still at the colliery, fell back, with every man for himself.

A Company, on the track running north east of Audregnies towards the spoil heap, was about to retire when two machine-guns began to fire on them. Captains Dyer, Joliffe and Massey, Lieutenant Matterson and about thirty men, with bayonets already fixed, charged them; in doing so they hoped to give the remaining men a chance to get away. They actually got more than 500 yards, the Germans melting away from them as they charged. Dyer, Massey and Joliffe were wounded and lay where they fell, with only some ten men surviving. Lieutenant Elliott of A Company rushed forward to pick up a wounded man, Private Miller, from the road, but was shot in both feet. Elliott managed to crawl to a deserted cottage and hid - in fact the occupants were hiding down a well. When the Germans found him and demanded his sword, he refused to surrender it; Leutnant Rogge (himself subsequently killed) of the 72nd Regiment told him to keep it.

Boger, seeing that his position was enveloped on both sides, ordered his men to retire to Audregnies Wood. At this time he was shot in the foot and in the right side.

Captain ER Jones saw some men of C Company pulling back from the main road; he gathered them to an embankment where there was better cover. They had to pull back still further, into the edge of the wood, soon after. He had about a dozen men with him, two of whom were young drummers. Coming across some Germans hiding behind corn stooks he opened fire with his revolver; both he and Drummer Hogan were killed instantly, and two others were mortally wounded. The long battle was nearly over.

Captain Shore (the only Captain left) with part of B Company were seen by a staff officer when they left the farm house they were holding because it was rapidly being destroyed. The staff officer gave orders that they were to go to the rear, where the two battalions were reforming. They kept going until they met up with the Norfolks; they were the only formed party of Cheshires to escape capture.

The time was now after 5pm and the shelling ceased, because the

German infantry had penetrated the Cheshires defensive perimeter almost everywhere and had got, in places, onto the main road.

Lieutenant-Colonel Boger lay in a field close to the road from Audregnies to Wiheries, unable to move. All about him were his dead and wounded men, but small parties were still fighting all over the battlefield and within the village and wood. At 6pm all fighting had ceased and the surviving Cheshires rounded up as prisoners, though some hundreds of wounded were left where they had fallen and would have to stay there for some time before help came to them.

Some Germans came across the wounded Colonel and the group of wounded near him and took his revolver and binoculars and broke the men's rifles; but left them where they were. In the dark Boger heard a man calling faintly in the distance and crawled over to the spot, finding Sergeant Dowling, who had both his legs smashed. Some time later a German officer found Boger and had him carried into a cottage; and shortly afterwards he was joined there by Dowling and both men were treated by a doctor. Dowling died as a prisoner in 1917.

1/Cheshire had done more than could have been expected of them and had done more than anyone to defy the attempt of von Kluck's IVth Corps to surround the BEF; they had served to halt the great drive of the 7th and 8th Divisions to the south. The Germans found it difficult to believe that their tremendous casualties had been caused by a few riflemen and vigorously demanded to know where they had hidden the machine-guns, as they were sure there must have been many deployed against them.

The salient was at last quiet.

That night a roll call was taken in a valley at St Wast, three miles north of Bavai, of those who had got away. Out of 1007 men and 27 officers who had taken part in the battle at Audregnies, only 192 men and six officers were able to answer their names. Lieutenant-Colonel Boger's Battalion had been destroyed, but as with so many others during those first months of the war, was soon reformed and 1/Cheshire became once again a fighting force. Its new commander, Lieutenant-Colonel Vandaleur, was himself seriously wounded near Bethune, captured, but then escaped back to England.

Field-Marshal Sir John French's BEF had gone to Mons expecting to take part in an advance; instead they had been forced to fight a two day defensive battle. The German casualties, even when compared with some of the great battles of later in the war, were staggering. In the Battle of Mons proper, on 23 August, the British had lost over 1600. On the second day, with the unexpected change in plans from a defensive stand to a hasty withdrawal, there were about a thousand casualties; except that on the left flank, the most vulnerable part of the operation, there were a further fifteen hundred from two battalions, some three squadrons of cavalry, a couple of batteries of artillery and some sappers. The grand total of 4,150 could be compared with the losses of, say, the 7th Division in First Ypres. In eighteen days this formation lost 356 officers and 9,644 other ranks, out of a total of 12,400 who had taken the field.

In the battle of the Mons salient six Victoria Crosses were won - and many more must have been deserved.

Postscript:

There are some interesting 'after the battle' stories of the stand of 1/Cheshire at Audregnies.

Boger and Sergeant Meachin escaped from the hospital where they had been taken. They reached Brussels and the hospital where Nurse Edith Cavell worked. She was famously executed by the Germans (her statue is just north of Trafalgar Square, opposite the National Portrait Gallery), Meachin escaped to Flushing and then Folkestone, but Boger was recaptured and imprisoned in Germany.

Lieutenant Frost, who was killed after he refused to surrender, was buried by the impressed Germans with full military honours.

Private F Woodier escaped from Osnabruck at his second attempt, in April 1918, and got to Holland. Private T Vaughan, who had tried to rescue CSM Francis under heavy fire, died in prison at Doebritz.

Captain ER Jones and Drummer Hogan, killed at Audregnies Wood, were buried with Private Garrard opposite the communal cemetery by the 66th Regiment. The Captain's watch and pistol were buried with him and a small cross was made by a German. His silver match box and some money were put in a haversack and they allowed Corporal Blake to take it to the church in Wiheries where some 60 prisoners were being held. Sergeant Raynor hid the silver box and gave it to Captain Lee Stuart when he escaped capture and made it to Holland (the Germans seem to have been extraordinarily careless about safeguarding their prisoners!). He eventually returned it to Jones' widow. A man and his daughter from the estaminet in Wiheries took up the body of Captain Jones from his shallow grave, took it into their home, thoroughly washed it, wrapped him in a clean sheet and reburied the gallant officer in the communal cemetery.

Finally there is the story of the Cheshires' miniature colour. This was a two foot by eighteen inches copy of the Regimental Colour made by the ladies of the Battalion in 1911 whilst it was in Ireland. It was brought to France, Drummer Baker being responsible for it (Regimental Colours could not be taken into active service). When the last little band of the Battalion was surrounded, Baker went into a house and hid the colour in its black case in the attic. He was taken prisoner by the Germans when he emerged from the house. Private Riley knew where the colour was, and whilst being tended for his wounds in the convent on the Rue d'Eglise, informed a nun. She, with a priest, went to the house of the Rue de l'Abbate, owned by M Alphonse Martin. The colour was hidden behind the choir stalls in the church. During the course of the war Fr Soudain became concerned about the safety of the hiding place (the Germans had had a tip off that the colour existed) and so it was, with the help of the schoolmaster, M Alphonse Vallee, hidden in the school roof.

On 15 November 1918 the Quartermaster, Captain Sprouke, accompanied by Captain Radcliffe, recovered the colour. On 29 October 1919, in an unavoidably rather low key ceremony, testimonials and an engraved rose bowl on an ebony stand were presented to the village and the three men who had safeguarded the colour for over four years of occupation - the priest, the schoolmaster and the secretary of the Commune, M Dupont. The colour was returned to the Regimental Depot in the castle at Chester; during that ceremony it was carried by Corporal 'Todger' Jones VC, DCM.

Drummer Baker, whose presence of mind had saved the colour, and who everyone thought was dead, arrived home from captivity in March 1919.

1 Bavay is the modern spelling of this town.

Chapter Five

TOURS

I would strongly urge that tourers should purchase the 1:100000 (purple) map, 111 Mons - Charleroi, published by the Belgian IGN. This will make the following of the tours that much easier.

I spent a long weekend following the exhaustive tours that Jack Horsfall has set out for this book. I found his achievement quite remarkable - firstly in identifying all the key sites in the battle on the ground today and secondly in coming up with such an ingenious arrangement of tours.

The battlefield of Mons was fought over what was even then a generally well built-up area. Although the maps and directions are as accurate as possible, this is undoubtedly a difficult battle to follow on the ground, but it is well worthwhile. In a car it is practically essential to have another person to act as a navigator, and one also requires a sunny disposition and a sense of humour! Indeed it is strongly recommended that you go on a drive around the area in order to become comfortable with your bearings. There are useful map shops in Mons (the only town I have had the fortune to come across, thus far, in Belgium with a full series of 1:25000 maps, for example) and it would be to your advantage if you invested in a number of these. Although an expensive exercise, it should be of benefit to your blood pressure, and should only increase your wonder that the BEF were able to find their way around at all, especially given that most of their maps were of a scale on the lines of 1:200000! It casts a whole new light, at least as far as I am concerned, on the difficulties faced by the competing armies as they fought the war of manoeuvre in those early days of the war in 1914.

Looking up to the Belfry at Mons.

TOUR No.1
Mons and the Nimy Bridges

Start Point: The Grand Place

It is almost always possible to find a place to park if you cruise around the Hotel de Ville and to the rear; the inner town is small enough to park and then walk, though there is a certain amount of high ground to be climbed up and down. The prospect might appear to be daunting, but a space can usually be found. Have a good quantity of Belgian coins for the parking meters, though the further away from the town centre you are the cheaper it becomes! Next to the entrance of the Hotel de Ville is the TOURIST OFFICE, from which you may obtain a variety of maps and guides to the museum and the battles around Mons.

The museum usually opens at midday; entrance costs about 60 BF. It covers both World Wars and is something that should not be missed. Amongst other items on display is a machine-gun of 1/Cheshire which was hidden after the battle at Audregnies - one feels if the Germans could not find that they did

1st Cheshires machine gun hidden on the battleground of Audregnies, now in the museum at Mons.

OFFICE DU TOURISME
DE LA VILLE DE MONS
22 GRAND PLACE
7000 MONS
tel.:065/335580
fax.:065/356336

not have much chance of finding the Battalion's miniature colour! There are a number of commemorative plaques on the walls at the entrance to the courtyard. After you have finished at the museum, turn right as you leave; tradition has it that you should rub the nose of the small brass monkey for luck. After a couple of hundred yards take a **The Town Hall (Hotel De Ville) Mons.**

'Lucky' Monkey outside Hotel De Ville

TO MAP 2 AND BRIDGES AT NIMY. AVE VICTOR MAISTRIAM

narrow steep street to the right, heading up to the Belfroi, the highest point in Mons and of great historical interest. One of the pamphlets you will have obtained from the Tourist Office gives you information about it.

In October 1952 the British and Canadian First World War memorial was erected here, but in 1986 it was removed to La Bascule (see Tour 2). There is a magnificent view over the town and surrounding countryside from the top.

Return to the car.

An excellent map shop may be found in the Grand Rue, which is along a pedestrianised street.

Mons is surrounded by a circular boulevard from which all roads to the suburbs. Be careful how you go, because if you miss your turning you are quite likely to have to go all the way around again. You need to look out for signposts to Nimy, Casteau, Soignies, Brussels, in that order; and you will be travelling anti-clockwise. Keep over to the right for the exit to Rue de Nimy; its name changes to Avenue Victor Maistriau de Bruxelles les Joeyeux (there's a mouthfull!).

Proceed slowly along this busy road; after you have crossed the bridge going over the railway cutting stop [1] in front of the row of houses. This is part of the battlefield of 4th Royal Fusiliers. On the left, below the road, was B Company, under the command of Captain Carey, based on the station [2].

1. Railway cutting
2. 'B' Coy. RF's Capt. Carey
3. Slip road to canal at new bridge
4. 'C' Coy RF's Capt. Ashburner

5. Lt. Holt R.E. killed at bridge
6. To 'D' Coy along lake bank
7. Exit to new road to Tertre

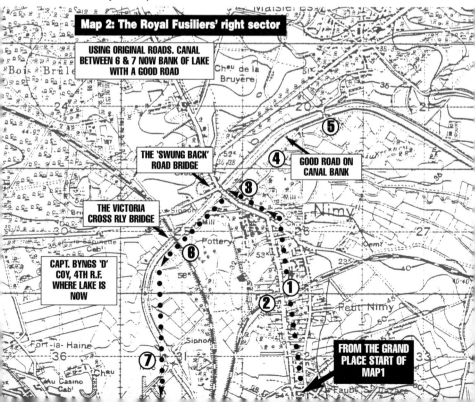

Map 2: The Royal Fusiliers' right sector

USING ORIGINAL ROADS. CANAL BETWEEN 6 & 7 NOW BANK OF LAKE WITH A GOOD ROAD

THE 'SWUNG BACK' ROAD BRIDGE

GOOD ROAD ON CANAL BANK

THE VICTORIA CROSS RLY BRIDGE

CAPT. BYNGS 'D' COY, 4TH R.F. WHERE LAKE IS NOW

FROM THE GRAND PLACE START OF MAP1

SLIP ROAD

The site of the old Nimy 'swing' Road Bridge. Slip road for access to the canal bank is on right of bridge, coming from Mons.

The railway bridge. Pte Godley's position at bottom right hand corner.

Perhaps 200 yards behind was Captain Cole and A Company, in reserve; they had entrenched a position, blocking this road. After the Germans had crossed the two bridges they proceeded along here, setting fire to those houses that were not already ablaze, pushing a group of terrified civilians in front of them and firing at the road block from the doorways. Captain Cole's men dared not open fire and consequently were forced to withdraw into Mons.

Some 500 yards in front are the bridges; this next part is not really suitable for a coach, which could pick up passengers in Nimy. Proceed slowly; as the road climbs to the bridge take the slip road on the right [3], which will bring you

Railway bridge at Nimy, Lt. Dease and Private Godley.

Site of 'swing' road bridge.

out on the south bank of the Canal du Centre.

This was Captain Ashburner's (C Company) sector [4] - from the railway bridge which may be seen to the left to about a thousand yards to your right, round the bend as far as Pont des Bragnons, where the left hand man of 4th Middlesex was.

The road bridge was a metal swinging one, and had been swung back to the British side. Defending it were two platoons under Captain Forester. This was the bridge to which a very brave German soldier, Musketier Oskar Niemeyer (84/Chasseurs) swam in order to release the swing mechanism and thereby allowed his comrades to cross the canal. Killed in the process, he is buried at St Symphorien.

The Fusiliers lined this bank, killing many of the massed enemy approaching from the far side, whilst they were in turn unmercifully shelled by German artillery on the upper slopes. Many of the Londoners casualties were suffered here, including Captains Ashburner and Bowden Smith and Lieutenants Smith and Mead.

Drive to the right until you reach the next bridge, which was the junction with

Rue des Bragnons Bridge where Lt Holt R.E. was killed, about to blow it up, looking from 'swing'road bridge.

View from Lt. Holt's (R.E) Bridge looking towards the road and railway bridges.

Memorial underneath the railway bridge to Lt Dease VC and Pte Godley VC.

the Middlesex. This was not destroyed and was the site of the first Royal Engineer casualties of the war [5] - the Germans rushed the demolition team and Lieutenant Holt was killed (buried at St Symphorien) and the rest of his section captured. Little has changed here in all the years apart from a new road on the far side; it was open land then, and suicidal for the Germans to attack in the manner which they did.

Turn round and drive to the railway bridge. The road between the road and railway bridge is called the *Quai des Anglais,* a tribute to the men of 1914. Underneath the bridge is a small plaque where there always seems to be a wreath of poppies. This is a memorial to the 4th Royal Fusiliers and the two Victoria Cross winners, Lieutenant Dease, who was killed here, and Private Godley, who remained with his machine-gun. This is not the original bridge, which was destroyed in 1940 by the retreating French and again in 1944 by the retreating Germans. However, understandably, it is in exactly the same place, similarly built and of similar dimensions; the buttresses on which the two machine-guns were almost certainly positioned are similar or identical to their predecessors. Climb up to the right hand side one (ie the eastern one) and you will then have the same view as Godley had as he repelled the enemy until he was wounded yet again and his machine-gun damaged.

The trench from which Lieutenant Dease made his heroic journeys to and from the machine-guns was about thirty or forty yards back down the track; it was in this vicinity that he was mortally wounded. Near here, in the gully on the west side, lay Lieutenant AF Day of 57 Fd Coy, wounded and eventually captured; he had waited in vain for an opportunity to destroy the bridge. Leutnant von Arnim, of the Death's Head Hussars, was brought across this bridge, wounded and a prisoner.

Pte Godley's view from his machine gun on the right buttress.

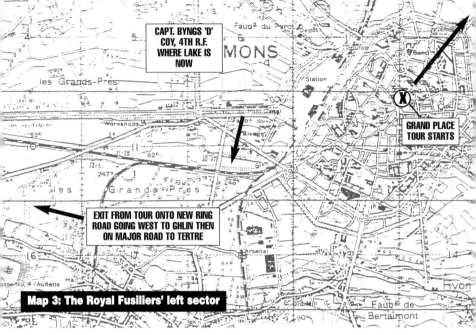

Map 3: The Royal Fusiliers' left sector

CAPT. BYNGS 'D' COY, 4TH R.F. WHERE LAKE IS NOW

Faub⁴ du Parc Depot

MONS

les Grands-Pres

Station

GRAND PLACE TOUR STARTS

EXIT FROM TOUR ONTO NEW RING ROAD GOING WEST TO GHLIN THEN ON MAJOR ROAD TO TERTRE

Follow the road under the railway bridge in a westerly direction, along the original canal bank; you will pass a large lake, drowning the site of B Company of 4/RF [6]. At the bottom, southern, end of the lake, you will come to a large quay. In the field to the left, to the south west, was the position of Lock No. 6. Drive slowly down the road, past the stockpile of sand, and it is possible to see that the railway line still comes down alongside that side of the old canal. Captain Harding's Company was here at the lock. A little further on are the railway embankments on the left over which Byng's men scampered in their withdrawal. Ahead is the road bridge going over the railway bridge which Byng blocked with drums of electric cable and barbed wire. The original road bridge was prepared for demolition by Corporal Pane of 57 Fd Coy and was the only one over the Canal du Centre between Obourg and Ghlin that was successfully destroyed. It is possible to appreciate the relative height of Mons from here and the open land, much of it now the lake, across which D Company fell back [7] in order to rejoin the Battalion.

Lt. Day R.E., wounded, waited here to blow up railway bridge.

The road leaving the lake going to the road bridge to Ghlin. Site of old bridge to the left.

Tour No 2: The First shots and the Battle for Mons.

The start point for this tour is off the Route de Wallonie; do not turn off this road for Mons, but at the Nimy road bridge junction turn left for Soignies and stop on the right, immediately over the roundabout, as the road climbs. This is the start point.

Proceed along the road, which is now quite wide, but in 1914 was considerably narrower, with a tram line on one side of its cobbled surface. There is a plaque on the wall of Maisieres church, on the left, to the first action in the war. The Headquarters of SHAPE (Supreme Headquarters Allied Powers Europe) is on the left. Stop at the traffic lights, where Rue Brisee crosses. The house on the corner in whose grounds there are numerous trees was there in 1914; the road on the right goes to St Denis and Obourg. It was in the grounds of the house that Major Tom Bridges with two troops of 4/DG, concealed by the trees, saw four German cavalrymen riding slowly towards them from Casteau at about 7am [1].

Further on there is a large white building, currently the *Le Medicis* restaurant. There is a memorial plaque to the Canadian Corps [3], which reached this point at 11am on 11 November 1918. Across the road there is a stone memorial cairn with a bronze plaque in front of it [2] which commemorates the 4/DGs' action here.

It was from approximately this place that Captain Hornby and his Troop

Road to Casteau and Soighies.

Canadian Corps Memorial on the wall of the building on the right.

gave chase to the German patrol and a few hundred yards more where Drummer Corporal Thomas dismounted and fired, some claim, the first British shot of the war; he claimed a hit.

Continue forward for approximately two miles, remaining wary of overshooting a minor crossroads [4]. It is open on the right hand side, but there is a large red brick building on the far left hand corner. This is the place known

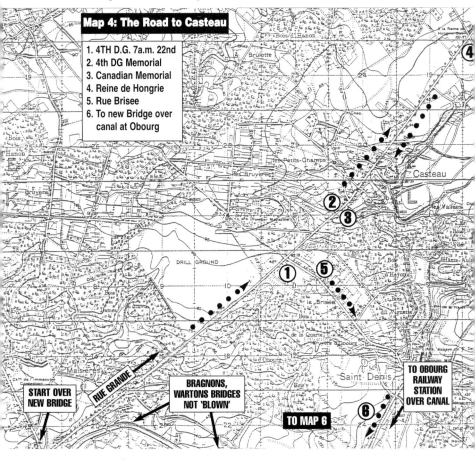

Map 4: The Road to Casteau

1. 4TH D.G. 7a.m. 22nd
2. 4th DG Memorial
3. Canadian Memorial
4. Reine de Hongrie
5. Rue Brisee
6. To new Bridge over canal at Obourg

START OVER NEW BRIDGE

RUE GRANDE

BRAGNONS, WARTONS BRIDGES NOT 'BLOWN'

TO MAP 6

TO OBOURG RAILWAY STATION OVER CANAL

as Reine de Hongrie (Queen of Hungary) - there is a small signpost on the right hand side stating this. It is here that a skirmish took place with the arrival of German reinforcements who were subsequently overcome, galloping away after losing men, dead, wounded and as prisoners.

[A short diversion, lasting about thirty minutes, can be taken to the small town of Soignies, about two miles further on. The communal cemetery lies about a mile from the start of the buildings and a few hundred yards from the church. There are a few British graves grouped together dating from 1918 and 1944; they are rarely visited. On Rue de la Station is the Chateau Brison, which was where von Kluck had his Headquarters from 22 - 25 August 1914.]

Drive back towards Mons, and this time turn left at the traffic lights, down the Rue Brisee [5], signposted to St Denis. This leads to the battlefield of 4/Middx and the other three battalions of 8 Brigade on Sunday 23 August. It is a narrow, winding road; all of this area would have been filled with German infantry, artillery and cavalry as they sought to cross the canal below.

Kluck's headquarters in Soignies.

At the village square by the church take the street to the right, down the hill to Obourg. A mile or so further on stop in the tiny village square, before the canal bridge; there is friendly pub by the church, where thirst may be slaked. From here it is only a short walk (or drive) down the Rue des Anglais to the canal and from there you will have a German view across the canal. It was from somewhere near here that the shot that killed Private Parr, the first British fatality at Mons, was fired. The original bridge ran from the bottom of this street to the railway station on the far side. This bridge should have been destroyed, but the demolition party arrived too late, with the Germans already on the far side. On the far side of the canal was Lieutenant Allison's party defending the railway station, with a section on its roof. Behind a barricade of sandbags and in overall defence of the canal bank sector was D Company and Captain Glass. Allison and Glass were wounded near here and taken prisoner.

Return to the village square and drive over the canal; immediately, once over the bridge [6], take the sharp left turn down and alongside it. This short street, the original, leads to a modern foot bridge. Go over this to the site of the station where a plaque has been placed on a memorial [1] made from the bricks of the old building and records the events there. The plaque used to be on the wall of the waiting room. This is the area of 4/Middx and 2/RIrR, the latter fighting with, and then relieving, the Middlesex.

Rejoin the main street and in less than a hundred yards take the concrete road to the right, which leads down to a large concrete factory. Drive past the factory (the canal is on the far side of it) and after about half a mile you will arrive at the Lock les Wartons [2], Lock No 5, on the Canal du Centre. There is a marvellous view of the canal and is the point where Captain Glass' D

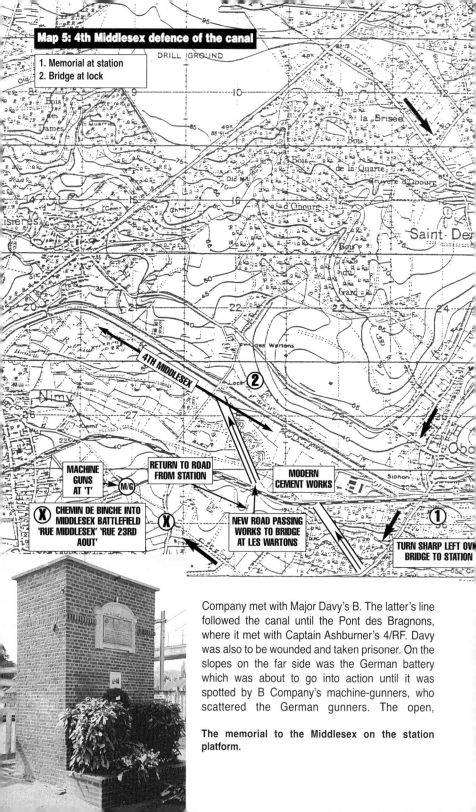

Map 5: 4th Middlesex defence of the canal

1. Memorial at station
2. Bridge at lock

DRILL GROUND

MACHINE GUNS AT 'T' (M/G)

RETURN TO ROAD FROM STATION

MODERN CEMENT WORKS

(X) **CHEMIN DE BINCHE INTO MIDDLESEX BATTLEFIELD 'RUE MIDDLESEX' 'RUE 23RD AOUT'**

(X) **NEW ROAD PASSING WORKS TO BRIDGE AT LES WARTONS**

(1) **TURN SHARP LEFT OV[ER] BRIDGE TO STATION**

4TH MIDDLESEX

(2) Lock

Company met with Major Davy's B. The latter's line followed the canal until the Pont des Bragnons, where it met with Captain Ashburner's 4/RF. Davy was also to be wounded and taken prisoner. On the slopes on the far side was the German battery which was about to go into action until it was spotted by B Company's machine-gunners, who scattered the German gunners. The open,

The memorial to the Middlesex on the station platform.

Lock No. 5, Les Wartons.

coverless sector which the Company had to hold is still quite obvious.

Return to the main road. Turn right into what is now a built up area; it then held very few houses, but the numerous trees made finding good fields of fire difficult. Almost immediately turn right, the Vieux Chemin de Binche, tree and house lined, which was the front line of the Middlesex and Royal Irish. C Company was entrenched along the left hand side where the hedge now is; at the first junction there is a wide road on the left, Chemin Chene aux l'Oasis and small, short lane on the right. This where Lieutenant Sloane Stanley had his two machine-guns, firing towards the wood; he was wounded and captured. Lieutenant Rushton was also positioned here with the two machine-guns of the Royal Irish. Long after the war, in the field behind the hedge, was found the remains of British soldiers and various pieces of military equipment, rifles and so forth. When planning this tour I met a man at this junction whose maternal grandmother's name was Stanley and came from Liverpool. His grandmother was here at the time when the bodies were uncovered and passed on the account to him.

If this tour is being done in a coach it is best to get out here and follow the next part on foot.

Further along the Vieux Chemin from this junction was A Company [1]; its commander, Major Abell, was killed here. B and D Companies moved up here to relieve the Middlesex. Take the first left, Rue Reve du Prophet and, almost immediately, stop. On the right is the Avenue du 4th Middlesex. Nothing could tell you better that you are in the heart of the Battalion's battle. Drive to the end of the road and turn left down Avenue 23rd du Aout. At the end is a T junction;

'T' junction on right at bungalow. Site of Lt Sloane Stanley's two machine guns.

1. Middlesex battlefield
2. Hospital on fire
3. Communal and Military Cemetery
4. Capt. Oliver's Convent
5. Middlesex HQ in hollow
6. La Bascule monuments
7. Chateau hospital
8. Gunpost on hilltop
9. Guns ambushed
10. 8 Brigade HQ in Hyon
11. Tourist sign board
12. Site of last battle

Brigade HQ at Mairie at Hyon

ORIGINAL TRACKS AND ROADS USED ALL GOOD FOR VEHICLES

MILITARY CEMETERY

OPTIONAL TOUR TO MILITARY GRAVES AT SPIENNES

Map 6: The retreat from the canal through Hyon

stop. Walk across the road and look over the fields - the battleground is still open. In there was the quarry where 4/Middx had their first Headquarters and the rough track going to the right, an extension to the avenue, is the route to the railway line. This was the route of C Company of the Royal Irish and is the line of withdrawal of B Company of 4/Middx. A great deal of close quarter fighting took place along and around here, as it was the line of the main German thrust across the canal from the north east. It is possible to walk up the track, but there are no physical reminders of the war, and your imagination will have to suffice for what went on here.

Return to the coach or take the car back to the junction on the Vieux Chemin.

The whole area came under intense bombardment; with your back to the machine-gun lane, look along and to the left of the Chemin de l'Oasis. Ahead

144

Avenue of the 4th Middlesex.

of you, on the left, is the Psychiatric Hospital [2] and, on the right, the communal cemetery. The hospital caught fire during the battle and some hundreds of patients fled from it, which must have added a quite macabre addition to the extraordinary scene. Fighting took place in and around the area of the cemetery.

Drive slowly down towards the hospital, keeping to the left at the fork; the cemetery wall runs alongside you; opposite is the large building which is the hospital, with a large sign board which informs you that it was part of the battle scene. Continue along the road, and at the bottom turn right and park at the small Café du Cimetiere.

Walk across the road and past the cemetery [3] gate. On the right is a memorial plaque to some heroes of the Resistance who continued to publish a clandestine newspaper throughout the Second World War. Take the left path that climbs the hill and leads to the British war cemetery on the left hand side. On the approach to this section of the cemetery you will pass, on the right, a gravestone to an English lady who 'mothered' Polish pilots during the Second World War. A little further on, on the left, is a very large French military plot, where men who had once served wished to be buried as soldiers. There are a variety of soldiers, men, members of the Resistance, who served in the Colonial Empire and in Europe and some who have died quite recently.

The psychiatric hospital was set on fire. Patients streamed down the hill towards the camera.

The cemetery at Mons.

Memorial plaque on cemetery wall, just to the right of the entrance and opposite the Pub.

The British plot has 382 graves and is split into two parts; the part on the right hand side of the road holds most of the 1914 casualties from all arms.

Amongst those who are buried here were those who died as Prisoners of War and a number who died after the war ended. The Germans treated the dead here in a fitting manner, burying the men with respect and setting out the plot well.

CSM H Rossington (V.B.21) of 1/Cheshire was wounded at Audregnies (see Tour 5) and taken prisoner. He died of his wounds somewhere near here on 11 October 1914. There are, somewhat to the surprise of the visitor, 74 Russians, who reached the Western Front via Vladivostok in 1916. They were part of four brigades which fought with the French and became known as the Russian Legion.

Private GT Beach (IV.C.14) was nineteen when he died as a prisoner in April 1917; he was in 2/Manchesters. One of the sappers involved in the attempts to blow the bridges lies here: Sapper Archibald (IX.E.11) of 56 Fd Coy, who died of his wounds on 6 September 1914. There are a number of men from the RFC and the RAF; Lieutenant Butler, aged 19, was shot down whilst serving with 3 Squadron of the newly formed RAF on 11 April 1918. Private McGrath (VII.B.9) was an American serving in the Canadian forces, captured and dying as a Prisoner of War on 9 October 1918, almost at the war's end. At the age of 42, he appears to be the oldest man here; and he left a widow in Chicago.

As you return to the cemetery gate, remember that the Middlesex and Royal Irish fought their way through the cemetery in close quarter combat.

At the gate turn right along the Chemin de la Procession. At the corner of the cemetery wall is the Chemin du Canon; on the left facing it are two tall grey houses and in between a short, muddy, open space. The Middlesex had their Headquarters in the cellars of the houses. Cross over and go to the far end of the open space and beyond you will look into a hollow [5] which has changed very little in all the years. At one time it held two sections from A Company of 4/Middx and Lieutenant Ferguson's men, part of B Company 2/RIrR. They came under heavy bombardment, and they, along with others, crossed the

4th Middlesex HQ was in the cellars of these houses in the Chemin du Canon.

fields heading south westwards, towards La Bascule.

You might wish to return to the car to do the next part, or to carry on walking. 500 yards along the Chemin de la Procession will bring you to a set of traffic lights and a complex road junction. Go sharp right, Rue Denant, and 200 yards on the right is the convent [4] where Captain Oliver with a few Middlesex from C Company came; this was where his horse was stabled. The building was already occupied by the Germans. Blowing the lock off the gate they entered and managed to evade the enemy, going on towards La Bascule. One can try and imagine the whole area on fire and strewn with dead and wounded men, with the survivors under constant fire and bombardment.

Turn around, or walk back, following the route taken by the shattered Middlesex men and that for the eventual withdrawal of 2/RIrR.

Drive away from the cemetery, leaving the pub on the right; at the T Junction and traffic lights turn left and then almost immediately turn right (Chemin des Mourdreux) which is a steep, short street. Ahead is a major road junction, La Bascule [6]. Some twenty yards before the junction take the slip road on the right and park. You will be looking down a hill with an industrial estate on the right and a major road on the left, going into Mons. Lock the car and bring your camera.

The road is very busy with traffic and is now well built up. Some of the

Captain Oliver's convent, already occupied by Germans.

houses (or their predecessors) were here then, used as protection by soldiers who knocked loopholes through their walls. Walk up to the crossroads and look around. On the far side, on the left of the junction, is the memorial that once stood in the grounds of the Belfry in Mons. On its left is the Chaussee de Beaumont; the wide road to the right (which you will cross) is the Chaussee de Binche. To the right is the main road into Mons and on the far side of it are the grounds surrounding the Chateau Gendebein [7], which is now the residence

of the commander of SHAPE - then it was being used as a hospital. Cross the street up which you have driven and on the corner is the cross memorial to the 2nd Royal Irish Regiment, dedicated by Field-Marshal Lord French on 11 November 1923.

This is the ground on which 2/RIrR and 1/Gordon Highlanders (GH) fought as 4/Middx withdrew. To the left of the monument, where the houses now stand, is the site of CQMS Fitzpatrick's valiant stand in the afternoon and evening with his small party - forty from the transport lines - which were firing down the slope up which you have just driven. He held on until 11pm, when he withdrew with his seventeen survivors. Captain Mellor and Lieutenant Shine of the Royal Irish were killed here; and it was also the site of Sergeant Whittington's position, who had managed to get the Battalion's last machine-gun working again.

Cross over the main road to the large memorial; incorporated within it is soil taken from the graves of those who were killed at Mons. Stand with your back to it. On the left were two guns of 23 Battery, which soon had to withdraw. It was whilst galloping to this place that Major Lyon was hit and fell from his horse; he was rescued by an Irishman and two Gordons, who came out of their trenches and got him to hospital. 1/GH were entrenched along the main road behind you, which skirts the hill, le Bois la Haut, with posts that stretched for a thousand yards also along the road to your right.

La Bascule. 2nd Royal Irish Regiment memorial.

Some 200 yards to the right, across the road and some four streets down, is the site of the Cremerie, a café, where the Gordons had a machine-gun, causing heavy losses as the Germans came up from the canal and Obourg. The Germans were coming towards you and the whole area was under severe bombardment. The chateau to your left (but hidden by trees) was on fire despite the Red Cross flags hanging from its windows; as the wounded were evacuated, some died in the ruins. One of these unfortunates was Major Maidlow, commanding 49 Battery - his grave is in the communal cemetery recently visited.

Return to the car, but before setting off look back up towards the main road. From there came Major Panter Downes and Lieutenant Shine with some thirty men, making a bayonet charge from the main road and across this slip road to repel the Germans coming up the hill, through fields full of cabbages. Lieutenant Shine was killed. Over the main road withdrew A Company of the

The German view advancing towards the Bois d' Haut and 8 Brigade's position. Middlesex, Royal Irish and Royal Fusiliers withdrew behind hill.

Royal Irish, by that stage having lost all their officers; preceding them had been 4/Middlesex, in the middle of the afternoon, and D Company of 2/RIrR, which had been almost wiped out in the area beyond the convent, had regrouped here before moving off to the rear.

Drive down to the end of the slip road, which joins on to the main road. On the opposite side is the gateway to the chateau and alongside it a narrow road to Hyon, the route of the British infantry. Because of the traffic flow it is necessary to turn right here, but keep left and take the first exit (after about a hundred yards) and return on the far side of the road, and take the narrow Hyon road.

This runs alongside the chateau wall, whilst to the right the ground drops away to a low-lying area, almost a water meadow. After a short while there is a fork in the road, stop; that on the left (or straight ahead) is an even more narrow, cobbled and uneven road, which was the route of the Middlesex, to which you shall return. In this vicinity the Royal Irish reorganised, meeting up with D Company which had already moved here; on the main road 1/GH were holding the Germans. The artillery had also retired down the cobbled road on the left, to look for new positions on the hill [8].

Take the right fork [9], which soon comes out in the tiny village square of Hyon [10]. To the right, the west of the village, the Germans had already arrived, coming through Mons as 4/RF and 4/Middx fell back. By 6 pm they were in the vicinity in some force. In the Mairie had been Brigadier-General Doran's 8 Brigade Headquarters. The Canadians came through here in 1918 and in 1944 the Americans - Major Tucker's 83rd Recce Battalion probably liberated the village.

This is quite a pleasant spot to stop for a picnic lunch should the spirit move you and the time be right.

On the far side of the square is the Rue des Canadiens and to its right the Rue des Americains.

[Should this be a coach tour the coach must take the Rue des Americains to Mesvin, then the road to Spiennes, joining on the eastern side the Chaussee de Beaumont. Turn left here and after about 200 yards take the Chemin de Bethleem on the left, where the party may meet up.]

If in a car, drive slowly down the Rue des Americains and take the narrow

The bridge at Hyon. Defended by Lt Tandy of the Royal Irish Regiment.

lane, first on the left, the Rue de Moulin au Bois. You are crossing the water meadow where there are two very narrow and old bridges. Lieutenant Tandy, with the survivors of A Company of the Royal Irish lined this lane, looking north, as the last of the Middlesex came through. Stop at the end and take a short walk to the left along the cobbled lane that you saw earlier. On the right you will see the entrance to a large chateau up on the hill; this is where the Gordons had their Headquarters.

At about 5.15pm Lieutenant Laing took some of B Company up the hill to get in touch with the Gordons on the top and on the other side, but he failed. There was heavy artillery and machine-gun fire from the north east. The Germans had arrived at about 6pm, but before they did Brigadier-General Doran came along this road with some of the Royal Irish, desperate to make contact with the Gordons, whilst in the background they could hear the battle going on with the Middlesex. However some Germans had got to this track and Brigadier-General Doran's large party turned round, going back down the bank and onto the open land.

There were two 18 pdrs still on the hill [8] and Lieutenant Hamilton of the Gordons went, from the far side of the hill, with his platoon to try and rescue them. On their way down the road on which you are standing they ran into a German roadblock [9]. Horses fell and guns went off the road; the infantry bayonet charged the Germans whilst others cleared the road of dead horses and got the guns back on to it. The guns were saved, but one can imagine only with great difficulty the confusion and the ferocious little battle that took place where you are now. The scene has changed remarkably little since 1914.

Return to your car and within a few yards, going to the right, you are at the corner of the wooded hill where there is a large notice board [11] erected by the Mons Tourist Board. Stop here. In front is open land. You are now on the Chemin de Bethleem and will take the right hand fork. If there is time, a goodish walk up the left hand road and up the hill will bring you to the flat area where the 18 pdrs were, with a good view over the battlefield. The site may be seen from the Chemin de Bethleem if you were to drive on for a few hundred yards.

BOIS D' HAUT

Looking toward la Bascule; 1st Gordons entrenched along this road on both sides, looking to the right.

The Royal Irish were entrenched along this road; Major St Leger and guns of XL Brigade were in the field, closer to the main road, 500 yards ahead.

Drive to the junction and stop [12]. The Germans were here by 8pm, being held off by the Gordons who had retired down the road and joining the Royal Irish and 2/RS (Royal Scots), the latter coming into the fight here. The guns were abandoned at one point but were regained and at 10pm the men of the three battalions, guarding the four guns, retired south west to Nouvelles. 8 Brigade were on their way to the second line of defence, leaving behind large numbers of Germans, many from Bremen, dead, wounded or exhausted in the fields behind them

Turn right and then take the next left, Rue Arthur Duquesne. On the left of this road were trenches held by the Gordons, on the right by the Royal Scots.

Looking from the hill on the Chemin de Bethleem. Royal Irish entrenched on this road looking away from camera towards the main road.

Scene of the last battle at Mons and recovery of abandoned guns. 8 Brigade retired towards Cambrai.

The original farm buildings were used by the British. At the T junction turn right, an unmade short street, Rue Nestor Dehon; St Symphorien Military Cemetery is at the bottom, at the junction of four lanes.

Victor and vanquished are buried here together on an ancient man-made mound. This cemetery was beautifully laid out by the Germans during the war, and in many ways it is the most unusual on the Western Front (as well as being the largest in the Mons area). From the imposing Germanic appearance of its entrance to the various burial plots there are numerous 'surprises'. Beside the British Cross of Sacrifice and memorial seat there are German memorials erected to the British. The German commandant, as his counterpart in Cambrai, worked hard to ensure respect for all of those who had fallen. This cemetery could easily take an hour to view.

Lieutenant Maurice Dease VC is in Plot V, to the left of the entrance. Major Abell of the Middlesex, killed early on in the battle, lies at the far end alongside the circular path; there are 85 of his Battalion here with him. Just in front of Lieutenant Dease is Lieutenant Holt, the first Royal Engineer killed, who died at the Nimy bridges. The first man to be killed, Private Parr, is in Plot I, at the bottom left hand side, and only a few feet away is the last man to be killed in Mons, Corporal Price.

Corporal Green, of 1/Wilts, was killed on 24 August at Ciply (Tour 3) and is buried in I.B.24; Private George Insley, RMLI, died as a PoW on 26 October 1918 (V.C.5). In IV.C.1 lies Corporal Charles Taylor, an old soldier who had fought in the South African Campaign as well as the North West Frontier in India in 1908. He was 31 when he died of wounds on 23 August whilst serving with 4/Middx.

You might like to take; the time to visit British soldiers buried in two nearby communal cemeteries, Spennes and Nouvelles. There lie a dozen or so men of 1918 who rarely benefit from a visit by a pilgrim to the battlefields.

TOUR No. 3
The Condé Canal and Locations in the Borinage.

This tour covers the eastern half of the Condé Canal as far west as Mariette and then goes into the mining villages south of Jemappes and the battlefields of Brigadier-General Shaw's 9 Brigade, Brigadier-General McCracken's 7

Graves in Saint Symphorien.

Brigade and the area into which Brigadier-General Haking's 5 Brigade was inserted between the 3rd and 5th Divisions.

Drive from the hotel on the Route de Wallonie heading for Mons. Take the turning signposted Ghlin and Mons, follow the route under the road, keeping right, and turn right at the roundabout for Ghlin. At the water tower and five road junction turn right at the crossroads, taking the road to Jemappes. This turning is a little tricky, it is the first road on the right, not the second, which tends to come back on you.

This is quite a difficult part of the tour because of the busy streets and the numerous crossings over railway lines, the drainage canal and autoroute, so follow the instructions with care, but be quite relaxed about taking a wrong turning and starting again. Being an urban area, and at the mercy of traffic planners, there is a tendency to put in one way streets where they were two way before - or even a new road. However, the instructions are as complete as possible and provide a clear enough guide of where you should be going; it would be useful to have a copy of the 1:20000 map, Mons-Givry 45/7-8.

Map 7: Jemappes and the retreat through Flenu

START AT MAJOR X ROADS AT GHLIN

CANAL NOW: AUTOROUTE

CAPT'S ROSS & YOUNG AND MR JOHN WHYTE

BRIDGES 9 & 12 NON EXISTANT BUT SITES THERE. ALL ROADS AND TRACKS OF TOUR ORIGINAL AND GOOD

1. Pont Gas Poste 'blown'
2. Lock No.2 Cpl. Jarvis VC
3. Capt Tullis 'D' Coy. Stops Germans
4. Out Posts RSF
5. 1st R.S.F. HQ
6. 'A' Coy 1st R.S.F
7. B &C Coys 1st R.S.F
8. Memorial to resistance
9. Pont Richebe not 'blown'
10. Maj Yatman HQ 1st N. Fus
11. R. J. Wright R.E. wins VC
12. Road bridge 'not blown'
13. Bridge house
14. School children
15. Capt John last to leave

16. Maj Yatman retires to Frameries
17. Jemappes Communal Cemetery
18. Running battle to Flenu
19. Flenu Cemetery
20. 2nd H.L.I 5th Brigade
21. 1st N.F.'s at Dawn 24th

COMMUNAL CEMETERY

2ND SOUTH LANCS BATTLEFIELD

COMMUNAL CEMETERY

All the roads and streets are quite narrow, more often than not, winding and often running through densely populated areas. They are easily negotiated by car and only in places 'tight' for a coach. The villages run into one another, it is hilly and very much like the mining districts of East Lancashire and West Yorkshire.

Proceed along the road, having negotiated the rather tricky crossroads. In the evening of 22 August Lieutenant-Colonel Douglas Smith brought his Battalion, 1/RSF (Royal Scots Fusiliers) up towards this spot, to go into line with 4/RF at Nimy, in readiness for the projected advance to the north east. However later that same day he was ordered to bring his men back to Jemappes and to take up positions along the Condé Canal; the advance had been put on hold.

Proceed slowly along this gentle road, noting the low lying land on each side (a little more difficult when the foliage is fully out on the trees). It was down this road that the German cavalry patrol came along in the early morning mist of Sunday 23 August, to be surprised by the Scots' machine-gunners and suffering casualties. The road bears left to the modern bridge [1]; there is a small turning to the right where it is possible to pull in and look back. The machine-guns were positioned here.

Drive over the bridge and park as soon as practicable. Walk back onto the bridge. Jemappes church is behind you and to the west is Jemappes station, where it stood in 1914. 1/RSF's battlefield stretched to 500 yards on either side of the bridge. The canal that you can see is the River Haine, which always ran by the canal, but has now been contained within concrete and stone banks.

Jemappes Station. Exactly where it was in 1914.

Unfortunately for all pilgrims to this battlefield the Condé Canal no longer exists. In 1969 the work commenced to make the new autoroute (to France and Brussels); whilst a large number of the old mine slagheaps were used as in-fill. All the bridges which the British fought to hold have now gone, as have the locks; however, many of the new bridges are near to where the old ones were, whilst the central bank of the Condé Canal remains. This forms the southern embankment of the autoroute, with the drainage canal beyond.

The bridge on which you are standing was the Pont Gas Poste [1]. On both sides of the canal, towards Mons on the one side and as far as the railway station on the other, about 500 yards either side, were B and C Companies [7]. To the west the bridge that you can see is Pont Richebe

Looking towards Lock No. 2, where Cpl Jarvis won his VC, and beyond to Pont Richebe.

[9], guarded by Captain Tullis' D Company, and Battalion Headquarters were up the hill behind the church. Just a little more than half way to Pont Richebe was the site of Lock No 2 [2] where Corporal Jarvis won his Victoria Cross. He was successful in blowing the bridge there whilst working under fire during the battle. It is a shame that the places where so much heroism was shown along the Condé Canal during 23 and 24 August are no longer there; nor anything to commemorate them. In the early hours of 23 August the church bell was ringing and the people were also heading towards the railway station to set off for their summer holidays or to spend the day in Mons.

On the land to the north, towards Ghlin, the German 6th Division had been attacking all morning. Lieutenant-Colonel Smith had withdrawn his posts to the Jemappes bank, but by midday the 20th Infantry Regiment had still not got across the canal. Captain Tullis' D Company had stopped them 200 yards short of it [3], somewhere to the left, beyond the modern car park. It was at the Lock that Captain Wright, the RE's adjutant, received his first wound and here Lieutenant Boulnois and Sergeant Smith blew up 'this' bridge (ie the one that stood on the site here) just after 1pm. Pont Richebe was not destroyed because the electric power in the house where Boulnois had connected his fuses had failed. Eventually the Germans streamed across it.

Rejoin your car and proceed down to a major road junction. Turn right and almost immediately left, up a narrow street and make for the main road towards the top of the hill; there is a small square with the Mairie on your right, and in the middle distance may be seen the church. At the main road turn right towards Hornu - this is the Avenue du Marechal Foch (on the left it becomes Avenue du Roi Albert). Proceed past several right turns until you come to a set of traffic lights and turn right down a narrow street, Rue Arthur Demerbe (extraordinarily enough on the other side of the road it is labelled Rue Richebe!). This road is a cul de sac. You will know if you overshoot, because there is a junction with a wide boulevard within a hundred yards or so. The street becomes increasingly more desolate as you descend down towards the old canal; after a crossroads, on the right is a short section of an old factory wall [8]. Stop and get out to look at the memorial here to members of the Resistance. The Resistance attacked the retreating German SS and Paratroopers with their small arms; the Germans, desperate to get away from the advancing allies, rounded up more than a dozen men and shot them here. A plaque outlines the story; in the bricks may be seen the bullet marks from the machine-guns that were used. The men were buried in Jemappes cemetery.

155

Part of old factory wall (factory demolished) which was the execution wall for 16 Belgian men shot by the Germans in September 1944. It is now a memorial.

The street ends at the railway line and here was Pont Richebe [9] which was not blown and the battleground of 1/RSF as they struggled to stem the enemy tide, gradually falling back up the road along which you have just come. The area was built up then, and perhaps some of the houses that have been passed were here at the time. The Fusiliers carried their retreat on into Flenu, which will be visited in due course.

Return to the main road and turn right and cross over the main boulevard, Chaussee de l'Esperance. The area is full of houses, but note how the ground on the right is low and broken once you have crossed the main boulevard. Take the second turning to the right, Rue Paul Pasture, signposted to Badour; this will bring us to the Mariette Bridge. Turn left at the first road at La Coubeterie (the little villages are blended into one another now), follow it round to the right and stop at the railway line [10].

This was where Major Yatman of the Northumberland Fusiliers (whose Headquarters was in the railway station) got a phone call from a British agent telling him of the progress of the Germans and where Lieutenant Dorman Smith had his barricade. The street on the other side of the railway led up to the old (lifting) Mariette Bridge [11].

Take the street alongside the railway and rejoin the main road before crossing the new bridge over the autoroute and take the first turning left after you get over it, with a sign indicating Quaregnon. You should be able to see the church of La Rivage below the embankment. Go into the village and turn left, back towards the autoroute; the large white wall in front of you, protecting the houses from the roar of the traffic, stands on the site of the bridge lifting gear [11]. Captain Wright strove to demolish it, but the electric leads were too short

The end of the street and site of 1st R.S.F's battle.

and the scale of the German fire made the task impossible. He was constantly shot at, whenever his head or hands showed themselves; he was working beneath the bridge; and he was already wounded. He fell exhausted into the canal, to be rescued by Sergeant Smith. His VC was richly deserved for his efforts that day, sadly never to be enjoyed, as he was killed on the Aisne three weeks later.

It was here that Sergeant Panter and his twelve men took up position in the Bridge house [13], which they had fortified. In the afternoon he and his men had to withdraw over the canal; by this time the Germans were getting over Pont Richebe, threatening to cut off Yatman's men.

There is a door in the white wall that leads onto the autoroute. You are standing more or less on the north bank of the canal and close to the site of Captain Wright's heroism. Sergeant Panter's house has gone, but the houses that you see (with your back to the wall) are either original or on the original site. Sergeant Johnston was killed here; looking up the street, there is a fork in the road, the left fork going towards Badour. It was up this road that Captain St John saw the terrified school children running across the road [14], behind whom the Germans advanced their position whilst the Northumberland Fusiliers were unable to fire. Remember that all the villages in this area were fully occupied by the inhabitants, who in the hours before the battle had been fêting the troops with flowers and chocolate and wine.

There were more than twenty British casualties here before Major Yatman withdrew; the Germans were slow to come across the intact bridge, fearful of British fire. They did bring a field gun up to the corner of the street.

Because of the Germans approaching from Pont Richebe, Yatman withdrew to the west of the railway station and then made his way to the hill top village of Frameries, whence he could see the withdrawal of 1/RSF, fighting up the hill to Flenu.

Retrace your route (there is a somewhat eccentric one way system in the village, but finding the escape route is a matter of common sense - even I managed it!) over the bridge and back up to the main road, the prolongation of Avenue Marechal Foch. Turn left and then turn right at the traffic lights (almost at the church, on your left) and head up the hill on Avenue Champ de Bataille. Take the third on the left, Rue Voie Berthe and then the third on the right, Rue de Ravin, which becomes the dark, tree-lined way to the cemetery, Jemappes Communal [17].

The British plot lies in front of you, close to the Belgian Memorial with its

Captain St John saw terrified schoool children running across this road.

howitzer and large commemorative plaque. The Belgian military section includes former military men and members of the Resistance, whilst one long plot holds those men who were shot against the wall situated close to Pont Richebe.

For all the fighting by British units in the area there are remarkably few graves - only nineteen in total. Of these nine are unidentified, and they are almost certainly 1914 casualties. Private Stevens of 4/RF died of wounds received at Nimy, whilst Private Marshall of 1/Lincoln was brought here from that battalion's battlefield in front of Cuesmes. The remainder of the named graves are from the last days of the war, clearly indicating the role of the Canadians in these parts. The Belgian plot is worth time to inspect it - old soldiers buried together whenever they died, many with the Belgian tricolour on their stone.

Return to the Avenue Champ de Bataille and turn left, continuing up the hill. At the traffic lights turn right (Rue de Quaregnon) and within a hundred yards you will be by the entrance to Flenu Communal Cemetery [19].

The British graves are in a special plot against the right hand wall. There are just thirteen graves, of which eight are unidentified, all thought to be Royal Scots Fusiliers. Above them on the wall is a memorial plaque showing a prone Scottish soldier firing his rifle.

Captain Allen Rose DSO is buried here; he had been reported wounded and captured, but died in enemy hands after his Battalion had withdrawn. Alongside him is his friend, Captain JE Young.

Also buried in the cemetery is John Whyte, an Irish soldier who married a local girl in 1920 whom he met in November 1918 before he went to Cologne with the occupation forces. His daughter (one of four children) and his grandson (Bernard Figue) are now my friends.

Return to the traffic lights and turn left, back along Avenue Champ de Bataille, heading for Frameries. All the way along this road the Scots continued with their fighting retreat.

Watch out for the town hall, several hundred yards or more on the left. There is a spectacular war memorial, designed on very similar lines to the Australian 2nd Division memorial at Mont St Quentin, near Peronne. The memorial here shows a Belgian soldier bayoneting the German eagle. In 1940, before the Germans arrived for the second time, the memorial was hidden down a coal mine; extensive searches left it undiscovered. Thus it avoided the fate of its Australian counterpart which was demolished during the German occupation of France. As part of their policy to subdue the local population the Germans also had the names and addresses of former British soldiers who had married and lived locally - they were soon rounded up.

Continue for half a mile or so, as the ground drops. At the bottom of the hill, and you have to drive slowly here, you will arrive at the old railway station and the Place de la Gare - the position of 1/RSF's last battle in the sector. The Germans gave up their close pursuit here and the Scots were able to withdraw into the outskirts of Frameries.

Just over the route of the old railway line there is a narrow turning to the left,

158

Rue Genes Trois: take it. You will know if you have gone too far if you come to the new flyover.

On the left you will see, after some distance, a large slag heap and remains of a coal mine's winding gear. The road takes you to the positions of the Northumberlands and 1/Lincoln of 9 Brigade and 2/Worcesters of 5 Brigade (the latter from Haig's Ist Corps). A mile to the right were 2/HLI [20], but they managed to stay out of the battle. They were withdrawn early on 24 August when Ist Corps retired. Their few casualties were caused by shell fire; whilst nearly at the houses in the vicinity were on fire as a consequence of the shelling. Major Yatman came from the right as he withdrew to Frameries from the Mariette Bridge.

Drive through the small settlement of La Garde, following the road as it bends to the left (ie ignore the right fork!). Along this road, right up to the railway line, were dug-in three companies of 2/Worcesters. They would stay there until early in the morning, when they withdrew with 5 Brigade.

Stay on this road, including the crossing of a major road, Rue de Grande-Bretagne, which goes (on the left) to Cuesmes. At this crossroads, to the left, were the Headquarters of 1/NF; the remainder of the Battalion came down the road towards you on the night of Sunday to meet up with Major Yatman and to take up positions there. There was a brewery on the right, where 1/RSF spent the night before retiring from the salient. These roads all existed in 1914 and seem to have altered little, apart from their surface and the fact that most of the housing was destroyed in the Second World War.

Proceed across the crossroads and at the next one turn left. Pont Donaire, the railway bridge, is still there and the communal cemetery is about a hundred yards further on the left; in fact the road is a cul de sac, degenerating into a track some distance beyond the cemetery [21].

It is a large cemetery, but there is no Cross of Sacrifice that indicates the site of the British burials. The plot is at the back of the old cemetery, on the left of the central path. The British are buried below a Belgian Memorial. There are nineteen men from 1914, but also another 67 unidentified and who must surely all be from the battle on Monday 24 August, when 9 Brigade fought here and 2/South Lancs lost so many men. These latter would all have been gathered in from isolated burials at the end of the war.

Amongst others to be found here are Captain Malcolm Leckie DSO, 1/NF's medical officer and Sergeant Groves of the same Battalion, wounded and captured but who died on 6 September 1914. There are a number of gunners from 109 Battery in Plot 1A; whilst Captain Cecil Holmes, 1/Lincoln, who died of his wounds two days after the battle, lies in Plot 3A.

This is, perhaps, a good place to stop for a picnic lunch, possibly eating on the hoof as you head for a good view over what was a particularly nasty part of the battlefield.

Proceed to the end of the street and the start of the track mentioned above. Walk along it for some 500 yards until it is crossed by another track. Look ahead and you will see a new autoroute, the R5 and a large slag heap in an area known as La Malogne. There and to the right on the open land is the battlefield of 2/South Lancs, where so many were killed or wounded as they retired on the 24th, coming this way towards Frameries and out of the salient. It is in this vicinity that Captain Travis Cook and his machine-guns mowed down the Brandenburgers, even though he had been wounded seven times and Sergeant Harrison wounded (and later captured). 2/South Lancs lost 300 men in the few hours of that morning, mainly victims to German machine-gun fire from the railway embankment, now gone, but approximately where the new motorway in front of you (in the direction of Cuesmes) now is.

On the left of the track (and to the left of the cemetery) had come 1/Lincoln earlier in the day, engaged in a fighting withdrawal and losing 160 men in those two hours of fierce fighting. At that time there were many coal mines; only the few remaining slag heaps and the odd, strangely forlorn, winding gears give any indication of this now.

Colonel von Brandis and Captain Liebenow of the Brandenburgers reported that their high casualties were due to numerous machine-guns - in fact it was mainly rifle fire. It can only be a short distance from where you are now that Private Tebbut of 1/Lincoln reported that his rifle had become too hot to hold and that he had never seen so many dead men in such a small area.

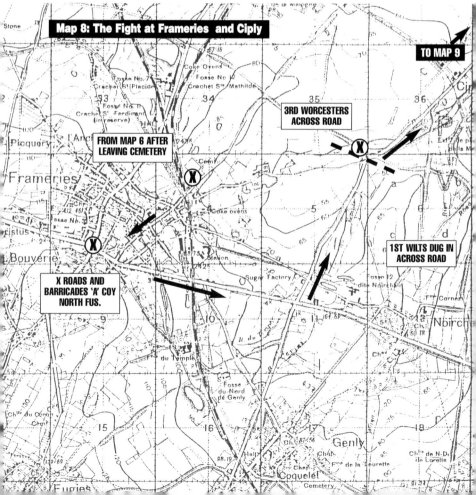

Map 8: The Fight at Frameries and Ciply

This battlefield is mostly unknown and forgotten, but on 24 August it was the site of some of the bloodiest fighting at Mons.

Return past the cemetery and at the crossroads proceed straight across, and then across the next one, climbing the hill. This is a main road running through Frameries, the Paturages to Norchain road. Turn right onto the busy road; go slowly and on the left, at the first major crossroads, you will see a large building on the far left hand corner, which is the hospital. Turn left and park where you can - if necessary in the hospital car park. Walk back to the crossroads.

This was the place where the barricades were erected. One was twenty-five yards or so down the street in front, the Rue des Allies. There were two more on either side, blocking the east west route.

Captain Sandilands of A Company 1/NF held the barrier facing you on the hill, taking up position after withdrawing up the street by the cemetery. 2/Worcesters Headquarters was on the left corner until they retired. It was here that the elderly lady insisted on going through the barricade to bring a doctor to the wounded lying in the hospital, despite the street being under bombardment and machine-gun fire. It is worthwhile re-reading the story of the battle at this point. Captain Leckie died here in the convent hospital. Not a lot has changed physically since then. The road behind you, going up the hill, was the main route for the British retirement from Frameries to Eugies, where 2/Worcesters had their roll called.

From here the tour moves towards Ciply and 7 Brigade's battle.

Return by going right at the crossroads, towards Noirchain and after some two kilometres you will come to a major crossroads, Carrefour de la Mort, turn left. Several hundred yards further on the road to Noirchain is Rue Brunehaut, the old Roman road, which was the route into the battle and for the withdrawal of 7 Brigade; it will be seen from the other end during the tour. On both sides of it 1/Wilts were dug in.

Proceed into Ciply, taking in the views on either side; at the major crossroads there (traffic lights - you will be turning right) try and find some space to stop. On the far left hand corner is the railway station and on the left,

The barricaded crossroads at Frameries. Hospital on the left. The road straight ahead goes down hill where an old lady insisted on going for a doctor. The British retreated towards the camera.

at the start of the road to Cuesmes and alongside the railway, was the sugar factory. A Company 3/Worcesters held both these positions. The Battalion was spread out mainly on the left hand side of the town and in its centre; C Company was behind you whilst the Battalion Headquarters was on the road to Cuesmes. The hill which the Royal Irish Fusiliers held may be seen about a mile away off to the right.

After turning right (towards Maubeuge) take the narrow road to Ciply, again to the right, within about a hundred yards. Almost immediately this road forks, take the right one that leads up the hill on top of which is the church and the Place du Ciply. Drive past and turn left down the hill and stop at the crossroads at the bottom. The narrow road to the right is Rue Brunehaut and opposite is Rue de Robiniere. You can drive down either

Ciply railway station.

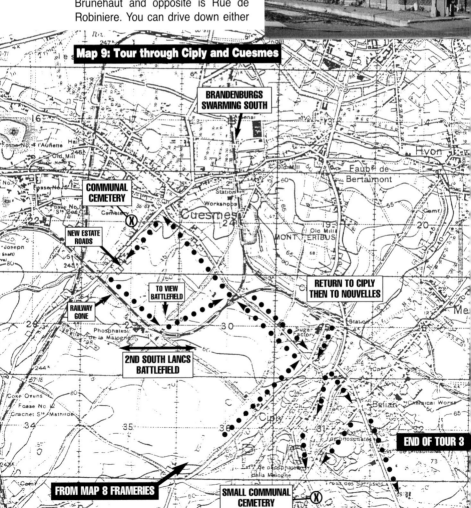

Map 9: Tour through Ciply and Cuesmes

BRANDENBURGS SWARMING SOUTH

COMMUNAL CEMETERY

NEW ESTATE ROADS

RAILWAY GONE

TO VIEW BATTLEFIELD

2ND SOUTH LANCS BATTLEFIELD

RETURN TO CIPLY THEN TO NOUVELLES

FROM MAP 8 FRAMERIES

SMALL COMMUNAL CEMETERY

END OF TOUR 3

of them; 500 yards along was the position of 1/Wilts, whose defensive line ran across to join the two tracks. It was there that Captain W Dawes and Private G Hibberd were killed (buried at Nouvelles CCE). These two roads connect at a crossroads (Lieutenant-Colonel Halstead had his horse shot from him close by): the tiny communal cemetery is along the southern part of Rue Brunehaut, a hundred yards or so down on the left.

Do take the trouble to visit this one; although sited in the middle of a battlefield there is only one British soldier buried here, at the far end against the wall. There is no visitors' book, no register, no Cross of Sacrifice, no comrade to share his eternal rest. Private John Levi Wright of 2/South Lancs, killed on 24 August 1914, the son of Walter and Eliza of 81, Clacton Road, Walthamstow, is the sole representative of the Battalion on this, one of its bloodiest battlefields.

All the narrow roads around here were choked with civilians trying to make their escape; whilst down the two tracks the Royal Irish came on their way out of the salient. This quiet hamlet must have presented a scene of utter confusion. It was down Rue Brunehaut that Captain Salis' D Company of 1/Wilts scrambled to safety; they were the last to retire and had to run in small groups because of the furious shelling all around them.

Drive back along the bottom road and turn left and then at the traffic lights head on towards Cuesmes. Head straight for the village square, which is dominated by a gigantic version of a miner's lamp sitting in the middle of the roundabout. On the left is the large police station and next to it is the Mairie. Drive between them and park at the rear.

In the Mairie Lieutenant-Colonel Ainslie of 1/NF had his Headquarters, the people of the village entertaining them royally, offering billets to the Geordies when they first arrived on the Saturday. On the left hand wall of the police station is a large memorial plaque to the Police Chief who was brutally put to death by the Germans in 1944.

Return to the car and drive along Rue de Frameries; within a couple of hundred yards is the communal cemetery. There are a number of men from 2/South Lancs buried here; the youngest of these is a drummer boy, James Price, aged 16. He was undoubtedly the youngest soldier to be killed in the war thus far, and possibly the only one so young

Lt. Col. Ainslie, C.O. 1st Northumberland Fusiliers. had his HQ here in the Mairie (Town Hall).

to be killed who had not lied about his age, such as Condon and Ross (both aged 14 when they were killed in 1915 and 1918 respectively). Price came from Mountain Ash in South Glamorgan. There are 38 unidentified here, probably 1914 casualties and including Lincolns and South Lancs, and a number of Canadians from 1918. Sergeant P Quinn DCM was killed on 9 November 1918 - the only thing sadder than these last gasp casualties of the war are the graves of those men who succumbed to wounds or disease after the Armistice.

Continue down Rue Frameries; just before the railway bridge take the

MOUNT EREBUS

The South Lancs battlefield. The Old railway line ran across the photograph from left to right. The local man is pointing to the site.

turning to the left (second turning after the cemetery), Avenue de la Grande Barre. Go to the end (several hundred yards away) and at the T Junction turn right. You are now at the south western edge of Cuesmes; a further hundred yards or so will bring you to a field with a small copse on the right. The railway embankment ran across here, and from it the Germans were able to pour fire on 2/South Lancs. If you proceed about fifty yards to the junction of some tracks, there are one or two cottages, you will see the new road crossing your front - this area is known as La Malogne and the other side of the road from the view that you had at Frameries cemetery. You are right on the battlefield and these fields saw the death of many of the South Lancs.

The final visit of the tour is to Nouvelles. Return on the same route to Ciply, but this time stay on the Maubeuge road. About a couple of kilometres after the traffic lights in Ciply take the left turn to Nouvelles and stop at the cemetery on the eastern side of the village, not far from the church.

There are only four 1914 burials. Two of them are men of 1/Wilts, killed at Ciply. Private DJ Carter of 20/Hussars was killed with 5 (Cavalry Brigade), guarding Ist Corps' retirement and Gunner Edward Nelmes was killed whilst serving with 29 Battery RFA.

[There is one further spot to go should you have the time or inclination: return to the crossroads in Frameries and turn left, going through Eugies to Sars la Bruyere. To the north of the village, and on the left hand side of the road, is the chateau (Chateau de la Roche) where Smith-Dorrien had his Headquarters and his fateful meeting with Field-Marshal French. A plaque in the hall commemorates the meeting there at 5am on 23 August when French told his recently arrived IInd Corps commander that there would be no advance.]

From here it is a matter of taking the reverse journey home, or possibly going on the R5 and picking up the autoroute or the road into Mons as relevant.

The South Lancs battlefield from the north side. You saw the south side at Frameries cemetery. The hill is an old slag heap. The new road is in front of it. The South Lancs were at and behind the new road.

SOUTH LANCS

GERMANS ATTACKING POSITION

TOUR No. 4
The Battles at Saint Ghislain and Wasmes, 23 and 24 August.

The touring proper starts at Hornu. Assuming that one is staying in a hotel in Tertre, proceed as follows: drive through Tertre; at the roundabout (La Rivierette - a restaurant of that name is on the far left corner) turn left for Saint Ghislain. Alternatively, this roundabout is reached by coming off the autoroute at Junction 25.

Continue to follow the signs for Saint Ghislain (at the next roundabout, for example, it is a right turn), cross over the autoroute and come into the town (via

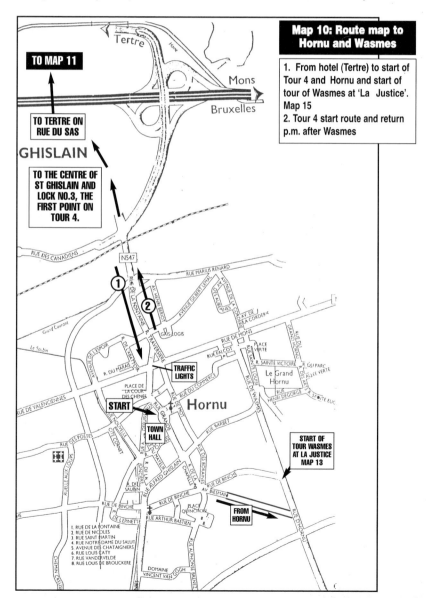

Map 10: Route map to Hornu and Wasmes

1. From hotel (Tertre) to start of Tour 4 and Hornu and start of tour of Wasmes at 'La Justice'. Map 15
2. Tour 4 start route and return p.m. after Wasmes

another roundabout). Almost immediately you will come into the centre of Saint Ghislain and the Grand Place. Ahead are the ruins of the church; drive straight past it and over the railway bridge; you are likely to be forced by the changes in road lay out to have to turn right instead of going over the bridge. At the end of this road go around the roundabout and come back up to the bridge and then turn right to go over it. At the traffic lights go straight ahead (you can get into the right hand lane) and then follow the road round (you have to bear right just before the main square). The town hall of Hornu is on the right, and there is a car park just beyond it. Park there.

Grand Place de Hornu.

This village saw two battalions of Brigadier-General Cuthbert's 13 Brigade come through here (then it was a village) going into the line on the Condé Canal

Hornu Town Hall with Belgian memorial to 32 killed in both wars. 2nd Duke of Wellington's plus half of 1st Royal West Kents and 17th Field Coy. R.E. had billets here.

and then returned when they were withdrawn on Sunday night 23/24 August. On Saturday 22 August 2/Duke of Wellington's found billets in the buildings surrounding the Grand Place. The scene here on that hot sunny Saturday must have been extraordinary; Belgians making a fuss of the first British soldiers that they had seen and they, tired after their long and dusty march, happily accepting the bottles of beer and wine thrust at them. They had hardly settled down when Captain Ozanne was ordered forward with his machine-guns to the north side of the railway embankment at Saint Ghislain. Also in the village were two companies of 1/RWK, the remainder of the Battalion already dispatched at Lock No 3 and the railway bridge over the canal. Also in the village were 17 Fd Coy.

Leave the square and drive back to the traffic lights, where you will turn right and almost immediately left, which places you back on the road by which you came to Hornu. Park by the side of the road a moment. This is the route by which the British entered the battle. Unfortunately this area was to suffer a far worse fate in May 1944. From here to the centre of Saint Ghislain the whole place was carpet bombed and destroyed by American Air Force bombers, thereby wiping out the largest railway junction in Belgium. They succeeded in destroying their target, but hundreds of civilians were also sacrificed. Quite remarkably the ornate and large railway station was about the only building that emerged unscathed.

Just before the railway bridge take a small road to the right, turn immediately left and park. This road, with its pavé, was the original that went over a railway crossing - the number of railway lines expanded considerably after the war.

Walk on to the bridge and appreciate the size of the junction. Off to the left is the ornate railway station.

Drive into Saint Ghislain and park by the church, or as close to it as you can, C Company of 2/Duke of Wellington's was held in reserve here in the Grand

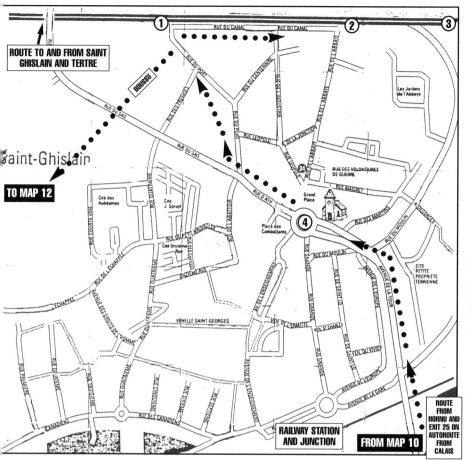

1. Site of lifting bridge
2. Site of Lock 3 lifting bridge
3. Site of railway bridge
4. Major Holland's plaque

ROUTE TO AND FROM SAINT
GHISLAIN AND TERTRE

Saint-Ghislain

TO MAP 12

RAILWAY STATION
AND JUNCTION

FROM MAP 10

ROUTE
FROM
HORNU AND
EXIT 25 ON
AUTOROUTE
FROM
CALAIS

The railway station in 1914, looking towards Hornu.

Place whilst other troops were a mile or so ahead at the Condé Canal. The street on the left is the Rue Grande, which leads to the station, whilst straight ahead, on the right hand corner of the Place des Combattants, is the Town Hall [4] with an information office. On a pillar in front of the restored ancient building, which escaped serious damage in the air raid, is a large bronze plaque commemorating Major CS Holland. He was killed whilst commanding 120 Battery RFA whilst they were in position on the canal bank.

Drive slowly past the Town Hall and take the first turning on the right, Rue du Port. Follow this road down to the bottom, when the road ends at right angles and narrows dramatically. Park near here. Currently, at No 97 (on the left hand side) lives M. Engelbert, the Royal British Legion representative in the town.

This was the original street to the lifting bridge [1] that was blown up by Lieutenant Godsell. The wall in front of you is a shield from the autoroute and was the south bank of the Condé Canal. This was the area covered by 2/Duke of Wellington's and 1/RWK. On the right, and running along the canal bank, is the large hospital used by the Germans in both World Wars (though it does not look very used now). The building is distinctly recognisable should you ever be driving along the autoroute.

The wall precludes seeing anything on the other side, but on the north side was B Company of 2/Duke of Wellington's in the large sheds. This was a port on the canal; here was the section of Dukes, under Sergeant Fittal, who were left on the wrong side after the bridge was blown. He and some of his men had to make their way across, eventually, by crossing via the ruins of the bridge.

Turn to the right along the very narrow road running in front of the hospital, and stop when the road bends sharply once more to the right. This is the site

Before the bombing.

Saint Ghislain church, which partly survived, the bombing, with a new one

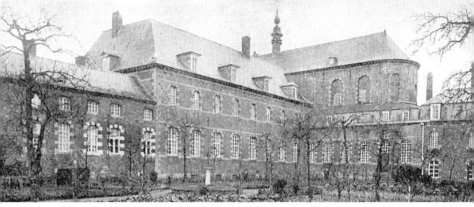

The old hospital at the top of Rue du Port and now alongside the autoroute.

of Lock No 3 [2] and the position of Major Townsend and A Company, 2/Duke of Wellington's. The bridge here was destroyed by Sergeant Payne. Along the length of canal bank over which you have driven were the four 18 pdr guns of 120 Battery; whilst along here was killed Private Thomas Shellabear, Lieutenant-Colonel Gibbs' (commanding 2/Duke of Wellington's) servant.

Some 500 yards away to the east is the new road bridge [3], then the site of a railway bridge, the location of Captain Ozanne's machine-guns and where Corporal Marsden showed so much heroism in replacing the explosive charges as they were blown off by German artillery fire; he was killed there. A tall contortionist might just be able to see it over the wall. This is the closest to the site that you will be able to get because of the complex nature of the fly-over arrangement of the roads.

200 West Kents went over the canal on this stretch early on the Sunday morning, but only 90 came back. It was beyond the railway bridge that Lieutenant O'Reilly's men fixed bayonets to fight a last stand as the Brandenburgers came over the bridge at Mariette, 1500 yards to the east.

Many of the wounded were taken into the hospital. Captain Ozanne, despite his wounds, managed to get away from it to join the last train at the station and escape capture. This was the bridge over which engines and coaches had been sent by the railway men in Hautrage to avoid the advancing enemy.

The next place to investigate is Boussu, on the left flank of 13 Brigade and right flank of 14 Brigade. Return along the hospital road and proceed up Rue du Port; take the first right, Rue des Preelles. Cross Rue Sas (the road by which you first entered Saint Ghislain) and proceed along Rue Quatrieme (signposted Boussu). It terminates at a T Junction roundabout - on the left the road goes to the ornate Saint Ghislain station; go right and at the next T Junction roundabout turn left, Rue du Moulin. After crossing the railway line the road takes a sharp turn to the right, and there is parking usually available by the (Boussu) railway station on your immediate right.

The railway station was always quite large. On 6 November 1918 a heavily loaded German ammunition train was standing here and was struck by a Canadian shell. The whole area for some hundreds of yards was completely flattened by the huge explosion.

During the weekend of the action in the salient the town was crowded with men from both brigades. Back over the railway crossing, on the right, a disused

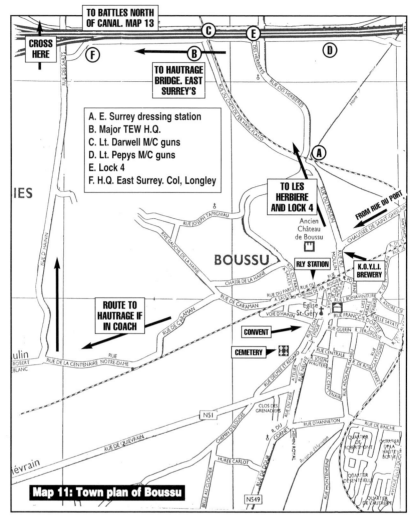

Map 11: Town plan of Boussu

Map labels:

- TO BATTLES NORTH OF CANAL. MAP 13
- CROSS HERE
- TO HAUTRAGE BRIDGE. EAST SURREY'S
- A. E. Surrey dressing station
- B. Major TEW H.Q.
- C. Lt. Darwell M/C guns
- D. Lt. Pepys M/C guns
- E. Lock 4
- F. H.Q. East Surrey. Col, Longley
- TO LES HERBIERE AND LOCK 4
- FROM RUE DU PORT
- Ancien Château de Boussu
- BOUSSU
- RLY STATION
- K.O.Y.L.I. BREWERY
- Eglise St-Géry
- CONVENT
- CEMETERY
- ROUTE TO HAUTRAGE IF IN COACH

factory now stands on the site of the brewery; this is where the KOYLIs were having their lunch when German shelling disturbed them and they were sent up to the line.

Walk into the town square. The very large building on the left is the convent where many British wounded were taken. Keep on the right hand side of the

The station in 1918 after the explosion of the munitions train.

tree-lined market place and a hundred yards beyond its right hand corner take a narrow street on the right. A few paces will bring you to a T Junction with a narrow, old street and the communal cemetery is a few yards away on the right. None of the 1914 men are buried here, but as presumably hardly anyone comes to visit it seems reasonable to take a few minutes to pay one's respects. Amongst those here are Private Henry Clarke (1/4 York & Lancs) who died of his wounds on 27 October 1918 whilst a prisoner; and Lieutenant Derek Webb, aged 19, of 107 Squadron RAF, who died of his wounds on 9 October 1918. Also buried here is M Leon Figue, MBE, the espionage and resistance hero who was executed by the Germans in 1943. There is a street in the centre of the town named after him.

Head back to your car, but the church is worth a visit, especially the quite magnificent medieval carved wooden altar screen now hanging on the north wall of the chancel. The tiny streets and rough cobbles are also highly evocative - presumably hardly changed at all since 1914.

Leave Boussu the same way by which you entered. A somewhat quaint notice on a very dilapidated brick wall on the left warns people that urinating against it will result in 'amendment'! At the T Junction roundabout go straight ahead and at the fork keep to the right, on Rue des Herbieres. Almost immediately you will go on a bridge over the River Haine and a railway. Stop a moment. A few yards to your left, where the track runs alongside the stream, was the dressing station [A] of the East Surreys; they were the right flanking Battalion of 14 Brigade. The railway loops to the left, heading north; their ammunition dump was on the left of the line a few hundred yards away.

Drive slowly forward; just before the modern bridge take the slip road to the left and stop at its end - the autoroute is ahead.

This is the site of the old lifting bridge [E], Lock No 4 at Les Herbieres, where so much took place in August 1914. The bridge was not blown, although it had been prepared for demolition, The enemy were fast approaching, but Lieutenant Pottinger of 17 Fd Coy RE was unable to ignite the charges; he fired at them with his revolver, but to no avail. He managed to escape capture in the dusk of the Sunday evening.

Go onto the bridge and look at 2/KOSBs battlefield straight ahead. 500 yards to the right, on the Boussu side of the bridge, was a white two-storey house where the Borderers put their two machine-guns (under the command of Lieutenant Pennyman), and further along was Lieutenant Pepys of the KOYLIs with his two guns [D]. On that side of the canal were C and A Companies

The slip road at the modern bridge and road on the right. Autoroute (Conde Canal) ahead. At the end of this old road was the site of the old lifting bridge at Lock 4, Les Herbieres.

(KOSB) and on the far side Major Chandos Leigh and CSM Wilson with D Company. There also was the cottage, associated with Major Coke (B Company) and the tablecloth episode. Signed by those who enjoyed a meal there, Coke recovered the tablecloth from the ruined cottage, where the ladies still lived, over four years later.

By late in the afternoon of the 23rd the Battalion had suffered more than a hundred casualties in those fields on the far side of the autoroute, amongst them Major Chandos Leigh, who was wounded and died in German captivity. When D Company was withdrawn over the Lock bridge the men were relieved by the KOYLI until they too were withdrawn in the hours of darkness.

[If in a coach, return to Boussu and take the road to Hainin; then turn right up Rue d'Hainin to cross over the autoroute.]

Turn left and set off along a narrow, concrete road that has a good surface but can be very uneven due to subsidence - drive slowly if you value your suspension! After a few hundred yards you will come to the railway bridge [C], which is in the same position as it was in 1914. Stop and get out.

Here was the site of the major battle of the East Surreys. Underneath the bridge a barge had been moored which they used to cross the canal. You can see the embankment where Lieutenant Darwell had his machine-guns on the western side and in the small wooded field Major Tew, the Battalion's second in command, had his Headquarters. Captain Campbell went over the bridge with a patrol early in the morning, and had gone as far as Hautrage railway station, where he saw the engineers getting up steam to evacuate the engines.

300 yards on the far side of the autoroute C Company was divided, with half on the right of the railway embankment, half on the left. Captains Benson and Campbell were brought back via the barge after being badly wounded, Benson subsequently dying - he is buried at Hautrage. After a bitter struggle the Germans managed to cross the embankment, from right to left; the East Surreys had 221 casualties over there.

Along the road on which you are driving Captain Minogue's D Company were dug-in.

The railway bridge was only partially destroyed. Corporal Barwick of 59 Fd Coy RE had used the electric exploder, but not all the charges went off.

Continue on the road along the side of which D Company was spread,

Corporal Barwick's bridge, Captain Campbell's barge underneath. Lt Darwell's machine guns were firing away from the camera.

EAST SURREY'S BATTLEFIELD

Site of the old lifting Pont d'Hautrage and 'B' Coy. The bridge was blown by Cpl Dorey R.E.

noting the wide open fields and occasional copse (this is true of both sides of the autoroute). At the junction with the main road, stop.

B Company (1/East Surrey) was deployed around here. This was the site of Lieutenant-Colonel Longley's Headquarters [F]. Half a mile to the left, and to the left of the road, was Captain Torrens with his A Company. Turn right to go over the new bridge. This has been built a few hundred yards to the east of the old lift bridge, Pont d'Hautrage. It was blown by Corporal Dorey of 59 Fd Coy, who was wounded in the head when he looked to see if his work had been successful.

When the autoroute was built in 1969 the buildings in this part on the north side were cleared for some hundreds of yards. Almost immediately you will come to an inverted fork in the road, take the left fork which brings you back towards the autoroute. This road will bring you to the north side of the lifting bridge, Pont d'Hautrage [10]. All the lifting mechanisms of the bridges of the canal were on the north bank. The road bends and comes to an end. This road and the bridge itself were guarded by B Company, which had a generally uneventful time, enduring the occasional shelling, but the main fighting was to their right. The enemy did not approach here until they had overcome the opposition near the railway bridge. Two hundred men were dug in here, but all

Map 13. The defence of the canal north of St Ghislain.

1. Site of lift bridge 'blown' by Lt Godsell
2. Site of Lock 3. Lifting bridge
3. Site of Rly Bridge. Captain Ozanne
4. Lt Pepys K.O.Y.L.I. machine guns
5. K.O.Y.L.I.'s in support
6. Site of bridge at Les Herbier
7. 'D' Coy East Surreys
8. H.Q. East Surrey Lt. Col. Longley
9. 'B' Coy East Surreys Capt. Flanagan
10. Site of Hautrage bridge
11. 'C' Coy East Surrey battlefield
12. Site of Major Coke's cottage
13. Battlefield of K.S.O.B.
14. German attack stopped here
15. Royal West Kent's 'Corner'
16. 3000 German casualties here
17. Major Yatman's bridge at Mariette

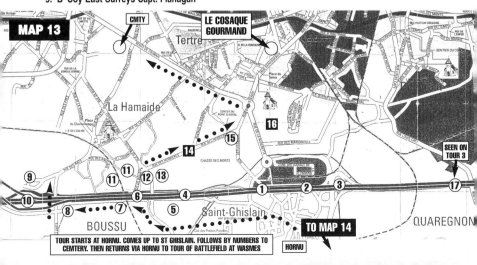

LT WARD'S CHARGE

Site of Capt Cambell and Lt Wynyard battle. Lt Ward's charge with sword here.

evidence of their presence has been obliterated.

Return to the main road and continue towards Hautrage on Rue des Bats. Ignore the first sharp turn to the right, but take the next one (there is a small grass 'island'), Rue des Anglais - though you will be hard pushed to find the street sign! It is a narrow road which brings you to a cul de sac to the west side of the railway embankment. This was the battlefield of the larger part of C Company [11], the others being on the eastern side. It is difficult to make it out, with the growth of the trees, the vegetation and some new housing. It was in this vicinity that Captains Benson and Campbell and Lieutenant Wynyard were killed or wounded. Lieutenant Ward was angered at seeing his commander wounded and lying on the ground; as the enemy came towards him he led his men in a charge, brandishing his sword, from the thin copse to the west and was killed. Lieutenant Morritt was wounded and subsequently captured here - many of the wounded were taken to the convent in Boussu.

The Germans crossed the embankment at approximately the point of the cul de sac, but they had to endure the machine-gun fire of Lieutenant Darwell from his position on the south bank as they did so.

Return to the island and turn right; proceed under the railway bridge and take the next right (Rue du Progress). Follow this road until you come to a crossroads and turn right. After about 500 yards there is a fork; turn right, which takes you around an 'island' on which is built a school. Follow the road until it ends - this is the old road to the north side of the old lifting bridge at Lock No 4 at Les Herbieres [6] which was not blown. You were on the south side earlier, before going under the railway bridge. To the right was a part of C Company, whilst that Battalion's machine-guns severely damaged the advancing Germans coming from your left (east). Close to this spot is the battlefield of the KOSBs [13], which suffered some hundred casualties on the Sunday afternoon.

Return and take the right hand fork around the island (ie keep the school on your left). Directly opposite is the road to Tertre, Rue des Herbieres. You are driving into the battlefield of 1/RWK [14]. Stop when convenient. Here, north of the canal, you have escaped the urbanisation that will have made your driving

From the north and 'C' Coy's battleground. Les Herbieres lift bridge at Lock 4. Site of Lt Pottinger's bridge. Not 'blown'.

Tertre
St-Ghislain

Battlefield of the K.O.S.B.'s.

thus far interesting, so to speak. The roads (probably now slightly wider) and the fields, apart from a few new houses, are much as they were then. About a mile ahead is the large roundabout, La Rivierette, which you used, if starting from Tertre, this morning. The road forms a V with Rue Defuisseaux (coming from the right) 200 yards or so short of the roundabout. Between these two roads A Company [15], under Captain Lister of 1/RWK, prevented any advance of the Germans from Tertre. They occupied that village in large numbers - regimental strength. On the (British) left, opposite Hautrage cemetery, was the 1st Battalion of the Brandenburgers; on the right, about half a mile from the centre of the village, was the 2nd Battalion, whilst a battalion of Fusiers was in the centre of the village. Lister had a difficult task to accomplish with his 200 men.

Drive up to the junction, turn left and stop at a convenient point. About a hundred yards down the road on the left was Lieutenant Gore's No 1 Platoon; behind you, on the left of Rue Des Hebieres, was Lieutenant Chitty's No 3 Platoon. At the corner on the right hand side of the road was Lieutenant Wilberforce-Bell's No 2 Platoon and in the field on the right, where a small stream crosses Rue Defuisseaux, was Lieutenant Anderson's No 4 Platoon. Some of the buildings were loopholed to provide a reasonably secure firing position. The Germans had an artillery battery close to the base that you may well be using in Tertre, Le Cosaque Gourmand. It was to Lieutenant Gore's position that four cyclists came pedalling furiously with news of the positions of the Germans in Tertre.

See Map
page 88

Royal West Kents battlefield. Former site of canal and other battles 1,000 yards away from camera. Germans advanced away from camera towards Saint Ghislain.

LT ANDERSON WAS KILLED
AND CAPT LISTER OF THE
1/RWK WOUNDED CLOSE TO
THIS CORNER

1/RWK WITHDREW
OVER CANAL

GERMAN ADVANCE

The German attack came at 8.30am from the right [16] and in overwhelming numbers towards Nos 2 and 4 Platoons: Lieutenant Anderson was killed and Captain Lister was quite quickly both wounded and captured. Close to where you are Private Donovan won his DCM [15], bringing in a wounded man under heavy fire. Lieutenant Gore survived this action, but was killed two months later. This action lasted until 11.30am, when the survivors withdrew to the bridge. The German advance had been stopped (amongst their casualties was Major Praeger, a battalion commander) and held some 400 yards from the canal. This is the battlefield that is so graphically described in Captain Bloem's military classic, *The Advance from Mons.*

Proceed to the roundabout and take the road to the left, Route de Tournai, and after about two kilometres or so you will see Hautrage Military Cemetery on the left (signposted before that with a CWGC sign). It is a quiet and secluded spot, and there is seating if you were thinking of having a picnic here.

The Germans laid out the cemetery, and as for the others that they established in France and Belgium, they did an excellent job. It makes one think about how their cemeteries in these countries might have looked if the end result of the war had been different. There are 538 German graves and 227 British; almost all of the British were killed in those two days of August 1914 and were gathered in from their hastily dug, battlefield, graves. The register identifies individual graves, but I found pleasure in examining all the British graves and spotting familiar names from the text. Amongst those here is Major Charles Stewart Holland, in the left plot, whose grave stands isolated. Corporal Marsden is to be found in I.D.12; he was the inventor of the Marsden Band Trestle, which facilitated bridge building. Private William Nicholson (I.A.13) joined the Cheshires when he was 16; he held the Long Service and Good Conduct Medal. Others buried here include Lieutenant Anderson of the Kents, Lieutenant Pepys of machine-gun fame, Major Strafford of 2/Duke of Wellington's and Sergeant Spence of D Company, 2/Duke of Wellington's, who won the DCM for his part in a magnificent bayonet charge at Wasmes, but who died of his wounds when a German captive. All of those who were killed (and who could be found) in the valiant stand at Wasmes, many buried where they fell, were reinterred here. Major Pack Beresford (1/RWK), buried at the time near a slag heap, was one of those whose body was not recovered.

The final stage of the tour is to Wasmes. In the withdrawal of the 5th Division on Monday 24 August, a costly rearguard action was fought there by battalions of 13 Brigade and 1/Dorsets of 15 Brigade.

The Battle at Wasmes
This battle was caused by the rapid German follow-up after the withdrawal of 9, 13 and 14 Brigades from the Condé Canal during the night of 23/24 August and the need for the exhausted and hungry men to stand and fight so that the survivors of those brigades might escape capture. This was a consequence of the decision that the BEF must leave the salient on Monday 24 August. It was to be the last battle fought by the battalions discussed in this tour, and thus it has been included as a mini tour in its own right to complement what has gone before.

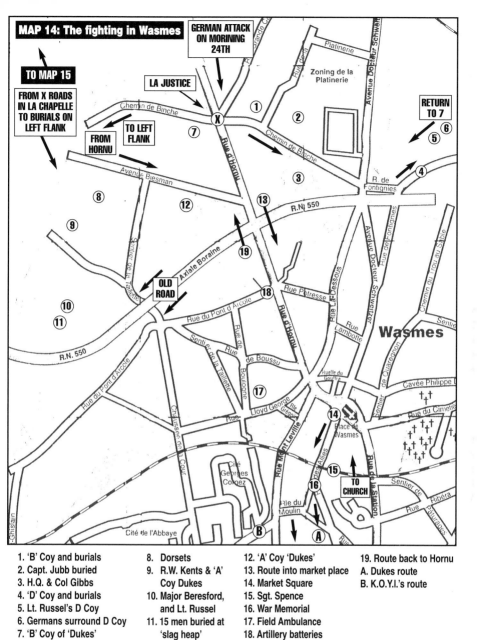

MAP 14: The fighting in Wasmes

GERMAN ATTACK ON MORNING 24TH

TO MAP 15

FROM X ROADS IN LA CHAPELLE TO BURIALS ON LEFT FLANK

LA JUSTICE

RETURN TO 7

FROM HORNU

TO LEFT FLANK

Chemin de Binche

Rue d'Hoxiu

Chemin de Binche

Avenue Biesman

R.N. 550

R.N. 550

OLD ROAD

Axiale Boraine

Rue du Pont d'Arcole

Sentier de la Taillette

Sentier de la Taillette

Rue de Boussu

Rue Boulogne

Rue Lloyd George

Rue Mont Leville

Cité Georges Cornez

Rue du Moulin

Cité de l'Abbaye

Place de Wasmes

Rue La Dessous

Rue Lambotte

Ruelle du Gouffre

Wasmes

TO CHURCH

Platinerie

Zoning de la Platinerie

Avenue Docteur Schweitzer

R. de Fontignies

Avenue de Fontignies

Rue de Fontignies

Chemin au Trou au Sable

Cavée Philippe

Rue du Cimetiè

1. 'B' Coy and burials	8. Dorsets	12. 'A' Coy 'Dukes'	19. Route back to Hornu
2. Capt. Jubb buried	9. R.W. Kents & 'A'	13. Route into market place	A. Dukes route
3. H.Q. & Col Gibbs	Coy Dukes	14. Market Square	B. K.O.Y.I.'s route
4. 'D' Coy and burials	10. Major Beresford,	15. Sgt. Spence	
5. Lt. Russel's D Coy	and Lt. Russel	16. War Memorial	
6. Germans surround D Coy	11. 15 men buried at	17. Field Ambulance	
7. 'B' Coy of 'Dukes'	'slag heap'	18. Artillery batteries	

To begin with, go to the Grand Place at Hornu as directed at the beginning of this tour. Proceed past the Town Hall, which is the road to Wasmes. At a multi road junction you want to head south east, on Avenue Biesman [12], which soon brings you to a road junction - try and stop before this and walk to the junction. Look down the straight road in front of you; at the bottom of the hill is

'La Justice' looking north: a longer view of Dukes' position and the German advance. Wasmes is towards camera.

the Place du Wasmes [14] - the church is visible - whilst beyond, as the road goes up the hill, there are numerous houses alongside it. This small mining town is full of narrow streets and surrounded by old coal mine workings and slag heaps. There are a lot of road and housing developments in progress, and the battlefield is difficult to see in detail. If there is the time it might be advantageous to park where you can and use the guide to take you around on foot; a sensible option to leave the car might be the town square.

If following the route by car, turn left and then almost immediately right (Chemin de Binche), and park.

This area is known as La Justice and was the centre of 2/Duke of Wellington's defence perimeter. Look north along Rue d'Hornu (the road up which you just turned) and along which Lieutenant-Colonel Gibbs, commanding 2/Duke of Wellington's, knew the Germans would come. He had spread the Battalion out on top of the ridge, from right to left, that protects Wasmes. All the fighting took place within a few hundred yards of the perimeter and in the streets going back to the market place. B Company [1] were dug-in just behind the crossroads on Chemin de Binche, the narrow road running from east to west. The company had trenches in the fields on the left (west) [7] of the crossroads as well as on the right. To the south east of the road Lieutenant-Colonel Gibbs had his Headquarters. There were a number of battlefield burials here.

Proceed eastwards on the Chemin de Binche; just before reaching the crossroads was the area where Lieutenant-Colonel Gibbs was wounded and subsequently captured (in C Company's lines) [3]. It is roughly in the large parking area, part of an industrial estate. In the same vicinity Lieutenant JHL Thompson received his mortal wound; he died on 17 September and was initially buried here before being removed to Hautrage. Half a company of 1/Bedford had somehow found themselves here in the early morning and by 5am had been all but wiped out by the bombardment. At midday a German

Lt. Russel's last stand (D Coy) at a slag heap in this field behind an old house.

Major Pack Beresford's battlefield on left flank of the defence of Wasmes. Many men were buried and lost. The hill is an old slag heap. Then, in 1914, on right at top of Rue de Pont D'Arcole.

aircraft dropped white discs in this area and an immediate burst of gunfire fell onto C Company, wounding many, including Major EN Townsend and the adjutant, Captain Denman-Jubb, who died from his wounds [2]. Major Stafford was also killed here.

[At this point the road becomes too small for a coach, so leave it here and walk, approximately 400 yards to the site to be examined.]

Drive straight across the crossroads and ignore the new road on the right. You should go straight up the narrow, original Rue de Fontignies and then go up the hill to the left. This road is both narrow and short. At the top there is a small crossroads with a very old house on the corner. Turn right into the field. On the left is the remains of a small slag heap. D Company was dug in on the right hand side of the uphill road [5] and some of the men that were killed were buried in that rough field. Here was Lieutenant Russel's platoon from D Company; surrounded, they made a valiant stand [6] and were wiped out. The Red Cross party after the battle found sixteen dead Germans, some still with bayonets in their body. Lieutenant Russel's body was taken to the left flank of the battlefield, along with Major Pack Beresford's and others of the West Kents [10 and 11]. Russel's body was found later and taken to Hautrage, but the Major's was never found.

This isolated and unexciting looking field was the scene of great heroism by both sides. It is doubtful whether anyone around here knows it.

Return to La Justice, cross Rue d'Hornu and take the western side of the Chemin de Binche. B Company was in defence in the field on the left - Lieutenant-Colonel Gibbs' semi-circular perimeter defence against the German advance from the north is now clear.

At the village and crossroads, there is a small island, go half way round it to the left and then right up a narrow street. [If you are in a coach park it on the wide road going left to Wasmes, because there is a maze of narrow and one way streets in the next part of the tour.] Ahead you will see new housing developments and after about 500 yards stop where the road veers to the left into a new housing estate. There are two very big slag heaps and you can see the new autoroute crossing the bridge ahead; below are the remains of the original cobbled road. That is Rue Pont d'Arcole. On the right, now totally lost, is the left flank of Lieutenant-Colonel Gibbs' perimeter and where two companies of 1/Dorset were[8]; they suffered 132 casualties. On the left [9]

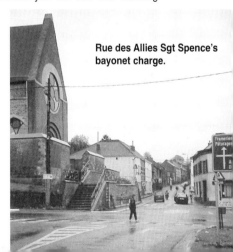

Rue des Allies Sgt Spence's bayonet charge.

179

was a company of 1/RWK where Major Pack Beresford and two of his officers, Captain Phillips and Lieutenant Broadwood were killed. The latter two were found in due course and are buried at Hautrage. It is possible that the gallant major is one of the unidentified at Hautrage. In the midst of this manmade desolation brave men fought and died. Do not try and progress down the cobbled road, you will regret it!

Go back the way you came and then turn right and return to the junction with Rue d'Hornu and turn right and into the Grand Place de Wasmes [14] and park.

Next to the church is Rue des Allies; walk up it. This is where Sergeant Spence led his bayonet charge [15], scattering the Germans, but receiving his fatal wound (and the DCM). At the top of the street is the war memorial [16], standing in the middle of the road, which has panels commemorating the British who fought here. Return to the square and then look up the hill down which you came, where British guns of 119 Fd Battery were positioned.

Return to base via Saint Ghislain. The Field Ambulance was on the left of the road as you head out of Wasmes.

As you drive through the centre of Saint Ghislain you might possibly stop for some shopping or a café stop; it is a pleasant enough place. The first casualty of 2/Duke of Wellington's was Sergeant Greenhalgh, who was struck by a shrapnel bullet on his way to the Condé Canal on the 22nd.

TOUR No. 5
The Battles of the Thulin Road and the Left Flank Guard: 23 and 24 August.

There is a fair amount of walking here, and so appropriate footwear is advisable.

Follow the route to Boussu (ie toward Saint Ghislain, over the autoroute, Rue Sas and then the small turning used on Tour 4, Rue Quatrieme, signposted Boussu). In this village use the circular road by the station, which should bring you on to the N51, signposted Quievrain. After three kilometres or so, turn left at the crossroads. After half a mile the road divides - take the right one which will bring you out in the large Market Place and the main church of Elouges.

Start Point: Elouges Church and Market Place.
Elouges has changed remarkably little since 1914. It was shelled on 24 August when it was full of British troops, but the church escaped with little damage. Almost all of 14 and 15 Brigades retired through it on their way to Bavai (Bavay), the 5th Division following its orders to avoid Maubeuge at all costs.

Go behind the church to the communal cemetery, on the left. As soon as you enter you will see the Cross of Sacrifice and the closely packed graves, set in a square in trenches. Buried here are 38 men of the flank guard. Most are of 1/Norfolks, but of the four officers of the Battalion killed on that Monday afternoon, only one is here: Captain EFV Briard, who came from Jersey. A

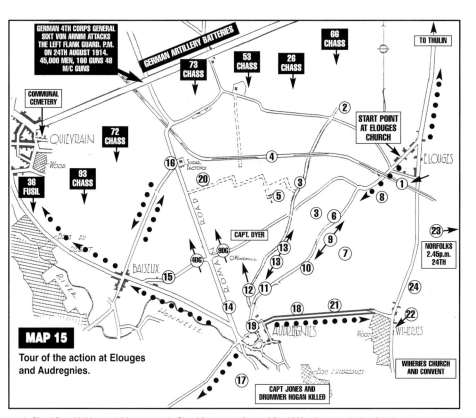

MAP 15

Tour of the action at Elouges and Audregnies.

Map labels:
- GERMAN 4TH CORPS GENERAL SIXT VON ARNIM ATTACKS THE LEFT FLANK GUARD. P.M. ON 24TH AUGUST 1914. 45,000 MEN, 160 GUNS 48 M/C GUNS
- GERMAN ARTILLERY BATTERIES
- 66 CHASS
- 53 CHASS
- 26 CHASS
- 73 CHASS
- TO THULIN
- COMMUNAL CEMETERY
- START POINT AT ELOUGES CHURCH
- QUIEVRAIN
- 72 CHASS
- ELOUGES
- Wood
- 93 CHASS
- 36 FUSIL
- Sugar Factory
- CAPT. DYER
- Bois du ...
- 9DG
- 4DG
- Windmill
- RIVER
- BAISEUX
- ROMAN ROAD
- NORFOLKS 2.45p.m. 24TH
- HONNELLE
- CAPT JONES AND DRUMMER HOGAN KILLED
- AUDREGNIES
- Wood
- WIHERIES
- Bois d'Audregnies
- WIHERIES CHURCH AND CONVENT

1. Cheshires 12.30 p.m. 24th	9. Cheshires on main road for 1000yrds	17. 'L' Bty R.H.A.
2. Norfolks 12.30 p.m. 24th	10. Lt Campbell killed	18. Col Boger wounded
3. Cavalry survivors	11. Cheshires machine guns	19. Capt Shore
4. Old railway embankment	12. Windmill bayonet charge	20. Cavalry veer right
5. Coal mine pits Chesh & Norfolk	13. Platoons of Cheshires	21. Wiheries cemetery
6. Light railway crosses road	14. Roman Rd 4DG & 9LN charge	22. 'Le Metro' now a meat shop
7. Cheshires last stand	15. Tom Bridges refuge	23. Norfolks 2.45 p.m. 24th
8. 119 Bty RFA two VC's won	16. Sugar factory	24. Road to Thulin

member of the heroic 119 Fd Bty is here, Driver Walter Atkinson, from Manchester. Private Thomas Rodger, 2/A & SH (Argyll and Sutherland Highlanders) was brought to this cemetery from Quievrain, about six miles away, where his Battalion was in reserve. The Battalion was part of 19 Brigade, which saw very little action on the 24th and whose early withdrawal forced Fergusson to form the left flank guard. Rodger must have been caught up in the Germans attack at Marchipoint; frustrated by the hold-up at Audregnies, they tried to get around on the left flank. Private Thomas Mason DCM was one of the few men in 1/Cheshire whose heroic actions were recognised.

Galloping battery hit here. Cheshires dug in along road coming from Elouges. Old track to Wiheries where the car is.

BATTERY HIT

CHESHIRES DUG IN

On the left of the road to Audregnies, just past the large colliery. Withdrawal route of 119 Battery. Two VCs won here.

Return to the car and take the first turning to the right after the church, heading for Audregnies. Go very slowly, traffic allowing, as it bends to the left, for you are now on the battlefield [1].

To the right on that morning were 18/Hussars, who withdrew over this road before the battle had really got under way. At the minor road junction ahead is the track going down to the right [2] along which Lieutenant-Colonel Ballard took his 1/Norfolks, taking up positions half a mile away, facing north west. The railway crossed the land here then; stop for a moment at the large coal mine and look to the north to see Ballard's view.

Here is the open land across which came some 3,000 fresh German troops of the 7th Division (13 Brigade); to the left of them came elements of the 72nd and 93rd Regiments (8th Division) and still further over came the 53rd Chasseurs and the 36th Fusiliers - all told, several thousand men of von Arnim's IV Corps. Kluck had finally turned south to drive the British into Maubeuge.

On the ridge, about three miles away, were massed sixteen batteries of artillery. In opposition were two battalions, a squadron and a half of cavalry and the eight field guns of 119 Battery and L Battery, RHA. The two infantry commanding officers, Ballard and Boger (1/Cheshire) must have seen this awe-inspiring sight and realised the implications for their men.

It is possible to follow the line of the old railway [4], which for a thousand yards or so goes north westerly, almost at right angles to the road, before it bends to the left towards the sugar factory. It is possible to make out the red bricks of the building in the far distance; closer to you, on the left of the old line, is a small copse with the remains of some buildings [5]. It is the old spoil tip where Lieutenant-Colonel Campbell sheltered with the survivors of his gallant squadron of 9/Lancers after their charge to the sugar factory. He rode back from there alone, across the shell and bullet drenched land to get further orders.

Go slowly forward. On the left hand side you will see an ancient pit which looks derelict; there is a space where you can park here. As the road climbs you should notice the remnants of a bridge which carried the light railway over the road from the spoil heap in the fields on your right. It was this area that saw the chaos caused when a shell hit a section of 119 Battery, creating a confusion of men, horses and gun and stampeding the Cheshires transport mules, taking shelter in the sunken road. It was here that Grenfell and Alexander laboured to get the guns shifted over the road and along the track towards Wiheries and relative safety. It is possible (though muddy) to walk up to the track of the old light railway line (do so on the north side) and to get a view over the area where this frenetic activity took place.

Continue forward and stop at a gap in the bank on the left hand side. This was the old track to Wiheries; there was a yellow gate [7] there in 1999. Walk

Looking from road - north to old colliery buildings in distance. Cavalry survivors came towards camera.

A small bridge over the railway from Audregnies toward Dour. Near here Lieutenant Campbell was killed.

along it. After a while the track is crossed by another, which was the old railway line [6] from Audregnies to Dour. Lieutenant Campbell of the Cheshires was killed here [10] whilst going forward to help B Company. Turn left along the old railway line for half a mile or so until a small bridge crosses the old light railway from the colliery. The guns of 119 Battery had to be shifted with care over here.

Return to the car and go forward until there is a sharp bend in the road; pull in at the little green triangular parking area. Walk back some 200 yards to the track going off to the left, by the two new houses.

Here were two cottages [11]; Lieutenant Randall had 1/Cheshire's two machine-guns behind the grass bank, firing into the advancing Germans. Walk up the track and at the ruins of the windmill, stop. Captain Dyer with three officers and thirty men made a bayonet charge here [12], going for some 500 yards from the main road to the left, driving the enemy back towards another windmill down the slope. Captain Joliffe, coming back for more men, was severely wounded here, his leg shattered. Only ten men survived the charge. The track marks the actual position of the forward platoons of the Cheshires [13], and their good firing position may be appreciated. 100 yards from the windmill were two platoons of A Company and at a similar distance was Captain Jackson with two from C Company. Beyond him were men under the command of Captains Dugmore and Jones. When you have walked enough along the Cheshires' forward line return to the main road. During the battle there were many German dead in the fields to your right. Near the windmill look towards the sugar factory and the land over which the cavalry charged; CSM Makin was struck on the head by a bullet just about here.

The farm [19] (Ferme de l'Abbaye) a few yards beyond your parked car held Captain Shore and half of B Company. The village is to the left.

Rejoin your car and slowly drive down the hill; take the first on the right. On the left is a large house which always seems to have the Belgian flag flying from its pole. As the road curves left, go straight on to an old and original pavéd road, Rue Brunehaut, a Roman road; park [14].

Walk up the road (ie to the north). On either side of it the cavalry formed up for their famous and historic charge at the German held sugar factory. Lieutenant-Colonel Campbell began his charge with 9/Lancers on the right of the track (then, of course, it was the 'main' road) and Lieutenant-Colonel Mullins and his 4/DG started his from the hollow to the left. The track is as straight as a die for almost four miles, and there is only a little wobble in Audregnies that prevents it being an even more considerable distance. If you

183

The windmill.

Cavalry charged towards camera.

happen to have a four wheel drive vehicle, carry on up it, otherwise walk. After some 500 yards there is a deeply sunken track crossing the Rue Brunehaut. The cavalry had to leap this hollow. The track crosses the battlefield in front of the positions of 1/Norfolks and 1/Cheshire and it was a natural feature for the Germans to gather themselves before their final assault. It must have been quite a sight to see the cursing and shouting Captain Dyer and his men as they drove the enemy back at the point of the bayonet back to this track - almost a ditch - from the windmill. On the other hand, it would not have competed with the noise and splendour of the massed cavalry coming over it as they made for the German machine-guns. Somewhere quite close to the left was the site where Major Tom Bridges, charging with 4/DG, had his horse shot from under him. He had already had quite an exciting time a day or so earlier on the Soignies road (Tour 2). Hit by his horse, he was knocked unconscious and rescued by two members of the RAMC and taken to a cottage [15].

Rejoin the car and take the road to Baisieux; after several hundred yards there is a small track to the right by which there are some old cottages. It is from one of these that Major Bridges escaped when he saw the Germans coming. Continue and then turn right at the crossroads in Baisieux; after a mile or so you will come out on the Rue Brunehaut and, opposite, the buildings that were once the sugar factory [16]. Turn right and park. Walk along the pavé track beyond the buildings, some of which stood then, which were occupied by German infantry and machine-gun. You can see the good positions occupied by the Cheshires and Norfolks on the ridge in front of Audregnies and the suicidal charge of the British cavalry coming towards you. Over on the left there is the old spoil heap where Captain Lucas Tooth of the Lancers stayed after his squadron had finished, helping a company of Norfolks to defend it whilst his Colonel raced across the fields to Audregnies. The long line of low trees denotes the railway line; the barbed wire fence [20] forced the cavalry to swerve left and right and pushed them alongside it. The German infantry were all along the fence. Behind you there is another view of the railway behind which was the German artillery. Captain Tooth won the DSO for his gallant work, but was killed on the Aisne a few weeks later.

Return to the crossroads in Baisieux and turn right to Quievrain. Take the third on the right in the village, by the water tower, and the large communal cemetery is only a couple of hundred yards away. The Cross of Sacrifice is on the left, close to the far wall. There are 43 British graves, but only one from the battle at Audregnies; the rest are mainly Canadians. Private John Clarke of 1/Cheshire died of his wounds on 2 September 1914. There is a crew from 98

Captain Shore's postion in Farm Hollow.

Major Tom Bridges' cottage down the lane to the left.

Squadron RAF, shot down on 30 October 1918. One of the Canadians, CSM Donald Mckenzie DCM MSM, from Ross Shire, was another to be killed almost at the war's end. 93 Germans were buried here, but as in so many communal cemeteries, they were removed at the war's end.

Return to Audregnies and take the right turn for Angre. Within a few yards the cemetery is to be found on the right. Look across the road [17] into the field to the south, where L Battery of the RA were for the first part of the action; it would of course become famous for the action at Nery, and one of the guns may be seen in the Imperial War Museum. It also saw service here.

The Cross of Sacrifice is against the wall; all the men in here were brought in long after the battle, originally buried where they fell or dying in the convent from their wounds. There are only some 40 buried here who were involved in the battle, 32 of whom are unidentified, but almost certainly Cheshires for the most part. The small numbers buried in the various cemeteries suggests that a large number must still be out there in the fields. If you have time, carry on to the communal cemetery at Angre, a mile or so away. The cemetery is on the right hand side at the beginning of the village, and there are 16 British burials there. None are directly connected with this battle, but it is difficult to imagine that anyone visits their graves, apart from some of the local people.

Return to the market square in Audregnies and park. This might be a good time to have your picnic.

In the late afternoon, as the Germans stormed the village, this place was crowded with Cheshires and the few Norfolks who had not been withdrawn with the Battalion but had been fighting at the colliery with the Lancers; many of them were wounded and a lot were taken prisoner. One of the houses here was the place where the Miniature Colour was first hidden before being taken to the church. The square has hardly altered (apart, most notably, from the road surface) since the war. There is a locally produced history of the events in the area, so that the local people are well informed. Walk down to the church, down the narrow street on the right. Nine men were buried in its garden, amongst them Lieutenant Campbell and Corporal Mallinson of the Royal Engineers. In 1953 they were removed and taken north to Cement House, near Langemark, in the Ypres Salient (as were those in Maisieres Churchyard, opposite Nimy). It is a pity that they could not have been left here under the care of the villagers.

The large house opposite the church was the small convent. Private Riley,

Cavalry swerved to the right along the line of trees. Railway embankment. Small copse on right, middle distance is the spoil heap.

RAILWAY EMBANKMENT

SPOIL HEAP

CAVALRY SWERVING TOWARDS SPOIL HEAP

wounded, was taken here, and it was he who told the sisters where the colour had been hidden. See page 130 for the whole of this remarkable story. Many of the prisoners were gathered here at the church before being marched away to captivity. A farmhouse Gite is opposite the church, identified by its badge.

Walk back to the market place and beyond the right hand side is the new and very large building of the Pensionnat St Bernard where many of the wounded were also taken.

Head for Wiheries, but remember that you are still travelling across the battlefield. Behind the buildings, in the fields on the left [18] is where Lieutenant-Colonel Bolger lay wounded with the injured Sergeant Dowling. They were eventually taken to the convent at Wiheries. The wood of Audregnies is on the right. It was in a field on the edge of this wood that a party commanded by Captain Ernest Jones and including Drummer Hogan saw a number of Germans hiding in the corn. They attacked them, but both Jones and Hogan were killed and were later buried by the Germans alongside the road, opposite the cemetery. Private Woods, who was present at the burial, managed to escape under the cover of dusk and hid in the field. Later he went into Wiheries, and at the village estaminet, Le Metro [22], they gave him food and clothing; in due course he made a remarkable escape back to England.

Stop by the communal cemetery [21]. There are only five men from the battle buried here - Jones and Hogan are buried side by side. Also here is Lieutenant Frost, whose bravery was so extraordinary, fighting to the last and surrounded by the enemy, that the Germans buried him at the place where he fell with full military honours. Later, after the war, his grave was found and he was brought here.

Drive into Wiheries; at the T Junction turn right and park alongside the farm wall. Opposite is a charcuterie [22], with an owner knowledgeable about events here in 1914. This used to be Le Metro; and the then tenant was Madame Julia Huvelle. She, her husband and daughter exhumed Captain Jones' body and brought it here and washed it and wrapped it in a white sheet; her daughter kept the Captain's wristwatch. They then reburied him in a proper grave in the cemetery and put a large cross above it.

Walk down the steep and narrow street on the left; the house which used to be the convent is opposite the church. Here were many of the British wounded, included Sergeant Dowling. He died in Rouen on his way home, having been repatriated. Here also were Lieutenant-Colonel Bolger and Sergeant Meachin. They made their escape and were sheltered, at great personal risk, by Madame Huvelle. The Germans knew they were hiding somewhere locally and threatened the Burgermaster with death. Madame Huvelle dressed them as civilians; knowing of Edith Cavell's rescue line, she got them away to her hospital in Brussels. Bolger's injuries made it difficult for him to walk, and he was recaptured when he was almost at the port of Flushing; Meachin managed to make it ashore to Folkestone.

The tour now goes to its last area of interest, the positions of 1/DCLI (Duke of Cornwall's Light Infantry). Turn around and go past the T Junction, leaving the road to Audregnies on the left [24]. Drive straight through Elouges; after a

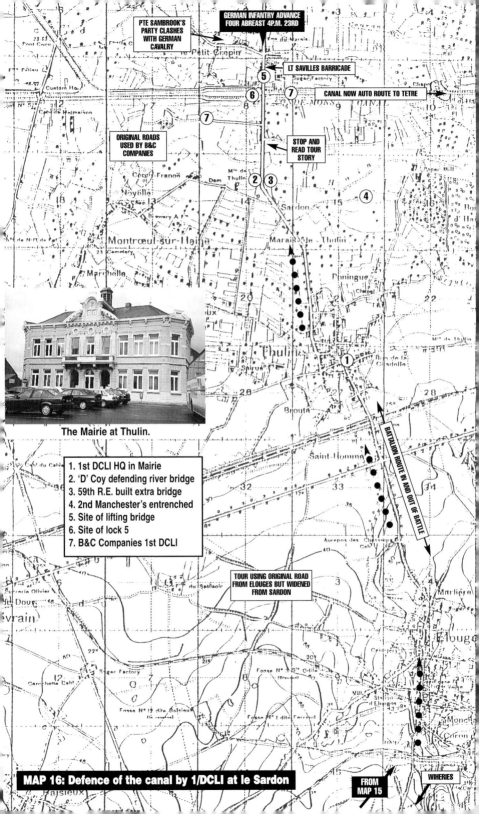

PTE SAMBROOK'S PARTY CLASHES WITH GERMAN CAVALRY

GERMAN INFANTRY ADVANCE FOUR ABREAST 4 P.M. 23RD

LT SAVILLES BARRICADE

⑤

⑥ CANAL NOW AUTO ROUTE TO TETRE

⑦

ORIGINAL ROADS USED BY B&C COMPANIES

⑦

STOP AND READ TOUR STORY

② ③

④

The Mairie at Thulin.

①

1. 1st DCLI HQ in Mairie
2. 'D' Coy defending river bridge
3. 59th R.E. built extra bridge
4. 2nd Manchester's entrenched
5. Site of lifting bridge
6. Site of lock 5
7. B&C Companies 1st DCLI

BATTALION ROUTE IN AND OUT OF BATTLE

TOUR USING ORIGINAL ROAD FROM ELOUGES BUT WIDENED FROM SARDON

WIHERIES

MAP 16: Defence of the canal by 1/DCLI at le Sardon

FROM MAP 15

mile or so turn left at the fork and then after another mile you will come to the wide main road. Turn left but then almost immediately take the right fork for Thulin; you should be able to see the church at the bottom of the slope a mile or so away. Drive into the centre and park at the big space behind the church. This was where the Cornwalls had their base; Lieutenant-Colonel Turner's Headquarters were in the Mairie [1], the big and ornate building. There is also a good auberge in the square, Le XIXeme.

Somewhat eccentrically the tour takes you along this battle in reverse, as it began on the far side of the canal.

Drive behind the church, and where the road joins the wide main road there is a small fork; the 50 yard long road to the right goes nowhere. Stop here. Once again the new road development has spoiled for us the view of the Cornwalls' battle at this point. This area is known as Le Sardon [2]. The short road is the old one along which Lieutenant-Colonel Turner's men went to defend the Thulin road lifting bridge. The road was blocked with traffic on the night of 23 August - with cavalry, guns and refugees, all heading south. Over on the right along the banks of the winding small River Haine were 2/Manchesters [4] and 2/Suffolks, in position in the water meadows for a mile or so from here. Their machine-guns were positioned so as to give Turner's men at the lifting bridge maximum support. Walk up the main road to the small, but now very wide, bridge over the River Haine. On the west side of the road the track and buildings still exist where D Company (Captain Woodham) was preparing the defences of the bridge. At that time there was a mill by the river. 59 Fd Coy had built another bridge to facilitate passage of the river. At 6pm on Sunday 23 August, 1/DCLI withdrew from the canal and took up positions on the south bank on both sides of the bridge [3]. Lieutenant Flint RE placed charges on the bridge on the Sunday night whilst the Germans were halted at the blown bridge over the canal. They brought a field gun up to it and were firing down the straight road. Each time the gun's flash was spotted, Flint and his men dived into the ditch. In due course a flying fragment from the bridge wounded him. When all the British had come back across the river bridge, it was destroyed.

19 Brigade had been a mile to the left, towards Condé; 1/Middx was nearest, at St Aybert, with the Argylls a mile or so beyond them.

This area has a lot of heavy traffic, so one needs to be cautious about stopping. Join the main road and go under the autoroute bridge; take the first turning to the left (but not on to the autoroute) and proceed along it for a hundred yards or so. Almost nothing has changed on this lane. The lifting bridge here was at Lock No 5 [6], which carried the road north. Lieutenant Saville, with No 6 Platoon built a road block on this side of the bridge [5] and then measured the distance up the straight road to where the railway line is still

At the hamlet of Sardon and Lt. Flint's bridge over the Haine. Car parked on it. Looking towards auto route (site of Lock No.5).

GERMAN CAVALRY PATROL

Lt Saville's position looking up
the road to Le Petit Crepin.

Private Sambrook's ditch.

visible - some 700 yards. Behind Saville was C Company [7] and the remainder of B. Lieutenant Benn's two machine-guns were at the bridge, sighted up the straight road.

Some two hundred yards up the main road, at a deep ditch that goes off at right angles to the one running alongside the road, was Private Sambrook and two men. It was there that he saw a German cavalry patrol riding unsuspectingly towards him. As the officer leading it came alongside he glanced down and saw Sambrook. Whilst attempting to draw his pistol, Sambrook shot him. His plumed helmet fell off, but his comrades gathered his horse's reins and they all dashed back up the road. However two terrified and wounded men had fallen onto the road, and were brought over the bridge into the British lines, quite convinced that they were going to be executed. The helmet with its bullet hole may be seen in the regimental museum in Bodmin.

Soon afterwards a larger body of cavalry came down the main road, but someone fired a rifle before the machine-guns could fire, sending the horsemen galloping back to safety.

The next excitement was at about 4pm, when a large body of infantry, four abreast, were seen coming down the road from the railway crossing. Lieutenant Benn's machine-guns and riflemen opened fire, devastating the attack.

Soon afterwards Lieutenant-Colonel Turner withdrew his men across the canal bridge; and later they were withdrawn to the river defences and the bridge was destroyed.

The action here was brief; the decision to withdraw out of Thulin was wise, for if they had remained much longer they might well have been trapped by the great German attack on the following day.

It is very easy from here to get onto the autoroute and head for home, via Calais, or for the other battlefields around Cambrai (some forty five minutes away) or the Somme. Of course, Waterloo is also nearby, as are the battlefields of Ramilles and Malplaquet.

Mons Selective Index.

Abell, Major WH, 44, 69, 143
Acland, Capt AN, 57, 97
Ainslie, Lt Col HS, 49, 163
Alexander, Major, VC, 121, 123, 182
Allenby, Maj Gen EH, 29, 41, 118
Allinson, Lt W, 43, 111
Allistone, Lt ABW, 62
Amiens, 25, 27
Angre, 123
Arnim, Lt von, 63, 137
Arnim, Gen Sixt von, 63
Ashburner, Capt, 43-44, 64, 136, 142
Audregnies, 121-126, 181-186.
Baisieux, 126, 181
Baker, Drummer, 130
Ballard, Lt Col CR, 121-127, 182
Bavai (Bavay), 106, 107, 111, 116
Bayly, Lt Col CGG, 28-29
Benn, Lt, 58, 97, 189
Benson, Capt JP, 54 - 55, 93 - 94,
    172, 174
Beresford, Major Pack, 68, 119, 176,
    179, 180
Bloem, Capt W, 28, 67, 176
Boger, Lt Col DC, 116, 121-130, 186
Bond, Lt Col, 93, 102
Booth, Major Sclater, 121
Boulnois, Lt PK, 65, 80-81, 155
Boussu, 54, 59, 68, 93, 98, 103,
    112, 169-171
Brandis, Colonel von, 116, 160
Bridges
    Pont de Bragnons, 44, 60, 142
    Pont Gas Poste, 154
    Pont d'Hautrage, 54, 55, 102
    Pont Mariette, 49, 84, 156
    Pont Richebe, 48, 65, 80, 81,
        86, 154, 155
Bridges, Major T, 37, 125, 126, 139,
    184
British Army
Corps
    I: 29, 31, 41, 105, 107
    II: 29, 32-33, 40, 79, 96, 105,
        107-109, 116
    Canadian Corps: 139
Divisions
    Cavalry: 29, 36, 117
    1st: 29, 31, 107

2nd: 29. 78. 99, 107, 113
3rd: 29, 33, 35, 43-51, 99, 105,
    107, 109, 117, 118, 121
4th: 106
5th: 29, 30, 51-59, 99, 105, 107,
    109, 117, 118, 121
7th: 130
Brigades
    1 Cavalry: 98, 123
    2 Cavalry: 36-37
    4 Cavalry: 38
    Independent: 29
    4 (Guards): 78
    5: 99, 111, 113, 114, 152, 159
    7: 35, 99, 109-110, 113, 116-
        121, 152, 161-164
    8: 35, 69-80, 99, 113, 141, 149
    9: 35, 75, 84, 113, 116, 152-161
    13: 35, 90, 112, 116-117, 118,166
    14: 38, 101, 112, 116, 118, 171
    15: 35, 59, 68, 98, 112, 117, 118
    19: 41, 104, 105, 117, 188
Royal Artillery
Royal Horse Artillery
Batteries
    D: 123
    E: 123
    L: 121, 123, 127, 182, 185
Royal Field Artillery
Brigades
    XXVII: 36, 48
    XL: 36, 76, 79
Batteries
    6: 76-77
    23: 76, 77, 148
    49: 76
    107: 36, 48, 75
    109: 113
    119: 121, 123, 126-127, 181, 182
    120: 36, 99, 119, 168
    123: 104
Royal Engineers
Field Companies
    17: 89, 93, 166, 171
    56: 59
    57: 59, 64-65, 74-75, 80, 137, 138
    59: 86, 102-103, 172-173, 188
The Cavalry
    2nd Dragoon Guards, 98
    4th (Royal Irish) Dragoon Guards,
        37, 121, 125-127, 139-141, 183
    5th Dragoon Guards, 123
    18th Hussars, 121, 182
    19th Hussars, 38, 51
    9th Lancers, 121, 125-127, 182, 183

Battalions
    2/Argyll and Sutherland
        Highlanders, 98, 181
    1/Bedfords, 112, 118
    1/Cheshires, 30, 98, 112, 121-
        129, 132-133, 182-186
    2/Connaught Rangers, 99, 111
    1/Dorsets, 30, 98, 112, 116, 119,
        179
    1/Duke of Cornwall's Light
        Infantry, 30, 55-57, 96-97,
        186-189
    2/Duke of Wellington's, 52, 67-68,
        89-90, 99-101, 111, 116,118,
        119-121, 166-169, 178-180
    1/East Surreys, 52-53, 93-96,
        101-103, 171, 172-174
    1/Gordon Highlanders, 30, 76-
        79, 148-151
    2/Highland Light Infantry, 99, 110
    1/Irish Guards, 78
    2/King's Own Scottish Borderers,
        30, 52-54, 63, 91-93, 101,
        111, 171, 174
    2/King's Own Yorkshire Light
        Infantry, 53, 54, 68, 93, 101-
        103, 111-112, 116, 170, 171
    1/Lincolns, 30, 75, 79, 99, 110, 113,
        114, 159-161
    2/Manchesters, 57, 96-97, 103,
        112,188
    4/Middlesex, 35, 38, 42, 44-47, 60-62,
        69-78, 131-137, 141-150
    1/Norfolks, 112, 121-127, 180-184
    1/Northumberland Fusiliers, 30, 49-51,
        65, 66, 81-86, 99, 110, 113, 114,
        156-157, 161, 163
    2/Ox and Bucks Light Infantry, 99, 110
    4/Royal Fusiliers, 30, 35, 43, 47-48,
        60, 62-65, 69-75, 99, 110, 134-
        137, 154
    2/Royal Irish Regiment, 60, 62, 69-79,
        110, 141-151, 163
    2/Royal Scots, 30, 76, 78, 99, 151-152
    1/Royal Scots Fusiliers, 48-49, 65,
        80-81, 86-87, 110, 154-157, 158
    2/Royal Welsh (Welch) Fusiliers, 98
    1/Royal West Kents, 30, 51-52, 54-55,
        66-67, 87, 89-90, 99, 111, 116,
        119, 166, 168, 174-176, 180
    1/Scottish Rifles, 98
    2/South Lancs, 110, 114-115, 159-
        161, 163-164
    2/Suffolks, 55, 57, 103, 188
    1/Wiltshires, 115, 161

2/Worcesters, 99, 111, 113, 159, 161
3/Worcesters, 110, 114-115, 162
5 Cyclist Company, 38, 51, 67
Recce Battalion, 83rd United States, 149
Royal Flying Corps, 27, 28
Squadrons
2:, 27, 28
3: 27
4: 27
5: 27, 28
Buchanan-Dunlop, Capt HD, 52
Bülow, Gen U von, 41-42, 105
Campbell, Capt, 55, 94-95, 172, 174
Campbell, Lt Col D, 125, 126, 182, 183
Canals
Condé, 21, 32, 35, 40, 43, 48, 50, 51, 54, 65, 102, 104, 105, 152, 167
du Centre, 21, 32, 35, 38, 69
Carter, Capt RC, 90
Casteau, 37, 139
Cemeteries
Angre Communal, 185
Cement House, 185
Ciply Communal, 163
Cuesmes Communal, 159, 163
Elouges Communal, 180-181
Flenu Communal, 158
Hautrage, 176
Jemappes Communal, 157-158
Nimy (Mons) Communal, 145
Nouvelles Communal, 163, 164
Quievrain Communal, 184-185
St Symphorien, 152
Tournai Communal, 29
Wiheries Communal, 186
Chateau Gendebien, 76, 148
Chetwode, Brig-Gen, 29
Ciply, 40, 99, 110, 113-116, 161-162
Coke, Major ES D'Ewes, 53-54, 172
Cole, Capt, 47-48, 135
Cox, Lt Col St J, 62, 72
Cuesmes, 49, 99, 110, 112, 113, 159, 163
Cuthbert, Brig-Gen, 90, 100
Darwell, Lieut TH, 55, 95, 172, 174
Day, Lieut AF, 65, 137
Davy, Major WHC, 43, 62, 69, 142
de Lisle, Brig-Gen, 125
Dease, Lt MJ, VC, 47, 64, 74, 75, 137, 152
Denison, Lieut BN, 93
Donovan, Pte, 68
Doran, Brig-Gen, 150

Drummond, Brig-Gen, 41
Dunlop, Capt B, 99-100
Dyer, Capt, 128, 183, 184
Elliott, Lieut, 128
Elouges, 59, 68, 103, 122, 123, 180-181
Fergusson, Maj Gen Sir C, 29, 116-118
Figue, Leon, MBE, 171
Fitzgerald, Capt, 60
Fitzpatrick, CQMS, 76, 77, 148
Flenu, 81, 110, 157
Flint, Lieut, 103
Forester, 47, 136
Forster, Capt, F, 64
Frameries, 40, 81, 86, 99, 110, 111, 113-116, 157, 160
French Army
Fifth Army, 26, 31, 39, 41, 105-106
Sordet's Cavalry Corps, 105, 106,
French, FM Sir J, 26, 99, 106
Frost, Lieut, 130, 186
Geard, Cpl F, 27
Gerachty, Capt, 91
German Army
Armies
First, 41, 105
Third (Saxon), 42
Corps
II (Cavalry): 57, 105
III: 38, 41, 65, 91, 109
IV: 41, 62, 91, 96, 129
IX: 38, 41, 47, 49, 80, 109
XII (Saxon): 39
Divisions
9th (Cavalry): 37, 57-59
5th: 67, 87
6th: 65, 155
7th: 96, 127, 182
8th: 96, 118, 127, 188
18th: 117
Regiments
4th Cuirassiers, 37
4th Brandenburg Grenadiers, 167
12th Brandenburg, 28, 87, 99, 175-176
24th, 113, 114-115
35th, 76
36th Fusiliers, 182
53rd (Chasseurs), 182
66th, 117, 130
72nd, 129
75th (Bremen), 79
84th (Schleswig-Holstein), 63, 76, 136
85th, 60, 76
86th (Bremen), 60, 76

93rd, 127, 182
Gibbs, Lt Col, 90, 100, 119, 169,178
Glass, Capt HEL, 43, 62, 141-142
Godley, Pte SF, VC, 75, 137
Godsell. Lieut, 91, 100, 168
Gore, Lieut, 67, 175, 176
Grand Reng, 31
Grenfell, Capt FO, VC, 125, 126-127, 182
Grierson, Lt Gen Sir M, 29
Haig, Major AE, 92
Haig, General Sir D, 29, 42
Haine, River, 54, 56, 96
Hainin, 57
Hamilton, Maj Gen HIW, 29, 113,114
Hamilton, Lieut IBN, 78
Hautrage, 38, 54, 55, 94, 174
Henderson, Brig-Gen Sir David, 27
Hepworth, Capt LF, 96
Heron, Pte, DCM, 80-81
Heubner, Colonel, 81
Hogan, Drummer, 128, 130, 186
Holland, Major CS, 36, 119, 168,176
Holmes, Cpl, 102
Halstead, Lt Col, 115, 163
Holt, Lieut HW, 60, 152
Hopkins, Major NJ, 59, 60
Hornby, Capt, 37-38, 139-141
Hornu, 111, 116, 165, 166
Howard, Major, 64
Hull, Lt Col, 43, 47, 62, 69, 73
Hutelle, Madame, 186
Hyon, 73, 76, 77, 78, 149-151
Innes, Capt, 49
James, Lt Col, 112
Jarvis, Cpl, VC, 65, 80-81, 155
Jemappes, 48, 50, 65, 66, 80, 104, 153, 155
Joffre, General Joseph, 27
Johnson, Sapper, 66
Jones, Capt ER, 128, 130, 186
Kitchener, FM Earl, 25, 105
Kluck, General A von, 38, 41-42, 105, 107, 141
Laidley, Lieut, 78
Lanrezac, General, 31, 99, 105-106
Le Cateau, 39
Le Petit Crepin, 38, 55, 57
Le Sardon, 97,188
Les Herbieres, 52, 54, 102, 174
Leigh, Major Chandos, 92, 93, 172
Liebnau, Capt, 116, 160
Lister, Capt GD, 51-52, 175, 176
Locks
Number 2, 48, 80, 81, 154

191

Number 3, 51, 52, 90, 169
Number 4, 43, 53, 93, 101, 171, 174
Number 5 (Les Wartons), 43,
141, 188
Number 6, 47, 74, 138
Lomax, Maj Gen SH, 29
Longley, Lt Col, 54, 55, 93, 173
Louvain (Leuven), 33
Lyon, Major, 76
Marlborough, Duke of, 21
Macdonald, Capt EW, 53
Mariette, 49, 65, 66, 81, 89, 152
Marsden, Capt, 89
Martyn, Lt Col A, 51, 89, 100
Marwitz, General von der, 105
Maubeuge, 25, 27, 106, 122
McCracken, Brig-Gen, 115
McMahon, Lt Col NR, 47, 74, 75
McMiking, Lt Col, 76
Meachin, CSM, 124, 130, 186
Mead Lieut, 63-64
Memorials
    2nd Australian Division, Mont St
        Quentin, 158
    2nd Royal Irish Regiment, 148
    4th Royal Fusiliers, 137
    Holland, Major CS, 168
    La Bascule, 147
    Resistance - Jemappes, 155
    Resistance - Nimy (Mons), 145
    Royal Scots Fusiliers, Flenu, 158
Miniature Colour (1/Cheshires),
    130, 185-186
Minogue, Capt MJ, 55, 172
Moltke, General Helmuth von,
    26, 27
Morritt, Lieut, 96, 103
Mullens, Lt Col, 125, 183
Mullins, Sgt, 102
Munro, Maj Gen CC, 29
Murray, Lt Gen Sir A, 41
Neary, Pte, 65 80
Niemeyer, Musketier Oscar, 75, 136
Nimy, 35, 36, 37, 45, 59, 64, 73, 74-
    75, 134-138, 144, 146
Nouvelles, 73, 151, 152, 164
Obourg, 21, 38, 43, 59, 60, 141
    Station, 47, 141
O'Kelly, Lieut, 89-90
Oliver, Capt, 44, 73
Ozanne, Capt WM, 52, 67-68, 89,
    99, 101, 166, 169
Panter, Sgt, 50-51, 66, 157
Panter-Downs, Major, 77, 148
Parr, Pte J, 47, 60, 141, 152

Parsons, Major, 38
Paturages, 40, 68, 87, 99, 111, 112, 116
Payne, Cpl A, 65, 100
Pennyman, Lieut JBW, 53, 90
Pepys, Lieut, 68, 93, 102, 171, 176
Petarel, Major, 97
Phillipeville, 39
Plan XVII, 24
Pommeroeul, 38, 55
Pottinger, Lieut, 101, 171
Price, Cpl, 152
Quaregnon, 49, 81, 86, 156
Queen of Hungary (Reine de
    Hongrie), 38, 140-141
Quievrain, 41, 123, 184
Redmond, Pte, 77
Rose, Capt, 49, 81, 158
Rushton, Lieut F, 73
Russel, Lieut, 118, 119, 179
St Aybert, 21, 98, 104, 188
St Ghislain, 66, 68, 90, 100, 166,
    169, 180
    Station, 166, 169
St John, Capt BT, 81-82
St Leger, Major, 72, 73, 76, 77, 79
St Symphorien, 78
Sambrook, Pte, 57, 58, 189
Sandilands, Capt, 113-114, 161
Sars la Bruyere, 40
Saville, Lieut, 56, 58, 188
Schlieffen Plan, 23-24
Shaw, Brig-Gen, 84, 114
Shellabear, Pte, 90
Shine, Lieut, 77, 148
Shore, Capt, 124, 128, 183
Simpson, Major, 76
Sloane-Stanley, Lieut LF, 44-45, 69,
    143
Smith, Sgt, 80-81, 84-86, 155, 156-
    157
Smith, Lt Col D, 48-49, 65, 80, 110,
    154, 155
Smith-Dorrien, Lt Gen Sir H, 29, 31,
    105, 109, 113, 164
Snow, Maj Gen T D'O, 106
Soignies, 139, 141
Sordet, General, 105, 106
Spears, Lieut, 39-40, 105-106
Spence, Sgt, 118-119, 180
Stephenson, Lt Col CM, 52
Tandy, Lieut AMS, 77, 150
Taylor, Cpl, 91
Taylor, Capt, 119-120
Tebbut, Pte, 113, 116
Terry, Capt, 74

Tertre, 52, 53, 67, 174, 175
Tew, Major HS, 55, 95, 96, 103
Thomas, Cpl, 37-38, 140
Thulin, 57, 58, 188, 189
Tooth, Capt L, 125, 126, 184
Tournai, 38
Travis-Cook, Capt, 115
Tullis, Capt, 49, 155
Tulloch, JAS, Lt Col, 59, 99, 100
Turner, Lt Col M, 55-56, 57, 93, 96-
    97, 98, 188, 189
Tweedie, Major, 78
Ville Pommeroeul, 56, 58, 97
Walker, Sgt, 102
Walker, Major G, 96
Wanliss, Lt Col, 115
Ward, Lieut, 95, 96
Wasmes, 68, 100, 102, 112, 116-
    120, 176-180
Waterfall, Lieut V, 28-29
Wetherall, Major, 112
Whittington, Sgt, 77
Whyte, John, 158
Wiheries, 129, 130, 182, 186
Williams, Cpl, 118-119
Wilson, Lt Col CS, 59
Wilson, Lt Gen Sir H, 25
Woodham, Capt, 57
Woods
    Audregnies, 128, 130, 186
    Badour, 51
    Boussu, 100
    Deduit, 127
    Haut, 76, 79
    Havre, 69
Woulfe-Flanagan, Capt EM, 55
Wright, Capt T, VC, 65, 80-81, 84-
    86, 155, 156-157
Wynward, Lieut, 94, 95, 174
Yate, Major CAL, VC, 102-103
Yatman, Major C, 49-51, 81, 86,
    156, 157, 159